WELL, IF YOU DON'T LIKE IT HERE, WHY DON'T'CHA LEAVE?

Memoirs of a Black Female Police Officer

Janet A. Garnett

Order this book online at www.trafford.com
or email orders@trafford.com

Most Trafford titles are also available at major online book retailers.

Print information available on the last page.

ISBN: 978-1-4251-8687-6 (sc)
ISBN: 978-1-4907-9742-7 (e)

Trafford rev. 09/16/2019

www.trafford.com

North America & international
toll-free: 1 888 232 4444 (USA & Canada)
fax: 812 355 4082

PREFACE TO THE PREFACE

THIS BOOK was actually completed and copywrited in late 2006. Since that time, several significant events have taken place, and are worth being referenced in order to complete the picture; (search for weapons of mass destruction, economic crises in America, Iranian nuclear development concerns, and the world-shaking phenomenon of Mr. Barack Obama). This book would have been outdated without some reference to these events. As one of those Black Americans who benefited during the 70's with certain closed doors being forced open to us by law, I can foresee some protest to the less than positive observances concerning our treatment in American society. Those same minds who declare, "I'm not prejudiced!" and who are going to vigorously point to Mr. Obama's nomination as President of the United States as proof, there are some concerns I feel obligated to point out.

Yes, I am VERY excited to see the chance for one of us to accomplish what I truly did not believe I would see in my lifetime...a democratically elected Black man to the highest office in the land. However, as I can tell you from the experiences we encountered as we also broke into new grounds for us: Number One – he is going to have to have the right to make mistakes. You see, we were fully aware of the number of unfriendly, hostile forces around us that were going to pop the champagne cork in celebration should we not succeed in our new supervisory positions. So we COULDN'T fail. And let me tell you that is a burden no human being should have to endure. As long as you're human, you're going to mess up here and there. It is your right to acknowledge and therefore fix it. All of the "Rev. Wright" business that Whites kept after and kept after Mr. Obama about was only part of the usual pampering and catering that they're used to. White Americans are more aware than we are that what Rev. Wright said was absolutely true, including the origination of some diseases this entire planet has had their suspicions about all along. No, the problem was the fact that he <u>said</u> it. You see, American society is used to expecting us to do what we have obligingly done all along...and that's pipe down, shut up, and let this society continue to tout its democracy and fairness to all. As long as you don't count what's being done to those "Negroes." And THAT was what the Rev. Wright "problem" was.

Look at Germany. Poor Germany is forever condemned in the public mind and eye because of a thirteen year period in its entire modern history. This is WITH them paying reparations to the state of Israel to the tune of about fourteen billion dollars a year, faithfully. I'm about 200% certain that at least 87% of the German populace could have easily said, "Look, I wasn't even around at that time! We weren't involved in that holocaust stuff. Why should _I_ have to pay for that stuff? Why should _I_ have to be held guilty?" etc. etc...but they're not doing that. And yet, on History Channel every other night of the week, there's some reference to the Holocaust and what was done to Jews in Nazi Germany. And our Jewish brethren are ALWAYS accommodated, sympathized with and listened to with reverent attention.

This country and its European tributaries are still benefiting to this very day from the African Slave Trade from the 1600's until the mid 1860's. Not only have we NEVER been given a dime for our labor, we don't even have the right to complain. If we ever bring up (even periodically) what happened to us, all we get is mocked, condemned and insulted.

In addition to being accorded the right to be a human being with all its frailties, Mr. Obama is also going to have to have the right to make unpopular decisions. That is supposed to be the standard of leadership. Let me tell you, I had been on my job in Atlanta, Georgia for quite a few years. When I was going into my 5th, 6th and 7th year there, I made some suggestions to upper management on how to better _accomplish our mission_, due to what I had observed over time. My ideas, I figured, were well thought out with all the possibilities, pro and con, well observed. I presented these ideas to the supervisors in that department, those who'd been there from 16 to 20+ years. They very kindly and patiently told me why my ideas wouldn't work and would not behoove the department to implement. They were the boss, I had to respect and carry out their wishes. Once I reached my 12th, 13th and 14th year there, I was actually able to see and understand what they were talking about. "Oh, this _wouldn't_ have been a good idea to carry out!" That's why we put the people whom we respect and reasonably trust in those positions.

It's pretty obvious that our Caucasian counterparts in this nation's history have had slammed home hard in their faces some unpleasant facts from the governing entities who <u>really</u> run this country. Those facts are that they too are just as much a bunch of useless, damn niggers to these entities as much as WE are. These last eight years they've experienced that the people _really_ running the show here don't give two dead flies about them anymore than they give two dead flies about us. They don't care whether you live or die anymore than they care whether WE live or die. They don't care if your children live or die anymore than if ours do. They...don't..._CARE._ ALL they care about is lining their pockets. And they don't <u>care</u> who gets hurt in the process. What other reason would there be for the nation to finally be willing to give the presidency to a Black man or a female candidate? Those who do have real representation in government are observing the fact that _they_ are in trouble. All this time they've been kicked back in their easy chair, smugly gloating about those "other people out there" who are going to end up fighting for scraps of meat in the street. They can finally see that they will be the "other people out there" if things continue as they are.

The pretext for war in Iraq which in 1991, was based on the accusation of the possibility of five dollar a gallon gasoline under Saddam. You can see whose leadership the steadily encroaching price is occurring under. It ain't Saddam...he's dead. You may as well realize that this $130 a barrel oil cost is not being paid by the oil executives. They've never had to pay full price for these barrels of oil. They always get it way under the stated price. But hey, who among those in power is doing anything about passing those savings onto us at the gas pumps?

If those elements still haunting the outer fringes, squatting on their haunches and digging their Bowie knives into the dirt (itching, hungry and anxious to turn back the clock) are allowed to have their way, then face the following facts. You've pretty much had your way, mostly covert, and kept things as they are in your closed door sessions. ALL of these oil executives, all of these hyper-powerful billionaires, and other reigning elites pretty much represent <u>you</u>, do they not? All of you guys who were destined to retire with a six-figure annual income from your Enrons and World Com's...that wasn't <u>us</u>!!! Our retirement income is around $17,000 to $24,000 depending upon your last job's salary and state of residence. That was <u>you</u> who got screwed by your fellows. That's you who have to go back to work and who can kiss that money goodbye. You put someone in office whose only mantra is exactly the same as General Ursus in "Beneath the Planet of the Apes," and that's "Invade! Invade! INVADE!!!" If Albert Gore (the truly elected President of the United States in 2000) were on duty September 11, 2001, may have come and gone as just another day. The price of gas would be a whopping, astounding $1.39 per gallon because we would be ON alternative fuels by now. He was instrumental in getting Black farmers a court-awarded fourteen billion dollars for discrimination. To date, under this current administration, those farmers have not yet been given a dime. If they had there could be more food crops grown to keep down the 'supposed' food shortage in the world. But they may not have gone for the genetically-altered seed that the corporations are driving hard for. That could also explain the reduction of our honeybee population. These same corporate executives are imposing genetically-altered seed sales to the Iraqis instead of the regular seeds they've used since 3000 B.C.

Now Iran is in their sights. In 2003, the Secret Service warned the president that constant threats and invasions of other countries at will, based on accusations that they harbor some type of weapons system, would only turn into a self-fulfilling prophecy. Subsequently, the accused nations who are 'guilty as charged' according to the U.S., will work with covert urgency to build a nuke or two for real.

What has this got to do with being a cop who is pretty much an average Joe or Jane? You'll be more or less pleasantly surprised (or outraged depending upon your level of awareness) when you note these observations based upon educated opinions and experiences. We all occupy <u>one</u> world. If there is another World War, fought with the unthinkable (nukes and other weapons of mass destruction), there will be precious little more space for survivors to occupy. I don't think we can haughtily figure that our territory will be untouched, much as we would like that not to be the case. As I named the title of this thesis, in order to save certain unsympathetic elements the trouble, should the truly unthinkable happen, you just might be hearing that same declaration yourself should you need a place to flee.

Nevertheless, this middle-aged girl is always mindful that "hope springs eternal." I am indeed highly encouraged and hopeful of a positive future for us and for this nation. Under truly NEW management, the United States may experience a healing and restoration of our reputation to the rest of the world. Think about it... the old way or best for <u>all</u> concerned way?

"WE DON'T <u>NEED ANOTHER</u> BLACK BITCH MAKIN' LIEUTENANT AROUND HERE!"[1]

---

[1]From a quote told to me in strictest 'sworn to silence' confession about what was overheard in one of those 'closed door' sessions among white police sergeants and lieutenants in my department.

CONTENTS

PREFACE

YOU KNOW, I recall my Grandmother's words to us years ago when we were, of course, much younger... "You know, you can keep doing what's wrong, and people get tired of it. But if you keep it up after you've been given chance after chance to stop...there comes a point to where finally GOD gets tired of it. And <u>HE</u> will step in and stop it <u>for</u> you!" Folks, in general – this is <u>not</u> meant to be a "belly-ache" session of "moanin' and complainin". Rather, in a further discussion of observances about THE on-going "problem" in this country (and the world) that everyone, including ourselves, are all trained to deny---the Race Problem---it is a hope and indeed an attempt to, prayerfully, give some sort of dissuasion away from that very problem continually enforced by the powers that be, and by all of us who have been swept up into perpetuating it if we wanted to be gainfully and lucratively employed.

INTRODUCTION

I CAME FROM A BACK GROUND (don't worry, I'll make this quick) of non-excuse-makers. Either you <u>did</u> or you <u>didn't</u>. You either succeeded or you failed. One of the main things I'm grateful to my mother's instilling in me when I was still in my early teens was that you cannot <u>trust anyone</u>. No, not meant to be felt in a negative fashion. But that "people fail us." They do indeed fail us all the time. She told me even SHE should not be looked at as being trusted 100% of the time...because, she said, you may be looking for me to pick you up from school...and if I have an accident or I get sick or something *happens* to me, I didn't do it. It's not that I *meant* to not pick you up. It's just circumstances beyond my control that kept me from doing it. People can *have* every intention of doing for you. But if things happen or something happens to them, they didn't do it! And since I had my eye on larger than life aims, being relegated to the usual menial things <u>we</u> (Black folks) had been relegated to was **not** in the cards for ME!

Thankfully, I think I can say, I grew up during the early '60's, when Dr. Martin Luther King, Malcolm X, Stokely Carmichael, H. Rap Brown, Dr. Ralph Bunch, Roy Wilkins, Jr., and all those freedom fighters and icons were alive, well and fully functioning. My folks had also alerted me to the types of things to expect as a young Black person out there in the world. I had always loved books. From the time I learned "See Spot Run" and on to my 1st & 2nd grade years, I always had a book with me. So when, at the age of about 5 or 6 yrs. old, I decided to make my own little book called, "Sony the Little Duck" on my own, no assignment or anything, I studiously made sure to have the blank page between the cover and the first page. Narration and pictures provided by me, of course. Page 1 thru 7, etc. And proudly took it to my 2nd grade teacher who was a "nice" young white lady. And my only reason for boring you with this is to point out the mind set of what I've seen is the same mind set of today among whites. And, thankfully, again I'd been advised by my folks about racism early enough so I wouldn't be shaken when I ran into it. Just suffice it to say that when Mrs. Nash saw that book that <u>I</u> had made, the expression on her face was as if a knife or a gun was pointing at her. My Mom and Grandmother proudly kept it in their mahogany desk drawer which lasted until the present days. Also, thankfully, as the '70's came on and the young white teachers who were coming to our schools to teach us, had much, <u>much</u> better reactions to my self-started writing projects. Yes, these were the younger generation hipsters who were themselves wearing dashikis, bandanas, multi-colored lens sun-glasses in the school, etc.

One very quick thing to note before I go on with the main body of this work is a story that my 6-yr-old little niece Imani, wants me to tell her over and over again. When I was in the 6th grade (in 1968) I brought home a "D" on my report card in Math. Now the teacher, Ms. Handy, was a very sweet, pleasant platinum haired, hefty-set open minded white lady who played soft ball with us at recess, and would bat the ball and run in between the bases, etc. AND she encouraged my love of reading and books with GIGANTIC sized volumes and encyclopedias that were school-only property that she would give to me to take home and bring back after enjoying my fill of them. Even so, I came home with *that* particular letter on my report card and my Mom went ballistic. "WHAT DO YOU MEAN BRINGING HOME A D ON YOUR REPORT CARD!!!?"

I protested, "Mom I didn't make that D for real, the teacher she was just mad at me 'cause me and Percy was fightin'!" Mom goes, "I DON'T WANNA HEAR IT!!!"

She called Ms. Handy at home, at her house. I could hear Mom emphasizing every word to her... "I- **A-P-O-L-O-G-I-I-I-ZE!!!! SHE CAN DO BETTER THAN THIS!!! SHE CAN DO BETTER THAN THIS!!! THIS WILL NOT HAPPEN AGAIN!!!**"

And on and on she went. Yes, you'd have thought I was in the Grassy Knoll in November of 1963, practically diapers and all. But she ended her talk with Ms. Handy with, **"SHE WILL NOT DO THIS AGAIN!!!"** And more of, "I APOLOGI-I-I-ZE!!!" Then I had to write a letter of apology to the teacher for getting a D in Math, saying that I was sorry, it wouldn't happen again, etc., etc. Well, folks, the outcome of that was that I was among those of my schoolmates who made the National Honor Society (1974), I skipped straight to Geometry from pre-algebra (because I thought I was no good in math) and passed with an A- ...the teacher, Harvey Banner, told me that I proved that you don't have to take Algebra first before Geometry, which was the way you normally did it, and I became good with numbers later on when I would advise people on tax preparation.

The only unhappy occurrence concerning us "stars" was that it was a Black female student, my best friend Wannah, who was the Number One student in ranking among the school body in graduation that year. The No. 2 student was a White female student. To the White female student went the prime and best scholarship awards that normally went to the No. 1 student. Wannah was left with a scholarship to Rochester University in New York, however with no other means for support, funding, provisions, housing, etc. In other words, "Yeah, be glad ya got THIS much out of us." But the White student, who's name I won't mention because I don't want to embarrass her since the "powers that be" were the ones who by-passed Wannah, and gave the best and the monies for support, etc., to her. No, I guess it didn't occur to anyone to properly protest.

The Basic Educational Opportunity Grants (B.E.O.G.) were in full operation during those years (the late 1970's) and my Mom promptly got ahold of, made out the schedule for and put me in to Jefferson Community College on that B.E.O.G. grant in 1975. I got my Associate of Arts Degree in 1978 (because I sort of wanted to work and earn some money in 1977). I made the Dean's List, and I mention this mainly to emphasize what good parenting will do...when parents were allowed to do it. Still having an "S" on my chest outlook on life, I was persuaded to join the Army in my graduation year...and had absolutely no other intent in mind BUT to make the Officer's ranks. I had to get a "life's lesson" on the sub-art of politics involved in that arena.

There were things I became exposed to during my military years that taught me quite a bit concerning the whys and wherefores at the root of certain "problem areas" in effect in the world, not just in attitudes about Black vs. White, so to speak. But also about Women vs. Men. In the end it's about _power_ and about who _is_ and who _isn't_ going to wield it. I <u>highly</u> recommend checking out Dr. Frances Cress Welsings' book, "The Isis Papers," which is a hard to put down analysis of certain desperate powers that be and their actions, attitudes and "problems" (and I do mean heavy emphasis on that particular word, "problems"). The things that whites in this society not only have done but continue to do to us is not based on just their having "problems" with people who've stayed in the oven too long. The only real provocation for their continued wrongs is their own guilty consciences.

Black men...you know how you observe the way Whites "lock their car doors, clutch their purses, fidget and quickly move away from you in the elevator, etc., etc." And you know it's because their thinking about you, "Mugger-rapist-killer...mugger-rapist-killer..." Stop and think about something for a moment. I've presented this anecdote to my younger co-workers some years ago. Let's say you and some other acquaintance of yours, be he supposed friend or otherwise, happen to see each other off to your respective destination somewhere. And let's say this acquaintance of yours doubles back to your place of residence and just cleans you out... I mean robs you of everything-and I mean EVERYTHING in your place, leaving only the floor boards in their place. There's a hole where even your kitchen sink once was. And then he's gone. You don't know what's happened yet. You haven't been home. Now, let's say you're happening down the street and you bump into your acquaintance. The one that just cleaned you out. HE doesn't know if you've been home yet. What do you expect his reaction to be to you??? You're probably wondering why he's acting so fidgety. And nervous. Eying you intently, as if he's expecting you to do something to him. Trying to shuffle back and away from you, mumbling indiscernible words to you. Folks, <u>THAT'S</u> the reason for their nervousness around you. It's not because of YOU. It's because of what's been done TO you that makes those people that do all of that clutching and ducking, and moving FAR away from you. And that fear is spurred on because of what they KNOW that THEY would do if they were us. And it sure wouldn't be to "Go Back Home!" For all of you readers who can't get off of that river in Egypt "Da-Nile", here are my memoirs as a never-say-die, "I'm gonna MAKE it,"! bright-eyed and open minded, successful young thing who "had to find out"..._some_ people will do <u>anything</u> to keep from having to acknowledge <u>you</u>. Even to their _own_ detriment. And as VonRunsted told Rommel (concerning Hitler's madness)... "There comes a point where you have to just stand back and watch with a kind of detached fascination at a man's rather enthusiastic determination to cut his own throat". (_sic_)

CHAPTER ONE

AND SO I'M HIRED

AFTER MY HONORABLE DISCHARGE from the U.S. Army in 1984 at the rank of 1st Lieutenant, chest all puffed out, "S" on my chest still, and ready to "show my stuff," I found that I couldn't get work. Period. I mean, I had managed to acquire my Bachelor of Arts Degree during my six years with the military, achieved the rank of a Commissioned Officer, didn't smoke, use drugs, or anything, had what I felt was a reasonably pleasant personality, was itching and hungry for work. I'd fallen in love, gotten a broken heart from a Georgia man, gotten over that, managed to not get pregnant. Didn't want any public assistance, anyway (I wasn't immune to all the negative insinuations about "welfare queens," etc.) I had too much going for me. I wanted to work. And I couldn't get work. It was the Ronald Reagan era. All of these companies owned by the same bunch of bigots who didn't want to have to hire us in the first place – NOW didn't <u>have</u> to...and they *weren't* hiring us. I had to watch every White high school drop out, regardless of whether he or she could barely grunt out their next sentence, get hired 15 times before I could even get seen. The PBS channels did a special in those years of '84 thru '86 profiling an Indiana Fire Department. They talked to the fire chief in charge of hiring personnel, and he told about how he'd been approached by certain higher ups and persons in powerful positions who told him, in private, "Hey, you don't have to hire _them_ anymore!" It was because this particular chief in charge of hiring was in the process of hiring some Black and other minority firemen. And the individual(s) said to him, "You don't _have_ to hire them now!" And the fire chief asked them, "What are you talkin' about?" He was hiring the best qualified candidates, and was not selecting based on race or otherwise. But this and these individuals were trying to dissuade him from hiring anymore Blacks and others like that on the force. And of course, when the PBS interviewers went to try to find these persons, they were disappeared, absentee, and when confronted or cornered, denied to the four winds any such conversation. It didn't surprise or shock me a bit. I _was_ very glad to see it being addressed.

Anyway, needless to say, the anger and frustration in me began to grow. You'll notice at this point that I'm telling about what WE Black folks have been going through that these supposed, "Angry White Males" keep purporting to be going through. It's as if it's <u>only</u> when the truth of things concerning how <u>they've</u> been covertly discriminating against US is _exposed_ and in particular, <u>CONFESSED</u> to by one of them that the _pretense_ of _their_ being discriminated against can be undone. Remember, **I** was still experiencing that good old standby excuse from them as being "too <u>overqualified</u>" for the jobs I was going for, as was told to most Blacks and all who had carefully and studiously gone to school to be qualified for these better paying, more prestigious positions. However, I was <u>never</u> too overqualified if it came to handing me a mop.

Nowadays, the clarion call for White hold-out and excuses for not hiring us is to arbitrarily label us ALL as being "Affirmative Action Hires", and as if _none_ of us are qualified _at all_ for anything paying over $5 bucks an hour, part time. It's one excuse after another. I found out to my ever increasing anger, myself, that these Whites were routinely being hired and started out at salaries of between $50,000 to $80,000 per year. I discovered this when I finally found _something_ to support myself with Manpower Temporary Services in 1986, and I was put to work in the mortgage banking nerve center in Louisville, Kentucky, which was home for me, since I'd run out of funds and _had_ to go back home. And these were Whites who hadn't even barely finished 9th grade. And here I was having to subsist on $4.30 an hour. Yes, even for 1986, embarrassingly low. Finally, in 1987, while on the TARC (Transit Authority of River City) bus, I overheard some riders talking about Atlanta, Georgia. "Aw, man, they got GOOD jobs in Atlanta. They got <u>good</u> jobs there! You can make $28,000 a year just working part-time there!"

Well, I let that sink in and seep into my little noodle, and then I determined, "I'm goin' to Atlanta!"

When my income tax return came I had $280 to my name. And that was what I purchased a Greyhound Bus ticket with, one-way, and went to "seek my fortune." Because, I ascertained, this wasn't makin' any sense. I had too much going for me. A college degree (B.A.), an Honorable Discharge at the rank of 1st Lieutenant, etc., etc...and I couldn't get work. The people on my job at the bank kept asking, "Do you have anything or anybody waiting there for you?" "No." "Do you at least have a place to stay?" "No." "You don't know anybody there?" "Nope. I'm not worried. God will take care of me." They were both amazed and a bit incredulous. But they all wished me well. I suppose it could have been looked upon as being very wreckless. But it would be an indicator of _how_ exasperated I was. AND pissed. And also – yes, I did have a very great faith that I would be provided for—by the Lord. The main thing was to get to the Land of Promise.

Upon my arrival, I was culture shocked at HOW fast one could get work there in Atlanta. Almost _every_ person I spoke with or made the acquaintance with there had some side line business, was a worker or a manager at another place of business, was in a position to take on another person for employment if so wanted…it was crazy! I had _four_ jobs in two weeks there! Finally, I found I was able to be selective, and took on the daytime, full-time or contract full-time positions available. By the way, let me mention. As of this date, now in 2006—I have _yet_ for my B.A. degree to pay off for me, or to be instrumental in my having been hired _anywhere_ that was long lasting and well paying.

Once again it was on public transit, their MARTA train, that I picked up the Transit Times leaflet in the slot, and it said they were recruiting for the MARTA police department. It was 1988 and the Democratic Convention was coming to Atlanta. The Metropolitan Atlanta Rapid Transit Authority was, therefore, needing to beef up its police force. A thing I noticed about Georgia…it seemed that _every agency_ and almost every company there had its own Police force. Georgia State, the colleges, the Georgia Building Authority, the Georgia World Congress Center, the Federal Reserve Bank, all the suburbs connecting to the main cities, the Post Office, the Federal Buildings, the private colleges & universities, and yes, the Transit Department. And hired I got, at the age of 31.

Chapter Two

AND NOW TO START

YOU KNOW, everybody likes to talk about the South. The South. The KuKlux South. When I was getting my Bachelor's degree at the University of San Francisco through an Army R.O.T.C. scholarship in 1979 through 1981 California, one of the R.O.T.C. Majors, when I told him I was thinking about relocating to Georgia, said, "I don't like the way you're treated in the South." Yes, that's right folks…laugh. Laugh heartily. Because supposedly "liberal" California was the first place I'd been in my life where I ran into real, true, raw, naked racism. You haven't seen people with problems toward those who've stayed in the oven too long like you do there. I had complained to my mother, when I was a little girl, "Oooo – the south, the south! The Ku Klux Klan!" etc., etc. And my Mom would say, "A Klan member is nothing but just an honest White man! He doesn't pretend to like you! He lets you know, up front, where you stand, that he hates and will do something to you if he gets the chance, etc." And when I got out on my own, I learned the value in dealing with an honest individual. Honesty. That's one virtue that will cause greater correction and healing that many other remedies. It's much, MUCH better to have a bottle of poison marked, "POISON," with the skull and the cross bones on the label than to have that same poison in a pitcher marked,

"Minute Maid or Kool-Aid." Because not knowing what it is when you get thirsty you will drink it. Then, you will surely die.

In Georgia...they give you a <u>job.</u> Quickly. It may not be excellent in pay, but at least you have a way to live. In the North, there's no concern whether you live or die. "Sorry, we don't have anything available! You'll have to take your 5 diplomas, your 3 degrees, your summa cum laude ranking in college and try somewhere else!" In the meantime, you return to that place later and there's a kid in there going, "Du-u-h-h! Du-u-uh, Ahhh, awww, uhmmm, uhuhuh" ...just so it's not one of <u>*you*</u>. And like Mahatma Gandhi said, "Poverty is the worst form of violence."

After the successful completion of the police academy in Marietta, Georgia, two of us were assigned to the Sergeant who oriented us into a few facts right away. Most of the bus calls we would be called to...the majority of the time, it is the <u>bus driver</u> who is the one who instigated the trouble in the first place. Not knowing how to talk to people. In fairness to them, though, yes, there *were* times when it was a drunk and/or disorderly rider. Treat people, he said, like we'd want to be treated, but within reason. That did and does cut down on a lot of negativity that could happen. Don't ever let them (the problem person we're dealing with) get away with calling you a "bitch," or otherwise cussing you out in front of people. Because if we let that go, the public will say, "Well MARTA police ain't shit!" and so on.

When we were assigned our actual FTO (field training officer) I was assigned a tough as nails, no nonsense street cop from one of Florida's police departments. She had relocated to Atlanta, also, because she had worked for them for five years, and they'd refused to promote her. And she told me how incredulous they were and how their jaws dropped open when she resigned from their department. One prime thing to keep in mind about all this, along with our less than positive experiences in the work world... when we would be hired aboard (on any job) we were gung ho all the way. Totally devoted. And trust me when I tell you...although we **know** how we've been done, and HOW unfairly we've been treated...when we actually get hired on to a job, we've always given our absolute best. And we, I repeat – WE get exasperated with those who complain and complain constantly about, "The White Man!" And we usually make ourselves scarce from those persons or just let them blow steam and then go on with business. I wish that my sharing this info would do some positive good for us in the minds of those in White America, but my experience and observation is that the more they see us being tolerant and non-complaining, the much more abuse we get.

Once I started full swing into the law enforcement world as a police officer, my first impressions were that I began to feel like "baby sitter of the world." For you literally had to be everything-to-everyone--guidance-counselor/parent/teacher/disciplinarian/marriage counselor/baby-sitter/mother/father/big sister/big brother/friend/advisor ---you name it. And then, of course, came learning how to effect arrests. With my FTO being a tough, aggressive, street cop the arrests were many. I had to get braced for and hardened against being too slack with some jokers out here. One of the things I noticed right away was that the same individual persons primarily got arrested over and over again! Yes, there were plenteous folks out there cutting up and doing this and that. But the same individuals (and almost always for the same offenses) kept and keep getting yanked up by us. Usually, it was because they couldn't stop drinking and getting drunk, or because they continually tried to jam/block or otherwise tamper with the faregates for the receipt of tokens, skilled pick-pockets, etc. When it came to persons who wanted to "put up resistance", for that time and era, it was only batons, and hands. You WERE NOT authorized to pull your gun on an unarmed individual. If he or she struck or fought you, you just had to strike and/or fight back. But that was the one thing I did and do like about our department. No guns to ever be drawn unless you were reasonably sure they were armed. This was 1988. With Atlanta's being well and reasonably integrated, the MARTA police force was well representative of such. When I was finally released to be on my own, thankfully, I was 31 years old and had, as such, a reasonable degree of maturity when it came to dealing with individuals as needed. You know, for the most part, my day was spent chatting with and becoming familiarized with vendors, patrons, faregate attendants and rail supervisors, bus drivers and bus supervisors. My direct supervisor at that time, on the North-East precinct line, was a reason-ably friendly natured young white guy about my age whose name was the same as a well-known singer. He was very country in his accent and talk. If you're familiar with those Hannah-Barbera cartoons of the mid 1960's just imagine Punkin' Puss, the cat, of the Hillbilly Bears, and that was him to the tee. While he may have had a friendly demeanor, though, he steadily and consistently underrated and gave me down right piss-poor, sorry evaluations on my performance. I know this is a case of "my side/his side" commentary. But no matter how hard I worked, how many suc-cessful arrests I made, had letters of thanks and so on from customers I served, I (and we began to notice) ALL Black females who worked for him – all got half-assed, so-so, screwed up evaluations from him. Evaluation systems for us at that time were based on the supervisors' being able to "articulate" in the narrative about you why you were worthy of a good rating. The rating system was based on "1" (lowest) to "6" (highest). All we could get were "2's" and "1's". The other Black men got "3's" and "4's". And the white guy on the squad got "5's" and "6's". And about all he spent his time doing was bothering the vendors around the patrol area and writing up papers/com-plaints about "improper" paperwork, or other improperly dotted "I's" and crossed "T's". The fact that those same vendors were always still there – AFTER being, to my humble opinion, unnecessarily jacked up, pointed to the fact that there wasn't any real reason to go out of one's way to bother them. This would point to a phenomenon that I began to notice was a routine occurrence whenever it came to Black people making an income that they could actually *live* on.

When I would ask Punkin' Puss what I had to _do_ to improve my evaluation, he would say, "Y'know, work hard. Do somethin' outta the ordinary. Make me look good." Well, during the course of the time with him, I had come up with the idea of posting the codes, signals, and other vital informational statistics like addresses to the stations, etc., on the wall of the staff room in order to save time and trouble in *trying* to locate that stuff, which was always in out of the way places, or else nowhere to be found. The sergeant praised me on this, and the entire departments began to do such. I was even the one who had to oversee the different precincts information gathering and posting up of this info. Later, as the system began to grow and more information needed to be gathered, the idea came up to put this all into a folder which would be placed in every staff room as a reference manual. Then, we got a white male officer who decided to come up with individual reduced sized "reference manuals" for us all to carry around with us. For that HE was paid. The rest of us, including me, were only thanked, but otherwise not compensated for that idea. It didn't occur to me that we *could* be, beyond evaluations. But <u>he</u> was. Speaking of evaluations, I was promised by Punkin' Puss that I would have this work reflected on my upcoming evaluations. Not only were they never referenced, this sergeant only came up with some *other* excuse everytime, to give me "1's" and "2's" in my ratings. Once it was, "Puts too much information in the police reports". Huh??? If you didn't put necessary information covering all that was necessary, it would be kicked back. One complaint (which proved to be totally unjustifiable) was from some prejudiced white guys not on the system over my not single-handedly tackling and thus fighting three men (all by myself) who had done nothing to them! Nothing ever came of their complaint about the three men...but Punkin' Puss's contention was that the white wise guys complained to him about my not attempting to tackle these dudes based on just their word alone. "But I'm glad you *didn't*!" he said. "Y'know, don't get hurt out here."

Yet, that was cause for acting like the <u>entire</u> evaluation period had to be lowered to those low ratings because of *that* only. I'd had perfect attendance throughout my first evaluation period, having taken one vacation period which you get with a leave slip turned in at least two weeks in advance. I was placed, not in category One for perfect attendance. Not even in category Two for being there most of the time. But in Category Three for missing days????? So, in other words...I don't have the right to even take vacation without being penalized in attendance? That was the only thing I could think of. By the way, your evaluation determined how much of a raise you got. Needless to say, mine was way down piss poor.

Being newly hired onto the force, and not wanting to make any waves, or appear to be difficult, I didn't do too much protesting as I probably should have. As it's called, you "go along to *get* along". Some of the fellows both from my academy class as well as some of the personnel already there for awhile were having their own difficulties. It seemed that Neal P. (who transferred to the sheriff's department and with better results) was a departmentally well-known dynamo. He was famed by all of us for single-handedly taking on two to three violent perpetrators at once, and downing them all. Neal had been assigned one of the white females from our academy class to train. She was a pretty timid individual who ended up immediately being allowed to transfer to the radio dispatch department. But the stories of how he had busted, caught, and successfully arrested (without getting hurt) several drug, gun and other illegal weapon carrying suspects by himself or with very little help enthralled us. We heard about how he had just taken on two more persons that he was going to have to struggle with and arrest while his trainee was literally quaking where she stood. Nonplussed, Neal, without complaint, simply told her, "Hold my hat!" and dived upon them without her assistance, and successfully made the arrest. Why wasn't he properly acknowledged by the department? We heard that instead, he was called on the carpet by the higher ranking officials (White, of course) and told, "Look—you're making it look like there's *crime* on MARTA! All these arrests…you're going to have to cut down." Yes, folks, you heard me right. He was <u>never</u> properly recognized or thanked for his bold daring, but instead, as I was to find out and learn later about the whole shebang here in these United States, such actions were NOT GOING TO BE RECOGNIZED or properly acknowledged—as long as it is coming from <u>US</u>! They *don't want to have to acknowledge* <u>**you.**</u> They only want to recognize <u>each other</u> for even the most miniscule of actions. I'll spell out several examples of such later in this memoir.

One White officer who was supposed to have saved somebody's life who was wayside (that's on the danger track way where the trains come) was immediately promoted to sergeant, paid a sum of money (we can't find out how much), placed on TV commercials, and basically had it "made in the shade" because of such. I found out later that things weren't as rushed and sudden as the "powers that be" had attempted to make it sound, in order to prop up "heroics" on that officer's part. Neal should have been thanked and rewarded. Instead, he was only castigated. He soon afterward, as was earlier mentioned, went to work at one of the county sheriff's departments.

Two other Black female officers came to work for Punkin' Puss, and had similar problems to mine. Being docked in attendance for authorized vacation (of COURSE this wasn't being done to anybody else), being given two's and one's in evaluation, one of them he even sexually harassed, and she made a complaint and was quickly given a small amount of money (to shut her up), and so on. Frieda, who was very dark complexioned, and also very sweet, and who single-handedly arrested mugs who'd looked like they'd axe-murdered their parents finally took some steps on her own to stop the unfair evaluations. About all she really succeeded in getting accomplished (after she bitterly complained to the Captain) was getting a "3" in her evaluation ratings, which was nearly unheard of for us Black female officers. The Whites got "4's", "5's" and "6's". Basically, for showing up, breathing, and going home. And their promotion to sergeant, then lieutenant, then precinct commander, was pretty much in the bag. Only excuse after excuse was come up with to keep from promoting <u>us.</u>

Well, in 1989 two very positive changes came about for us on the whole. Number one, apparently some "tired of being shat on" officers decided to take on the department for the lopsided evaluation unfairnesses. Not only were we arbitrarily being discriminated against because of who we were, but those sergeants who did not have a command of the English language and therefore were unable to articulate why we should be given higher numbers, was also a factor in our being held back in pay and promotion.

I'm convinced some sort of legal action was about to be taken, because the above mentioned complaint had *been* being made for awhile, and no action had been taken. Yet, we who'd experienced lower raises were suddenly notified in a memorandum that due to some kind of (well explained) 'glitch in the paperwork, thus, error to be corrected,' a lump sum payment amounting to about $2,340 there or abouts was to be made to the officers on the attached list. My name, included. I *knew* it was because the department had been caught and exposed, and now they were trying to cover their tracks real quick.

The second great occurrence was that the department was now going to allow us police officers the right to choose the precincts we wanted to work out of, rather than just being assigned to one. It was a right similar to the bus drivers' right to choose garages to work out of. We were overcome with joy. The one's of us who'd been suffering the punishments of working in the Northeast Precincts with their politics, babying and coddling to the wealthy persons in that area quickly transferred *outta* there! We went to work the South and West lines. And Oh, what a difference a location makes! As well as better and fairer supervisors to work for. Things quickly and wonderfully improved for a lot of us. You could understand the lousy, screwed up evaluations if we were sorry, lazy, didn't know how to talk to people, ended up with complaint after complaint from the public, had regularly beaten up or victimized people, or otherwise been a thorn in the side of the department. But we had committed none of those infractions as far as the paying, riding public went. When I would try to talk to my fellow co-workers and ask them their opinion about what on earth was I doing wrong, they all pretty much told me the same thing: "Janet—you're a *threat* to them. You're intelligent. You write wonderful reports. You sound beautiful on the radio. When you were first heard on Radio, everybody was saying, 'Who's that?' You sounded so articulate. You've got a college degree...**you** should be the one to be sergeant. And these ol' dumb necks...they see you as a threat. That's why they keep doing you like they're doing you." Although that was awfully complimentary, I still wasn't going to be the one to challenge or be a pain to my higher ups. And I still wanted to get my raises and a good evaluation. And these folks were *still* my supervisors, although I did find myself beginning to get a growing, seething, writhing bitterness rising in me. Again, no matter *how* many times I would ask *them* what I needed to do to get better evaluations, and I would be told, "Oh, make me look good...do this and that..." etc., when I would DO these things – with gusto, and meet all their demands, when my evaluation came, I found that not only had those 'done with gusto things' been totally not acknowledged...they had come up with *something else* to downgrade me for. In case you think that maybe I <u>had</u> screwed up in one or another type of something, let me tell you as a former supervisor, myself...if you're genuinely "screwing up" in a particular area it's the supervisor's job to alert you to it. In order to give you time to fix it, adjust it, stop it, or whatever. This is so you won't get a screwed up evaluation. No, this joker was just plain *inventing* stuff to downgrade me about, and catching me totally by surprise. If it was something I was really doing wrong, then why didn't you say something about it before?

I was staying in a rooming house in the Ashby Street area near Ashby MARTA station during the first eighteen months with the department. And unfortunately while I was living there my room was entered and I had some of my police equipment stolen, which I had to agree to allow the department to deduct payment for it from my paycheck The amount was about $65 or so per pay period, and until the $1,868, there or abouts, that was due was satisfied. Needless to say, this incident was also showing up on my evaluation as, "failing to take care of department equipment", although I was the victim of theft. As far as they or *he* was concerned, it was my fault.

CHAPTER THREE

AND NOW I BECOME RESURRECTED

AS THOSE OF US who chose to "get the hell out of the Northeast precinct" as we put it, we experienced a new and positive rebirth as far as the damaged reputations some of us had been saddled with while up north. We had new supervisors, newer and better put evaluations, and a much more positive work environment. And now I come to the Star of this police story shedding light show. Lieutenant Carol Downin. Yes, it's Downin, not "Downing". The name is Irish, she told me. Yet she's still African-American, like most of the rest of us who have Irish and Scottish surnames. When I went to work for her at the Five Points location she was still Sergeant Downin. And Corporal Paul Reed was the assistant supervisor. She and Cpl. Reed had a lengthy talk with me at roll call when we who had transferred there were part of her new squad. She talked about the severely damaged reputation I had managed, somehow, to end up with from the Northeast line. It seemed that I had been talked about and presented as the biggest "Fuck Up" MARTA had ever seen, no doubt spurred and encouraged by the likes of Punkin Puss and his ilk. Sgt. Downin told me, "You've been talked about more than the Man in the Moon!" Although, as we were all very aware, those officers who had gone on calls with me, and I on calls with them, had no real problems or difficulties to complain about concerning me. Oh, sure, there are going to be minor disagreements about some things here and there. That's with any place. However, the tiniest disagreement that may have occurred (with only one individual on Punkin Puss's squad) was greatly highlighted up and magnified, so that the word went out that none of the other officers wanted to work with me. Sgt. Downin told me that she had taken the time to meet with some of the officers out there and talk to them about me. She said that in reality, although I was reputed to be the worst thing to happen to MARTA in its history, and that they were reluctant to work with me, when it came to our having no choice, having been dispatched together to some calls, that when it came actually working with me, they never did experience any problems or difficulties. "So, I don't know how you ended up with this reputation, and we're going to have to see what we can do to undo it." In the meantime, there were officers who did manage to justifiably earn their bad reputations, primarily the ones who couldn't be depended upon to back up their fellow officers on dangerous calls. And the racists. But mostly, the real problem was faulty supervisors. The ones who would write you up for miniscule mistakes simply because some really racist lieutenant and above wanted you written up. And the immediate Black sergeants or corporals wouldn't have the balls enough to stand up to them and tell them "No." But then, that was the way they ensured their promotions. Which leads me to another type of person there—and that was the White officers who weren't "white", so to speak. That is, they were White, descriptively, but when it came to being foul racists, and unfair in their practices toward others who were minorities or women, they weren't. These guys either never or barely got promoted, thanks to their not playing Ball with their entrenched department heads who wanted "certain things done," shall we say. One of these White officers was married to a Black woman. "Oh, my God!" the other Black officers would joke... "You can sneak around with us, but you're NOT supposed to MARRY us!" And of course, this was to mimic the sentiments of dominant White society. The other two that I was aware of were both from my academy class. One did NOT have those "vibes" coming out of him that some Whites, try as they might to hide it, usually exude when they're around us. And he was very, very quiet. Did his job excellently. The other had graduated at the top of the class. When we finally went to an exam system for the promotion to sergeant and above, he also passed at the top of that. But the department sabotaged (that's right) his chances and reputation, I believe by attempting to insinuate that he had failed some kind of psychological evaluation. Anybody who knows him knows that's bunk. We all ascertained that it was because the higher ranking department officials knew that they would never be able to "control" him. In other words, if one of the racist lieutenants or captains were to pull him aside and tell him to "write him/or her up" over something that was in reality truly unjustified, they knew John wouldn't do it. And since he'd scored too high for them to refuse him the promotion, this was the only thing they could resort to in order to boot him out of his chance for promotion. Speaking of the exam system for promotion to sergeant and above, it was supposedly handled through the one of the college systems there. And each and every time they would give the exam, for some reason or another, the department would claim that there was something "wrong" with the results and it would have to be taken again. This happened again and again. One of the Black lieutenants confided to me that what it was, every time they got the results back, when those persons passed it whom they did not want to make sergeant/and when those persons failed, whom they did want to make sergeant, the test would be given again. And again. And again, as necessary, until the scores could either be tampered with, or some kind of fluke could get their desired ones over.

Even so, the less than desirable officers to work with, as was earlier described, had managed to play political handball with the higher ups, and were able to be assigned nice cushy assignments or be able to lay low for the most part. But of them, it was spoken in hushed tones (we'll get to the "blue wall of silence" later) that it was prayed to God to _never_ have to go on a call with one of them because you couldn't depend on them to get to a call with you and give you back up. I was always running to my calls whenever we had a "hot" call given… "fare evader," "gun or knife violation/possession," "fight in progress," and so on. Of course you're nervous. Of course you're a little scared. The veterans out there will tell you, "If anyone says out here that they're _not_ scared, they're either lying or crazy." However, especially due to my prior military orientation, I did not want the reputation of arriving too slowly at a hot call. That's my co-worker out there. I will not be caught in a situation where I have to try to explain where I was! And those few officers during that recovery period of mine who did have some sympathy for me, as far as my terrible reputation, attempted to prep me up by telling me about how among themselves they always said, "Well I would rather go on a call with Janet than with so and so. Because, at least, SHE'S coming to back you up!"

When I was in full swing with Sgt. Downin, I'd been put in the squad car to drive on my own, for the very first time, because I supposedly wasn't supposed to know how to do it when I was up North. I was given more responsibilities, and to my great joy, a chance to expand my experience in greater areas with the department. When Sgt. Downin finally took the time to thoroughly examine all my records from up North, she held a meeting/conference with Captain Neely, another White sergeant, and me. She began to actually bristle at some of the things she found that had been done to me when I was working up there. There were only minor things I had been aware of that I knew wasn't right. But she found more things in the records, and questioned more things that were incidences of omission as well as commission on the part of that Sergeant. She held the meeting for more than two hours going over the fact that I had never been assigned to things by him that I needed to be assigned to if I was going to get out of probation. There were tasks that we all were required to do that he also never put me to, supposedly because I would have left a mushroom cloud over where MARTA once stood if I got my grubby little paws on it. I was downgraded for never being assigned to mobile patrol, etc., etc. And then evaluated accordingly for never having performed those tasks. She was livid. "How the HELL can she be given "1's" all the way across the board if he's never going to assign it to her??? How are you gonna punish her with a screwed up evaluation for not doing thus and such if you're <u>never</u> going to put her ass on it??? Wait a minute, Janet, did he EVER put you in a car?"

"No, sarge."

"Why <u>not</u>?"

"Because, supposedly, I don't know how to drive."

"You've got a car of your own, don't you?"

"Yeah!"

"So what was the problem?"

"Well, they think I may not be able to handle <u>that</u> car!"

"Why didn't he assign some of his own training officers to you in the car, then? He <u>knows</u> you *have* to drive the squad car if you're going to even keep this job!"

"Well, supposedly, none of them wanted to ride with me. I guess they thought I'd kill 'em!"

"Doesn't he have FTO's on his squad?"

"Yes, but what I heard, was that they didn't want to get with me."

"Wait a minute, Janet. He's the boss. <u>He's</u> the sergeant. He should have *ordered* those jokers to ride in the car with you!"

"Well, according to what *else* I was told by one of the guys who was in my corner, if he'd have done that, they would have called in, sick."

And by now, her voice fully raised, "IF IT WAS AS BAD AS <u>THAT</u> – **HE SHOULD HAVE** RIDDEN IN THE CAR WITH YOU!"

"Well, he did."

"How much time did he spend in the car with you?"

"He rode with me one time."

"How did he say you did?"

"He said I did real good."

"But then he never put you back in it?"

"Uhhh—no."

And Sergeant Downin was telling the Captain and fellow Sergeant, "That ain't right! That just ain't right!" Then it came out afterwards that along with my retained low pay due to bad evaluation that I was now having to come out of my own salary over $130 per month to pay for stolen police equipment in what was supposed to be a reasonably secure, bolted front and back door rooming house. She was just aghast and speechless. To see that all this had been done, plus the fact that I was having pay deducted for a theft. She and the Captain went off together to speak in hushed tones, and I overheard him telling her, basically agreeing that I'd been screwed numerous ways to one, and something needed to be done about it. I heard him telling her, "Let <u>me</u> see what <u>I</u> can do." And she approached me with the Captain walking a bit behind her. She came up very close to me and said in a very low tone, "I don't like what I've seen here, and neither does the Captain. We're going to see what we can do here because…" and coming even closer to my face and saying even lower…"we think you've been punished enough."

First, they assigned me to the squad car. On my own. My friends on the force told me that when they heard my voice over Radio for the first time on mobile patrol, they dropped their jaws and slowly turned their heads toward each other, a smile of happiness in my behalf coming over their face, and saying simultaneously, "Is that JANET!?" And she and Corporal Reed both worked on building up my confidence in myself, because the powers that be sure had me worked over in the self-assurance department. I said, "I sure don't know my way around the city very well. That's why I bought a car, so that I could get familiarized with these streets. What if I get lost?" "Get lost," they said. "That's the only way you're going to learn anyway. Just go on ahead and get lost. Call out on radio for one of us (either her or the corporal), tell us to change to the alternate channel, we'll go there, you tell us where you are, and we'll direct you onto familiar territory."

Next, was the amount of money being demanded of me to pay the department for the stolen equipment. They reduced the amount of money I had to give them every pay period down to $22.00. As the amount of money due began to reach the total amount, the corporal in charge of the finances for supply argued for my case to the department, and the balance, which was close to about $150 or so more was forgiven. Then they started working on my techniques and the way I dealt with folks. Since my FTO was a street cop and very able, her method of dealing with people was to grab them on up and take them in. So I did likewise. I always kept in the back of my mind that they could nut up and swing on me any given time, and the fact that I was spared this to any real violent fashion (because some surely <u>did</u> resist) I attributed my success at staying unhurt, thus far, to the protection of the Lord. Well, when Sgt. Downin and Cpl. Reed weighed in on this they said, "Now one thing, Garnett. You are small. You're gonna have to stop grabbin' these folks!" Cpl. Reed continued, "Yeah, you're not being paid to engage in Championship Wrestling! Just do your job, do what you need to do, and if you <u>have</u> to, <u>then</u> affect your arrest."

So that's how it went. I now had a more positive atmosphere with more positive people to work for. They were in my corner. I didn't have to keep one eye trained on perpetrators, and another eye on hostile supervisors out to burn me. It became a very satisfying time. And that was only because of not being weighted down with deliberate unfairnesses. Sgt. Downin had said to me during this period and of my recalling Punkin Puss's antics, "Garnett, he fucked you. He KNOWS he fucked you. But there is a God." And I knew she meant that He would get things straightened out for me and all of us as far as eventual just desserts would go. In His own time and in His own way. For the time being, though, I had to learn to not complain about the past. As Les Brown had put it, "Why complain? Because whoever you're complaining to, number one they don't *care*. And number two, they glad it's *you*!"

CHAPTER FOUR

IN FULL SWING

AS THE TIME BEGAN TO TURN INTO YEARS, Sgt. Downin had become Lt. Downin. I went to work for a Sgt. F, a Black sergeant who was the biggest kiss-ass this side of the Camptown Ladies singin' that song, "Doo Dah", and working along with squad members of his who were devoted and hard working good people to work with. When it came time for evaluations again, he too had begun to give me some poor rated numbers. When I asked him why, he was not able to adequately explain why. In fact, he only repeated his down-grading sentences in the narrative about me. If you're familiar with the old, "In Living Color" show that starred the Wayans', you'll recall Damon Wayans' character where he used all these 60 and 70 dollar complicated words, and didn't know what the hell he was talking about. Well that was Sgt. F. He'd attempt to talk a good sounding speech, but made little sense. He was also very young. In addition to giving me a badly justified low rating, he also pulled some dirty little stunts like calling me at home while I was on vacation and about a non-emergency situation, which would have been the only justification for doing it. And then tell me to call a police property room, or something like that (which he should have and could have done) while I'm off. Of course, I would practically be yelling at him, because not only was my family at home and I was supposed to be unbothered visiting with them, but because I knew that he knew better. However, as I was told in private, another officer in the precinct at work during the time of the call told me that she said to him, "I can't believe you called that girl at home while on vacation." And he'd just laugh. Another more mature sergeant I later went to work for, when I told him of this incident said, "He knew better than to do that." Well, with my trying to give the benefit of the doubt way of thinking, I told the older sergeant that I chalked up what F had done as due to his being thoughtless and immature. "NO, Janet," he said. "He KNEW better. He knows he was in the wrong." And still, with my forgiving heart, I said, a-a-a-h-h-h, he's just immature. And again, with very deliberate, measured tones, firmly emphasized one word at a time, "NO, JANET...HE—WAS—HARRASSING—YOU." Some time afterwards, though, I was told by another officer friendly toward me and in my corner that F was doing something with the paperwork in his office, and she overheard him nearly whispering to himself, "I sure am glad I've got Garnett here and handling this." And the officer there said to him, "Oh. You found out Garnett's not a fuck-up after all!" And she said that he had confessed in resigned tones, "Yeah, I guess I was just listening to what everybody else said about her and I was just evaluating her by what they said." But I knew in my gut that he was only talking about Punkin Puss. And that apparently, he'd inspired him to hand me those insults. Afterwards, he too improved my evaluations.

MARTA began to want to have on hand at the precinct a "paddy wagon" for the transport of multiple prisoners. I was now driving just about everything on wheels MARTA police department had. Even vehicles I had no idea of how to drive, like 3 speed Cushman scooters, which I had to learn in about 20 minutes how to operate. The rickety-rackety paddy wagon was some poor bread truck shaped van with non-stable mirrors on the side, and NO WINDOWS except for the driver's side and windshield. It was IMPOSSIBLE to see where one was going or what was coming. And I had to drive that freaker every single day from downtown Five Points all the way up to Lindbergh Headquarters by way of the expressway to pick up and deliver inter- department mail. I literally had to change lanes on prayer... "Please don't let nuthin' be comin'/Please don't let nuthin' be comin'/Please don't let nuthin' be comin'...ahhhh, relief," as I had moved into a right lane safely. Because as I said, the side mirrors jiggled out of place because of the motion, and you *could not see a thing* if it was coming on your passenger side or from behind you. I finally decided to take some action before one of us killed ourselves in that thing. I stole away and drove to the Radio repair shop which was on DeKalb Avenue at the time, and talked some of the repairmen there into graciously allowing use of their screw driver and repair expertise in tightening those mirrors. Next, after talking with some higher department heads, they OK'd the purchase of two of those small concave mirrors to attach inside the main side mirrors. That helped things *a lot*...for everybody.

Ever since I had been first assigned to the car, it seemed that things occurred where I was always in it *all the time*! And, of course, the car was a highly desired assignment to have (apart from being asked to do lunch runs for everybody), as you were riding and rolling instead of having to be on your feet. It seemed I had the reputation of being where I was supposed to be, instead of "all over creation" as it was suspected of my fellow squad members. No amount of work, calls, or assignments seemed too much to me…I was so anxious to be of "use" and to satisfy my supervisors…who were NOW evaluating me accordingly.

One of my Sergeants had joked about my report writing style. Since I was the known "writer", having aspirations as such, he told me that my initial reports, when I was new on the job, read like a thrilling novel. He said, "You know, it's like, 'It was a cool summer day! His hand ran down her silken thigh…her chest heaved with anticipation…' You know, it's like a novel. I'll be hanging on (demonstrating with a leaned over posture as if reading an adventure story's climax) to see what happened next! Just tell the facts. 'This happened/that was who it happened to/this is where/then what the circumstances were. That's all!" Of course, he was exaggerating some bit. Due to my wanting to leave no detail out, I was as thorough and careful with my descriptions as possible. But I thereafter fixed it, and put in "just the facts." He would then, several times afterward when he saw me, grin and lull on… "It was a co-o-o-l summer breeze! He placed his hand upon her heaving sun drenched shoulder…!" Apologists for Punkin Puss' earlier mentioned downgrading me with the comment, "Puts too much information in the police reports," this was when I was still in training with my FTO, and I hadn't even gone to work for him yet. Apparently, the word must have gone out, no doubt with affectionate humor from our area, and P P's getting wind of it, used it as a stab against me when he was looking for things to find wrong with me. He never aggrieved over my reports, apart from minor nuances to either change or add to, which was common in almost all report writing, and they were always passed on with his approval. I went to work for three various supervisors during this period from 1989 until 1991. After LT. Downin and CPL. Reed would patiently listen to me blow off steam about how I'd been done up North, and some of my co-workers began to disengage me in my tirades about it, I began to pick up on that fact that I should concentrate my thoughts AND speech on more positivity. My severely damaged reputation was becoming repaired. I was doing my job with nearly no trouble, either from "perps," which is what we called out criminals and arrestees, or from the general public with whom I found more and more joy to be around, as well as my fellow MARTA employees.

One of my police co-workers, Ronald, whom everybody called, "Tee," had always been a regular source of encouragement for me during my "rough" period. When things had begun to improve for me under LT. Downin and I was in to about my third year there he told me the following in private: "You know, Janet, just look around the department. ALL the folks who had downed you, talked about you all crazy, said you were 'this' and you were 'that' (I knew he meant the guys on my squad), they're all gone now…" They *did* end up leaving or being released from MARTA for everything from sickness to questionable actions in their duties. "And _you're_ still here! See, everything works out! God sees to that!" I got little pick ups like that during my opening year there, as if God _was_ holding my hand and bracing me up not to fall down. I had said at that time to one fellow employee, "You know, I'm working so hard. I'm doing so much. And nobody seems to be watching." I cannot recall whether this was one of the bus drivers, faregate attendants, or what. But I guess the message they gave me was what counted. Because I'll remember the rest of my days that the answer seemed to be from Him on high, rather than from the employee who told me, and that was, "Don't worry, Janet...<u>Somebody's</u> watching."

Chapter Five

ARRESTEES AND THEIR VARYING GRIPES

I FIGURE *SOMEWHERE* ALONG THE WAY YOU ALL ARE WONDERING, "Is she <u>ever</u> gonna talk about <u>arrests</u> and dangerous moments on the job from *<u>criminals</u>*???" Yes, I am, and do I have some doosies to tell you about as far as <u>who</u> my back up came from during these years. When it came to my first dealings with placing handcuffs on people I felt a sinking feeling of discomfort within my chest. Here we were catching, holding and then depriving an individual of their freedom of movement. The cause for that individual's arrest was being publicly drunk and disorderly. To my layperson's way of thinking, why couldn't we just send them on their way? I had some things to learn, and had some re-orienting of thought that had to occur. When persons have to call the police, think about the circumstances—normally, anyway. You've got some joker out with or around you. There's nothing else you can do with this individual. Talk is no good. Actions are too risky for you the civilian public to take with him. He can't be reasonably negotiated with to come to some satisfactory conclusion for all sides. You decide to call the police. When WE arrive, that's it. All talk is over. It's, "Sir, come with me!" "I ain't goin' no goddamn where!" Then out comes our hands, grabbed up is the individual, carried out, escorted out, led out, whatever, and once again, "SIR! Come with me!" And because MOST persons out there may or will do you bodily harm for violating/touching their person, that's why we need: 1) Legal authorization to do so, by way of the badge which symbolizes the right and duty the issuing entity gives us the AUTHORITY to do: And 2) Varying degrees of weapons or restraining tools to use only on an escalating degree—all the way up to the service revolver or semi-automatic handgun in the taking of a life if need be. As one of our police academy instructors put it, "You—have the authorization to take someone's life if absolutely necessary. The State is giving you the right to kill someone if you have to." As is already granted, you better be able to absolutely justify it if you do. Trust me, I'm fully aware of the rash of police shootings of unarmed Blacks by squadrons of White officers over wallets, combs, cell phones and pagers. The real reason for all of this is the absence of accountability the powers that be keep refusing to hold them in. If you've got somebody who has issues, whether it be toward certain groups or certain spouses, that's going to show in their work. The problem is with the governing authorities that keep letting them walk. If they knew punishment was certain, the incidences of this would be greatly reduced. To date, the only action I've seen taken against an officer was the Black one at the Atlanta Hartsfield-Jackson Airport where the White woman caught him on her side view mirror, which spun him completely around and injured him. His only response, instead of shooting her 15 times which would have happened had she been Black and he'd been White, was to pull her out of her car, throw her to the ground and handcuff her. The powers that be QUICKLY came to HER defense, made the department drop all charges against her, and the officer was fired. If he'd shot her, do you think all the forces above that ALWAYS LOOK OUT FOR WHITE OFFICERS WHO KILL BLACKS UNJUSTIFIABLY would have looked out for him???

When the local Atlanta news channels showed the tape of the incident, the part where he was hooked by the mirror, after he cursing out tirade to him, was blanked out. It just resumed where he was taking her out of the car and throwing her to the ground.

He should talk to the $2 million dollar man in Los Angeles. That White police officer was given $2 million dollars for complaining about being shown punching a handcuffed sixteen year old Black youth in the face. He said, "You didn't show any Black officers doing anything!" And he was compensated for that! On with the arrestee gripes.

My FTO had to orientate me on a few procedures when it came to making the decision to effect an arrest. As I mentioned earlier, we're not there to talk or negotiate, per se, we're there to de-escalate or end a particular problem involving persons who are armed, violent, intoxicated, etc. Our job is not to continue the talk. That can and usually does come afterwards...but only after you've compelled the offending party or parties to come with you, out of the area, to a neutral location, etc. After all parties either have or are cooperating—then you can allow those sides' views to be heard. Sometimes it's a dispute over something both lay claim to—and they can't wait for Judge Wopner to decide. Or it's a "he said/she said" situation, and if no injuries or violence was involved you can let them work it out later, separate the two until one goes one way and the other another. If it's a fight, you generally have to arrest or cite both parties equally and let a judge figure it out at court. Sometimes you can haul the arrestee in for an offense right there. Or, if you decide under some circumstances you can be lenient, you can give them a "copy of charges," which is a formal writing and ticket of arrest, but the person doesn't have to go to jail and spend some time in a cell. If you deem they can be trusted to show up for court, you schedule them for up to two weeks later for a specific date and time. We would usually do this for people who 1)had a swell & cooperative attitude: 2)were gainfully employed and we didn't want to put their job on the line: 3)had kids to take care of, and if you took him/her away you had to await another relative or near guardian to come and get them. That could take *time*. Otherwise, the Department of Family & Children's Services (DEFACS) would have to be notified and the child or children taken *there*. And that would be something you *really* wouldn't want to have to do that. Talk about victimizing the innocent.

And then, there are those "winners"...people that stand up in the train seats, or who move back to the rear of the bus they've been ordered off of, and yell, threaten, curse and want to fight. A quick word about those subjects who are armed with guns. I always give all thanks and ALL credit to the Lord for my protection on ALL my hot or dangerous calls. I noticed that those persons who we took guns off of were, when disarmed, among the most polite, gentle, cooperative and docile people you'd ever want to deal with. The ones who *weren't* armed with *anything* – either gun, knife, or whatever—the ones who were just relying on their own bare dukes... THEY were the ones that it would take between five to seven of us to get subdued. There were some big guys out there that would put up a horrendous fight. And some little guys whom the men on the force had most of their horror stories about having to actually fight. You've heard of the "little man" syndrome. Some rather big cats on the force, over 6 feet tall, talked about how they would rather have to fight two or three big dudes rather than one little short man. Because the short, little men whom if they determined to fight, would put up Hell on Earth, literally. And several officers have corroborated such. Oh, now they would eventually get the small man subdued and taken in, but that would be after that little man had literally "kicked the ass" of three of those bigger men than himself, and all by himself!

It's a mess dealing with girls. And teenaged girls. And teenagers, period. No, it doesn't have to culminate in pulling one's gun on them—if they're unarmed. They're just young, they don't understand the implications of some things, plus they're fit, agile, able bodied, fast, sturdy and smart. I've shared with people on so many occasions that when I was in my thirties, their sharp, sarcastic tongues didn't *bother* me like they do today. I'd just patiently deal with it. But now that I'm a cranky ol' middle-ager, I'm at the age now where I *can't STAND* a disrespectful young person. It does things to the nape of my neck now that I'm almost 50.

When we were required in the early part of 2000 to be put through pepper spray training one of the mandates of it, you'll note, was that WE had to be sprayed with that mess first. When it happened, I could appreciate the fact that we had to be introduced to *how bad* that stuff is! I wouldn't use it on Hitler if he were still around! That wasn't how my co-workers felt—"Man, I'd make Hitler EAT that shit!" I figured, "Oh, *now* I see why we have to experience that first." Because, I felt, if we didn't know how bad it was, we might be willing to spray anybody too soon. And also, I guess what the varying departments were really wanting to do was get us prepared and braced for it should there be any back splash from it.

And I truly felt the way that I claimed. That I wasn't gonna use that on ANYBODY! I was just going to use the old methods as required...baton, hold-ing techniques, etc. However, when I reached the age of 45 in 2002, those smart mouthed little 14 and 15 year olds had me out and readied (well not with the safety latch disengaged, anyway) with the spray as I chased them out of the station, with my yelling out to them, "I'm about to spray you like a little cockroach!!!" Ooooo, I would be bristling, so!

When we would be bringing in those persons under arrest (and again, usu-ally for being intoxicated, refusing to leave the station or refusing to exit the bus they were causing strife aboard, etc.), we would hear a prime clarion call among the arrestees:

"Y'all don't do **White folks** like that!" And that was due to the fact that our beat assignment areas were in largely African-American parts of town, thus, the trouble-makers would be, largely, Black folks, yes. I, for one, just couldn't see arbi-trarily yanking up and arresting a fare-evader. You could have 1000 arrests a week if you arrested ALL of them. I *will* say for argument's sake, that when I was up North, we were *required* to give fare evaders the option to pay or leave the station. Remember, that was the wealthier (and thus, Whiter) part of town. I took that op-tion and ran with it when I was working the downtown and West part of Atlanta. When I would spy them through our staff room glass jumping the gates, I would go out, confront, and make them go back out. Then tell them to pay or leave. If they put up an argument or got belligerent, I'd order them to exit the station. Upon their refusal to leave, I would give them a Criminal Trespass Warning, which was leave or be arrested. Then and only then would I effect an arrest. For something more tangible, in my view, than for attempting to dodge $1.25, which is what the fare was at that time. I was not the only officer who felt like that, by the way. Some people talked about how nearly embarrassed they'd be if, standing in court with Atlanta Police, DeKalb Police, etc. who had rapists, burglars, muggers, child abusers in front of the judge, her we'd come with somebody and when the judge asked the charge... "A dollar twenty-five."

When it was then that they would start that Malcolm X speech tirade of theirs, it would fall on deaf ears... "Ya can't do the time, don't do the crime." "Yeah, yeah, yeah." Or as I would tell them, "Hey, I gave you chance after chance to leave. You wouldn't go, Man! What was I supposed to do!?" I'd say I've personally experienced only four people who admitted they were wrong and silently accepted their being placed under arrest. As for the rest, another thing I learned was that people used to breaking the law have a different way of thinking from most of the rest of us. THEY did NOTHING wrong. Whether it's punch a spouse in the face, beat and rob an elderly person, hang a dog or a cat for their own personal sadistic delight, 3 Card Monte cheat people out of their money, or what have you, it's never _them_ that's to blame for their misfortune at being arrested and put behind bars. It's the fault of the victim they robbed or hurt, or, <u>especially,</u> it's OUR fault for catching and arresting them.

When I was briefly on Morning Watch (that's 10:30pm until 06:30am) I would listen in the patrol unit to the talk radio shows, and I heard John Walsh, crook finder extraordinaire, interviewed. At some point the interviewer asked Mr. Walsh if he'd ever gotten threats/death threats, etc. from the people captured due to his show's efforts.

"Constantly," he said, "constantly."

John Walsh, I learned later, is one of the few American citizens authorized to carry a gun _anywhere he goes_. Even places <u>we</u> can't carry a gun, i.e., aboard airplanes, in Federal Courts and other courtrooms, etc. He gets that many threats. Because, as John Walsh explained, "The criminals aren't thinking along the lines that _we're_ thinking. In other words <u>their</u> way of thinking is, 'I'm not in prison because I kidnapped, raped, and killed five little kids…I'm in prison because _John Walsh put me here!_' "

Some of the angry epithets and complaints loudly shouted at us from our arrestees were sometimes quite humorous. "Y'all don't do that when the WHITE MAN does it!"

"Y'all Uncle Tom Sambos!" "White Man's Fool! White Man's <u>tool</u>! <u>YASSUH, BOSS!!!</u>" We'd be silently laughing ourselves to coughs, some of them would be so hilarious.

One BIG pain in rear was having to arrest juveniles. Mainly because the paperwork involved that you had to complete was _crushing_. And then there was the matter of attempting to reach their parents to notify them of their being in our custody. You had to rely on the juvenile to give you their parents' correct name and where they worked so that you could hunt them down, and so on. Sometimes we were blessed in being able to contact their parent and then turn the youngster over to them, rather than take them into custody if their offense wasn't too serious. And then there were times when the parent would angrily tell us that they couldn't keep taking off work because of their wayward kid. I don't know what a whole heck of a lot of officers are experiencing these days, but at least in the late 1980's through early 2000, much of what <u>I</u> experienced was parents telling us to do what we had to do. No, they weren't negligent, uncaring parents. They were just not apologists… "MY boy would _never_ do such a thing!!!" I found also that a _lot_ of parents seemed unable to control their youngsters then-a-days as well as nowadays. When I would be on foot patrol on the platforms (where persons awaited the arrival of the trains) I would observe their bratty little tots climbing and running over seats, dashing too and fro on the platforms (always dangerous), and risking possible accident or injury. Their parents would appear powerless to stop them. I'm guessing it's because of busy-bodies who feel it's their business to interfere if you *might* have to swack them in public.

There's a reason why we're told in the scriptures we shall "swack his butt with the rod and save his soul from Hell" (*sic*). NO-O-O-O-O, I'm not talking about kicking them down steps, blacking both of their eyes, breaking bones or putting out your cigarette in their palms. And I'm not talking about killing them over clumsy mistakes and accidents that occur with small folks. But for <u>willful defiance</u>, and refusal to obey your orders, if they can't/won't or don't obey you from verbal command, and the defiance and or disrespect toward you continues, then as Rev. Joyce Meyer (whose teaching tapes I own dozens of) puts it: "Take junior out of the store (or whatever public place): Take junior out to the car: Take your switch or your belt: Take junior's pants down: And go to work. Then take junior back into the store: If junior's behavior continues...repeat steps One through Five." (*sic*). That's NOT child abuse. My best friend, Veronica A., I do believe, correctly observed the fact that Dr. Spock is probably responsible for more damaged and screwed up, disobedient children (and as a result), screwed up, twisted up adult generation of today than anybody we know. HE *never had any children* to raise. HE is not <u>qualified</u> to tell you and me how to raise *ours*. "Now, now, now...you never spank your children! It's due to anger...you're bigger than he is...you're teaching him it's alright to bully!" (*sic*) BULLSHPIT! (torn up spelling, mine). It's NOT about anger. It's not about bullying. It's because children *are* very smart, very clever, and they *know* how far they are able and allowed to go before you reach the point of no return. They're constantly observing what you do, what you care about, what your limit is, how to get what they want (ice cream, toys, TV programs, et. al.). But they also want to know you care enough to NOT let them have their way <u>all the time</u>...that there are *some* things they can't get by with. And you DON'T handle the situation by bribing, buying, negotiating or other types of stuff that is not appropriate for someone who's six years old and existing due to your feeding, sheltering, nurturing, clothing, caring, and yes—indulging him, largely, because it *does* give parents a great deal of satisfaction in seeing their child happy and carefree, playing with his toys, enjoying ice cream, etc. But you have to realize that this "Time Out" mess is only creating little monsters that will turn into BIG monsters that eventually, WE have to get called to deal with. There's an African proverb that goes, "If you give a child EVERYTHING he wants, he will hate you." Take a lesson from that, Folks. When well meaning busy bodies hear *your* child moaning, wailing, and *shrieking* as though he is dying, because you finally had to sting those little legs, it just tears at their heartstrings, doesn't it? As the Scripture puts it, "He may scream as though he is dying. But he won't die." If you will please note...if you take away a toy that he is playing with...he will scream as though he is dying. If you forbid him to go outside and play...he screams as though he is dying. Haven't you noticed that? And if you swing at his face and MISS...he screams as though he's dying. That's the child's natural reaction. People, would you please note...you are <u>not</u> his buddy. He is not <u>your</u> buddy. He's your <u>child</u>. <u>You</u> are the parent. You are not there for him to dictate to <u>you</u> how things will go. It's an authority figure to a subordinate situation. That's it. Once you tell him to do something or not to do it, you have _no business_ worrying in the back of your mind, "Ohhh, is he gonna obey me? Do I have to sit outside his window to make sure he minds/stays/doesn't sneak someone in," etc., etc.

What's this stuff about, "It's MY room, Mom...stay out!" If you let that little squid command you and YOU obey...what do you THINK you're going to end up with?

Before you all think I'm Adolph Sister, let me tell you—my six year old neice walks on her aunt's back with spike-healed shoes. She's a wonderful, somewhat spoiled little joy who does find ways to ease in things she wants to do or have. Yes, she does. And this is with an ultra-religious father who's one of those "Papa don't take no mess" types. He believes in the belt. Yes, he has had to use it. And she loves her daddy, madly. When he goes outside to smoke his beloved Dominican and Honduran cigars by Fuente, Davidoff, and Perdomo, she's planted at the door, "Daddy, are you comin' in yet?" "In a minute 'Mani." When they're playing with her Milton Bradley games, every time he wins, she balls up her little fist and punches him in the arm. In fact she punches on him so much that he told his wife to buy her one of those punch-bob dolls (the inflatable big red nose types). When I told her I always had funny feelings about those things, that it might instill some taste for aggression (I don't know _everything_—surprise, huh?), she told me, yeah, well he's tired of her punching on _him_!" Yet, her daddy and mommy won't take any kind of disobedience. She's been brought up with, "Yes, Ma'am" and "No, SIR," because she's been trained so. But, yes, with her auntie (me), I have to take her aside and whisper in her ear, "I'ma tell your Mommy on you..." "I'ma tell your Daddy on you..." And finally, when she gets wise to that, I just resort to threatening to not buy anymore popsicles to share with her. Then she goes, "OK, OK, OK, OK, OK, OK, OK!!!"

One of the most unruly young people we once had was a very tall sixteen year old young man who had nothing but mouth, sass, and defiance at everything, making the disciplinarian "parent" come out in the Sergeant who was backing me up on that call. When we were able to contact his mother (with great difficulty due to his deliberate wrong information he was giving us), I heard a resigned, protective, apologetic-in-his defense voice on the phone. When I made the unthinking mistake of asking her if she was aware of the large sum of money he had on his person (I had named the amount—dumb me), she again, sighed and hesitatingly said yes, she was aware of it. We knew she was lying. But she was trying to protect him. Some time after we cleared that call, the Sergeant and I looked at each other and almost simultaneously said together, "I see why that young man is like he is!" Non-discipline and non-accountability from his parent. The most egregious types of youths that we inevitably end up having to take into our custody are the one whose parents agonizingly say, "But he was never spanked! I just don't understand why he's this way!" That's IT, Lady! Because _he was never spanked_.

I didn't say nearly _killed_. And, yes, there is child abuse. Don't get me wrong. However, some of us would talk among each other, never mind other officers, but other department employees, period. They would point to each one of us, one by one while saying, "Look, you, you, him, her and me...we got out butts...BEAT! And WE didn't grow up to be problem people or criminals! WE ain't psychopaths!" And the generations before mine, and some with me now...they got beatings. Not spankings...BEATINGS. They all, with perfect love and adoration of their parents and grandparents, calmly say that the discipline they got would be considered child abuse today. "If my parents were alive today, and they *beat their kids* today the way they beat us then...they would get fifty years in prison."

Our "tour guides" were primarily homeless, habitual fare-gate stuffers several of whom were hopelessly hooked on the crack cocaine epidemic, and had full blown AIDS. They hustled their living and paid for their habit by "employing" themselves as self-appointed MARTA tour guides. Whenever we would see them we would chase them off the system, whereby they would haunt the outer fringes of the stations, awaiting business. What they would do was approach an obvious tourist, particularly those who had luggage. They would engage themselves to the visitors, offer to show them around, carry their bags for them, answer questions, direct them to hotels, etc. When their services were no longer needed they would *lean on* the visitors for tips. The tourists and sightseers usually paid—and well. However, these guys were not, necessarily Honest Injuns...sometimes the people would get pick-pocketed, the twenty dollar bill they would absent-mindedly be holding in their hand as they looked for smaller bills would get snatched, and so on. A surprising number of tourists would seek us out to report a robbery, only for us to find out that the circumstances were that one of the "tour guides" had finished his services, was waiting for his tip, and when the tourist didn't have anything smaller than a $20, the "tour guide" would say, "Well, wait here while I take your twenty and get change." Of course, they wouldn't see him again. And we would say, "You mean you gave a complete stranger a twenty dollar bill?" And they would flounder and struggle to make an explanation, themselves, while we would just look at them and slowly shake our head.

I mean, we're talking about homeless, grungily clothed, odorous, unshaven, clearly disheveled men with a visible layer of grime on them...and you're *trusting* them? Their victims in this matter that I'm aware of were too embarrassed to continue with their complaint.

We had free MARTA publications around the station and in display racks in some hotels that were out in the open for the taking. One of the security guards at the Hyatt Hotel told me about how those "tour guides" were taking those free magazines and selling them for $3.00 apiece! Geez, don't you see at the top left corner the word, "FREE"?? Well, it was the same with some of the hotel brochures, as well.

When it came to stuffing the fare-gates, even the token machines, what was done was to either jam a thick wad of paper or paper towels up into the base where the tokens or change was to come out, and when it would be stuck, they'd come back later, remove the wad, and their booty would come tumbling out. Or, they would stick a slug into the coin/token receptor of the fare-gates, causing the token or quarters to jam in there. Then they would come back and actually _suck_ the change and tokens out of the receptor.

The department, then redesigned the fare-gates with one side of the receptors removed, making it impossible to suck them out. And when the Revenue Agents would do their daily fare collections out of the machines, the regular routing was to check way up into the base for any paper jams. One time we got a report that some winner had stuck a used syringe needle up into the base of the token machine. Thankfully, no one was pierced from this. There had been an ominous note attached to the syringe that read, "Welcome to the world of AIDS." So we had to just work according to each new risk that appeared here and there at ongoing times.

The precinct that I truly enjoyed working out of (and which I remained at the longest during my tenure at MARTA) was Five Points. Due to its size, its central-ized location for the linking up of all trains from all directions, North, South, East & West, and dozens of different bus routes operating out of it, you were so busy that the time to change watches (that's quittin' time) arrived in what seemed to be thirty minutes. And I was still experiencing ever increasing recovery and betterment of my reputation, so that I was at last, no longer considered an "F" up by anybody anymore.

CHAPTER SIX

GEE, DADDY, WHY DON'T THEY LIKE US?

I HAD MENTIONED in my opening statement to these memoirs that a "certain problem," not necessarily exclusive to the U.S., yet having at its base the holding of Power by a certain group, was something I hoped this writing might help to redress. You're not going to be a Black person in these United States and NOT run into this "problem" in *every* capacity. It's like going down to the beach and expecting not to encounter any sand. It's here and it's permeated through every fiber and fabric of this continent. And quit talking about the South! As Malcolm X pointed out, "As long as you're south of the Canadian border, you're South!"

A thing that we would all like an answer to is, "Just what does make for these things, and why *is* one group finding it necessary to continue unprovoked offenses against the other?" Let's see if Dr. G. can answer it for y'all. If you're going to kill a tree, striking off branches is not the answer. That's called "pruning," and you know what happens to pruned vines and green growth...it only grows back quicker, stronger, and fuller. To kill the tree, *you have to go down to the ROOT*. And so, here are some roots, or better, the Beginning. No, not THAT beginning--with Adam & Eve. But the origin of this particular "problem."

You have to go back to the decline of the ancient Roman Empire. Rome was a multi-racial nation. You had Roman Asia, Roman Africa, and Roman Britain. Due to the fact that the history books had been, along with the rest of the dark skinned world, "colonized," MANY historical personages of Black, African, or other dark skinned hue have either been left out of the history books, or been replaced with Caucasian identities. My reason for bringing this to your attention is the fact that Rome had *several* Black emperors, such as Macrinus, Claudius Albinus, Pocennius Niger, and the most famous, Lucius Septimius Severus. The young Roman ruler Honorius, who reigned in 1880 in Italy, if you can find his real picture, has distinct Negroid features, although his skin is very light. As I said, Rome was multi-cultural, with Black emperors as well as others of varying origins and complexions.

As it was becoming time for other powers to come upon the scene, such as the Muslims and the Crusaders, certain Germanic tribes who had been biding *their* time, took their opportunity to invade the Empire. There were three large Germanic barbarian hordes that swept out of Germany and into Rome, itself in 459 A.D., and these were the Jutes, Vandals, and Angles. The Vandals took on Roman Africa and massacred more than 200,000 persons, and did such a world wide infamous job of damage and destruction that their name, "Vandal" became synonymous for wanton wreckage of property. Keep in mind, ancient North Africa, which is what comprised much of Roman Africa, was <u>MUCH</u> Blacker in those days than it is today. The degree and amount of rape of the womenfolk there was SO pervasive that the entire region from Morocco to Palestine lightened up in complexion, almost overnight.

The Angles originated out of Denmark, and were so hated by their conquered victims that they were described by Briton and Roman alike as being "from Hell." The Angles (who would later be known as Anglo-Saxons) invaded Roman Britain and pushed the native Britons out of their native soil into Cornwall, Wales, and the north of France. And then the Angles forbade the original British natives back onto their own old common ground. In fact, the name "Wales" is the Angle/Saxon word originally, "Wayerlash," which means, "Foreigner." So the native Britons were called "foreigners" in their own original land. Keep a side thought...the folks who invaded (sorry) "discovered" America in the 1600's, after massacring the Native Americans here, pushed and barged their way into California and Texas, later. California and Texas initially belonged to Mexico. But now, the descendants of those very Anglo's now have ownership of those states, and when the original Hispanic inhabitants of it attempt to enter back into lands that they once did own, their called, "Illegal Immigrants." Hawaii, a kingdom of its own, met a similar fate from these Anglo-Caucasians in the mid 1800's, with King Kamayah-maya and his wife, the Queen, penned up and held up in their palace as prisoners under the White American advance and permanent settling in. Now you have a short history lesson on WHY White Anglo-Saxon Protestants (WASP's) are *so* universally despised...once they come to visit, they don't like to go home.

A particular type of damage was done by these tribes to all the art work and sculptures of the Roman Empire's great ones in the land. This included Egypt, as well. They found all these statues with African and "Negroid" features...full lips, flat nose, heavy chin, curly hair arranged in rows of knots. What the Vandals and Angles did was to knock off the noses and chip the lips of these statues so as to hide their "Negroid" strain. This was so they could claim they were "Whites." Yes, that's a fact. If you'll look at all those statues, obelisks, bas reliefs, and sculptures that we have from that period and beyond, the noses have been damaged. Even when Napoleon later found the Great Sphinx buried in the sands of ancient Egypt, he had one of his Arab artillerymen take careful aim at the nose and blow it off. That's why it, too, has similar damage. The beginnings of White Supremacy and its effort to claim that THEY did everything, invented <u>everything</u>, and accomplished <u>everything</u>, while the people inside of our skin were purported to have done <u>nothing</u> had begun. <u>Everything</u> under the sun has been resorted to in order to perpetuate that belief. They **WON'T** acknowledge great feats and accomplishments by you and me. Even after they later got into the ancient African kingdoms such as Mali, Songhai, Benin, Timbuktu, Ghana, ancient Zimbabwe with its own Great Wall constructed more than one thousand years ago...any place they find US, they <u>quickly</u> worked to either hide it, or try to find some fictionalized "white" source from somewhere for it. I found in some older books out of that period, authored by Whites, who when they couldn't hide the fact that Africa had civilizations and kingdoms, tried to at least claim their rulers were "White." I noticed the word in these books was always italicized, "*white*" kings. But when you read the famous Arab traveler, Ibn Battuta's writings about his travels into those regions of Mali, Songhai, Timbuktu, etc., HE always describes the inhabitants AND their kings as being Black, <u>Black.</u> The Zimbabwe great wall had South African Apartheid Whites so discomfited that they said some Greeks just *had* to have made their way down there and built it...because, they said, WE just weren't capable of such. The brick is so firmly in place and solid, that without mortar, they're held in solidly.

The giant stone heads found in Central Mexico with obvious African racial or "Negroid" strain, if you will, belong to the Olemec period in Mexico's history, also thousands of years old. Some of the stupidest excuses have been resorted to by White history deniers to the point of assininity. "The stone heads in Central Mexico got those features because they rolled downhill, and that's what flattened their lips and noses," they tried to pass off. The otherwise intact features on the Great Sphinx they said, "possibly became that way because it was really a lion's head, but with the rains that came on Egypt, the features melded and smoothed out to—well—*that*." There were coins struck and issued by Hannibal, the terror of Rome in 218 B.C. that bear the image of an African raced man on one side, and an elephant on the other. The most commonly accepted statue of Hannibal comes to us from Greece...and ALL experts will tell you that is NOT Hannibal, himself, but an ideal representation of a hero-type as far as Greeks are concerned. The early Carthaginians were great merchants who were hard-headed, hard-nosed *businessmen*, who had little to no use for indulging in artistry during their day. They left practically ALL their artwork to the Greeks inhabiting the isles that the Carthaginians had domination of during the time. That's why much of the coinage and statues done of Hannibal, Hamilcar Barca, the Lightening (Hannibal's father), and other nobles of Carthage look like Greeks. The little artwork done by the actual Carthaginians themselves, are of gods and goddesses.

When Hannibal was occupying Rome, he had to have the coinage struck to pay his troops done, himself, while there. Thus, the images are of clearly Black, African men. The White writers who came upon these claimed that they weren't of Hannibal, but of Hannibal's elephant driver. Folks...coins, medals, and commemorative medallions are NOT struck in honor of the guy who sweeps the camel turds off the street...they're struck in honor of the Big, Bad Man or Woman. They <u>know</u> this. And they know <u>better than</u> WE do. There's just this <u>pretense</u> that nobody did <u>anything</u> worthwhile EXCEPT them. And anything that messes with that pretense has to be dealt with or destroyed. And since it's a matter of one woman's word (because that's what will be implied...that I'm coming up with all of this out of the blue), then go to *other* sources for your proof. And since it's likely that it will be implied that OUR word isn't good enough (in other words, from Black writers), go to other lands and histories from *their* sources. France had a popular play about Hannibal and the Black Numidian prince, Massinissa, who joined Rome's side and helped Scipio the Younger defeat Hannibal's forces. It was called, "Salaambo," and played around the late 1700's. The actors are Blacks. I had mentioned the earlier Black Roman emperors, such as Septimius Serverus. He ruled Rome in 168 A.D. The Roman song writers of his day joked about him and nicknamed him, "Hannibal's later day revenge," because another Black African had taken over Rome...although *he* proved to be one of the most energetic defenders of the Empire, and a real Roman patriot. He was the one who put a stop to the Praetorian Guard who had become permanently encamped in Rome, and were literally selling the empire through extortion to the highest bidding emperor. <u>Place</u> of birth was important to people at that time. The other Blacks who had ruled Rome were born in other Roman provinces, such as Caesarea, Palestine, the surrounding isles, etc. Dick Gregory, in the '70's had made mention of the fact that when Hannibal invaded Rome he put "soul" into those Italians... "That's why their cookin's so good!"

Any place they find <u>us</u> in ancient history and it's not insulting, embarrassing, or about being slaves, *things are done* to quickly get rid of the evidence. There are Black rulers in 1500's through 1800's Central and South America, such as Rafael Carrerra, dictator of Guatemala and five adjoining countries, and Simon Bolivar for whom Bolivia is named after... whose portraits have been doctored so as to Caucasianize them, or else they're left out of the history books here in these United States. But you can tell when they haven't been able to either erase them or hide their identity...their importance is simply negated or else their very existence is questioned. With Hannibal, the general whose strategies were so brilliant, that modern day military academies were teaching his techniques, his exploits were suddenly described in dismissive tones in a recent book I read, where it was said, "Well it was *just ambush!*"

With Aesop, world famed for his fables, "The Tortoise and the Hare," "The Fox and the Grapes," et.al., his name is just a Greek variation of the word, "Ethiop." And when the "powers that be" were no longer able to deny *that* fact, now they want to deny whether Aesop even really existed in the first place. There is a similar historical personage described in the Holy Qu'ran named, Lukman or Lokman. And he was another Ethiopian wise man who told humorous stories, advised wise men, and was honored in Arabia, to the point that he was so mentioned in their Holy Book.

After these Germanic tribes conquered the Roman Empire, which was that part of the then known world, they held onto the learned ones (mathematicians, scientists, geographers, writers, etc.) and made them teach them how to read, write, etc. When the tribe members learned what they were able they told the learned ones, "Alright, get out!" and either killed them or dropped them into their growing slave colonies (because we're going down through history now, as we get to the 1400's). These Angle-Saxons and so on *still* did not want to have to acknowledge that they <u>had</u> to rely on the conquered Blacks and so on to show them how to do everything. And what you get is the biggest cover up ("calypso"—Greek for "cover up") in world history, as far as the dominating group either forgetting, or better still, *pretending* to forget what they <u>knew</u> they had seen of our African civilizations, and knowing fully well <u>WHO</u> was and <u>is</u> responsible for all these inventions of modern convenience that we enjoy today. I just can't help believing that the "<u>uncovering</u>" of this ("apo"— Greek for "<u>undo</u>", and thus "apo-calypso")—the Apocalypse, or "Uncovering"—is at least part, if not most, of the Revelation of the Age due to come. Once again, if they can't claim somebody White originated it, then it's just not talked about. The Railway brake, the steam boiler furnace, the pencil sharpener, the automatic traffic light, the machine that puts out a complete and finished shoe, the Evaporating Pan (which revolutionized the sugar refining industry), the gas mask, the lawn sprinkler, the cigarette rolling device, the machine that sends messages through the air by the use of electricity, the camera lenses that film wildlife and insects way up close like what you see on National Geographic (and the same inventor, LeRoy Flourant, has his high-powered cameral lenses onboard NASA's Space mission satellites and shuttles), the elevator, the typewriter, even ice cream, potato chips, and the Pillsbury Doughboy—come up with by a Black advertising woman who also came up with the Secret deodorant commercial—"Strong enough for a man, made for a woman," as well as Coca Cola—invented by Black domestic worker women for their harried and tired, overworked White employers...the list is very, <u>very</u> long. But we get ZERO credit for these things.

The Cotton Gin was <u>never</u> invented by any Eli Whitney. The slaves he owned invented it. HE just got the credit (and subsequent monies) for it. It was <u>never</u> any Dr. Henry Gatling who invented the Gatling Gun in 1867...it was six Chicago Blacks who invented that gun. They took it to General Pershing who was pursuing the famous Mexican bandit Pancho Villa. General Pershing complimented the Six, saying, "This is the finest piece of work I've ever seen!" U.S. Government officials then gave the gun to England for use in the Anglo-Zulu war in 1879, and that gun turned the tide of the war in England's favor. Because prior to that, these "naked savages" as the British had called the Zulus were handing them the *worst* defeats England ever suffered as a modern army against, "primitive, dark skinned men."

WE won't ever get the credit for these achievements and inventions. The Black inventors of these things, with the exception of George Washington Carver and Madam C.J. Walker, always died in poverty and obscurity. Once again, the powers that be KNOW this, but it's covered up.

So you get down to our day. With the same attitudes prevailing, every time any of us does something that can't be put down, or have the importance of it negated— do you see a genuine congratulatory attitude from our White counterparts...or do you see a low and seething unexplainable hostility growing within and finally coming out of them? Just remember White America's reaction to Rev. Jesse Jackson's bringing those hostages back with those amazing successes. Was he congratulated? Was he thanked? Or did you see Whites go into hypercritical hysterics? You'd have thought that he'd just tried to blow up the White House or something. Instead, he was only accused and accused, and insulted, booed when he went on the Wall Street Floor, he got *death threats*, for God's sake, and now it's just plain and simply taboo for them to ever mention his successes overseas... "Aww, he's just tryin' to get publicity," etc. Anybody else, and they could be Charles Manson, they'd be lauded and applauded. If they'd done, partially, what he'd accomplished, they'd have had the TV movie made about him, he'd have received accolades, been loved and congratulated, there'd have been parades in New York, etc.

And to prove how intensely determined they are to keep up this façade of denial, as the anger and accusations against Rev. Jackson reached their fever pitch when he had a second success at bringing hostages back (and Pres. Ronald Reagan said, "Jesse Jackson *may have broken* the LAW!"), it was finally New York Governor Mario Cuomo who went on TV and said, "Look, this is happening to him because of his race...and that's it!" Governor Cuomo, who had been governor of New York forever, was not re-elected to office that next term. Governor Pitaki was sworn in, in his place. Likewise, Governor Jerry Brown of California simultaneously acknowledged that what was happening to him was because of "race, and nothing other." That year spelled the end of *his* term, as well. Governor Pete Wilson was sworn in. And he had been Governor of California for a long time, as well. The point I'm spelling out here is that Whites will penalize their fellow Whites for either taking OUR side, or not playing ball and pretending like, "WE'RE not doing anything to you people!" as they continue their "catching the wind"-like innocence game. It's not ever supposed to be acknowledged that Racism is in the play. It's for every other reason in the world BUT that.

Getting back to the body of this thing, this is a quick *real history* teaching lesson here in order for you to know what makes our "lighter counterpart" tick. If you know root causes, and root psychological motivations, then the actions of the other party will not only come as no surprise to you...*you may find yourself properly equipped* to deal with any occasion of this type that arrives. Sun Tzu, in his centuries' old book, "The Art of War" had said, "If you know your enemy, and if you know yourself, you've won the battle 100% of the time." It literally translates, "Know thy enemy—know thyself—one hundred battles—one hundred victories." If you know only your enemy and not yourself, or vice-versa, you've won the battle 50% of the time. In case my White readers are starting to take this as an "up in arms" publication piece, let's get a few facts straight, right now. In this nation's entire history, you've only had "Kill Whitey" types among us for *real* during the slavery period...because things were just impossible for us then. After Emancipation, they did decide to forgive and forget. But the Whites couldn't. Number one, they were afraid. Thomas Jefferson (yes the one openly acknowledging his Black mistress, as if none of the other names on the Declaration of Independence weren't cohabitating with them) had met in private with his fellow Whites to talk about the day when these Black enslaved human beings would become freed, yet felt, "The Negroes will NEVER forgive the ten thousand times ten thousand crimes we've committed against them!" Oh, but we did, we just weren't welcome to participate in American Business, make a living without getting lynched if we became *too* successful, and were generally maneuvered right back into a state of slavery, just not in name. We kept our cool, and in return suffered a *thousand* provocations from Whites, spurred on to this day, quite simply I believed due to their guilty consciences.

You all KEEP looking for us to nut up and come after you, while you sleep in your beds. And it HASN'T HAPPENED. We cannot count acts of individual vandalism which victimizes MY Grandmother, just like your Grandmother by hooligans. No, I'm talking about this awaited for *en masse* scale of screaming angry Black citizens converging on suburban America in righteous vengeance! It hasn't happened, you wonder why it hasn't happened, and I believe your guilt and paranoia, try as you might to deny that there's any reason for you to have it, is steadily causing you to lose your minds with fear everyday.

There was (and is) a great and intensive desire among Anglo-European Americans to christen themselves as the beginning of all things, and to have no end. They presupposed and attempted to prove to the world that EVERYTHING from the beginning of Civilization to ALL inventions, as previously mentioned, of modern convenience was created by White people. Yet, the deeper they dug into the sands of time and into the ancient of ancients to the tens of thousands of years ago, all they could find was us. The world's first primitive abacus (multiplication table principally used in China) was found in what is now Zaire formerly called the Congo in central Africa. Among other disappointments the Whites of that time suffered was when Howard Carter discovered King Tut's tomb in Egypt. If you can get hold of J.A. Rogers' books, "Sex and Race, vol. 1 thru 3," and "World's Great Men of Color," vol. 1 & 2, you will be in for a virtual buried treasure chest *full* of Black and African historical personages from the B.C. period until the 20th Century. He points out quite a few astounding and unforgiveably hidden facts about our origins and continued achievements. What J.A. Rogers pointed out was how after the Carter expedition uncovered all that finery and majesty dating back to 1300 B.C. the local native Egyptian populace (who had been forbidden anywhere near the tombsite—more odious and audacious barging in actions on the part of the Angle-Saxons!) were finding themselves, in spite of all the insults they'd suffered at their hands, actually beginning to feel sorry for the Whites. Carter and the rest had emerged from the tomb gloomy, depressed, obviously heartbroken and in the dourest mood. Because, the modern Egyptians observed, this White man wants, *desperately*, to place himself as the progenitor of nations and he *can't do it.* The deeper he digs, the sadder he becomes.

Well, that didn't stop denial packed Whites from coming up with a solution for themselves. THEY will become Black and Semitic—THEY will become "Black but comely, O ye daughters of Egypt!" If anyone is mentioned as "Hamitic," or even "Black," THEY will be the one the ancients are talking about. The way this was accomplished was for the Caucasians to approach all these current day people of those regions of the world (the Middle East, Northern Africa, Morocco, Algeria, the inhabitants of Jordan, the Sinai Peninsula, etc., and get them to agree to THEIR racial designations and definitions. MANY of these people so approached were blacker than Black. Jet black. Coal black. You know, that *bluish* black color in pigment. And the Whites got them to agree to be categorized as Semitic or Hamitic, which was really, they said, of Caucasian racial belonging. So these people, in one land after another, were told they were really *Caucasian*...just anything but a Negro. *They* were a totally (and undesirable) *other* race. If you want proof of this racial farcity, J.A. Rogers provided a copy of National Geographic's article and pictures from that period, about late 1889, thereabouts. There is a picture of one of the inhabitants of the northern Arabian penninsula. He's as jet black as any full-blooded Black man can be. With everted lips. The caption underneath the picture says, "This is an inhabitant of the northern Arabian lands who is of Hamitic racial origin, but not a Negro." The powers that be at that time did all they could to lump persons *they* designated as "Negroes," into something small in numbers, totally undesirable as a racial member, "stunted and stunted in growth," they said, and other not so positive attributes. J.A. Rogers says of this article, "Take these same Black people (the ones in pictures like these wearing turbans and swaddling clothes), dress them in American made clothes, and these same scientists attempting to list them as "Hamitic," therefore, "White" –will *declare* that they are "Negroes."

What was being done as a result of getting these native peoples' OK to be classified as *White*, was that whenever pictures or drawings of the inhabitants of those regions were placed in American history books, or text books, they were always shown to be clearly Caucasians. The drawings of the ancient Egyptians building pyramids were of Whites. Actors and actresses portraying ancient Egyptians and Northern Africans were all played by Whites. You'll notice today that whenever there's U.S. news coverage of Egypt, Morocco, Arabia, and the inhabitants of Jordan, etc., the camera keeps jumping around, showing the people, then stopping and resuming again, etc. What they're doing is picking out the lightest, fairest skinned people and showing *them* to us, giving the impression that *everybody* over there is light skinned.

The people of Ethiopia were approached in like manner during that period. But what the Ethiopians did when they were told they were *really White* was to say, "Well then, you don't mind us moving next door, marrying your daughter..."

"NO, now **WAIT** a minute!" was the obvious response, and the Ethiopians, among all those other people got to stay designated as Black and "Negro"!

WHY am I bringing all this up, you say? Because, as I mentioned, if the _root causes_ of these things are brought to the open, I won't have to spend a whole heck of a lot of _time_ making like I'm trying to look for an answer as to _why_ the actions of *some* people are a recurring, on-going, regular occurrence. In all fairness to all parties concerned, there are those among our White counterparts who do heroically break ranks with the bandwagon jumpers among their own, and either don't support what their fellows are doing, or sometimes bring recorded information to the public for exposure. Although, to me, there's *little* change in that "glass ceiling" action, at least such "pants being caught down" exposure is priceless in verifying what we've been saying all these decades.

I had mentioned that Whites are more aware than we are about the real truth of what history has to offer us. There's a MARKED difference between our Northern White "Buddies" supposedly, Liberal—and our Southern "Sworn Enemies" in the Conservative Red states. When I was in my Army ROTC class at University of San Francisco I had done a paper on Hannibal, complete with photo copied pictures of the coins he had struck and issued to pay his troops in 219 B.C. I had also mentioned in the paper that the "Carthaginians were descendants of the Phoenicians, a Negroid people who were great merchants and seafarers." The Captain over that class was a White guy who had always been very cordial, joking and friendly with me. But whenever he saw me afterwards from the receipt of that paper, his demeanor and the expression on his face was if I was pointing a gun at him. And I began to experience a preview of what was to come later on in my job situations whereby I wasn't willing to "stay in my place."

When I was overseas in Germany (in 1978) I had been riding in the back of the deuce and half, as we called them (2 and a half ton trucks) and I was reading J.A. Rogers' book, "World's Great Men of Color," which I had brought along with me. A southern, "country boy," White Corporal asked me what I was reading. I tossed the book to him. He looked at the front of the book for some seconds in silence. And then, without even opening the cover, he said (with that perfect Southern drawl), "Did you know that the first university made by man was in Africa?" Of course, he was talking about the University of Sankore which was in the heart of Timbuktu in the 1500's. Students from as far as India and China went there *in _those years_*. What this told me was that apparently, White people in general are most likely *more aware* and more knowledgeable of our *real* history than WE are. But, the marked difference between this White Northerner and White Southerner's reactions to MY knowing it was what stood out in my mind. That "good ol' boy, 'neck' didn't mind me knowing it, while that pretended "liberal" from California acted as if it was the end of the world when he saw that I knew what *I* wasn't supposed to know. Again, IF you know what makes some people tick, then not only will you not be surprised, confused, or taken aback when some unexplainable response or action comes from them...why, you <u>may</u> actually become armed with a knowledge of a way to <u>fight</u> it. Undo it. Catch it in its tracks. Make it walk the plank.

CHAPTER SEVEN

BACK TO THE THIN BLUE LINE

DURING MY YEARS ON PATROL WITH MARTA P.D., the precincts changed up their precinct name coverage as the system began to grow and expand. We were now North Precinct, South Precinct, East Precinct, West Precinct, and later, the Airport Precinct, which was previously under the South Precinct's coverage. Some short time before that, though, as more and more officers were being hired, you guessed it, more and more of those officers were Black, and the force was becoming much Blacker. The upper leadership, however, was still being kept disproportionately White—that is Lieutenant Level and above. It was going to become harder and harder for certain determined "forces" at work to keep it that way. From the Chief on High came a new status rating all of a sudden. This was about 1991. First, all "skeeter wings," as we called our little one-stripe insignia (depicting senior rated foot patrolman) was done away with. Then, there would be no more Corporals. There were a large number of Black Corporals, and only three of them were White. The three were considered pretty much unpromotable—one, because he was married to a Black woman. We all <u>knew</u> his truck was pretty much chucked. The second because, well, let's say he was a bit on the "big" side. Yours truly ain't no anorexic nervosa, herself, so I have to word that cautiously! And the third because to say he was a bit "scary" may be the kindest way I can put it. When he went to his beat assignment you wouldn't see him anymore all day until time to change the watch. And it was from the bank of Corporals that the next Sergeants would be chosen. So in knocking everybody back down to the rank of "officer" only, no rank, no status, it would be easier to choose who was wanted by the upper leadership instead of who was most qualified. That was when we went to Sergeant's exams, and with the "situations" that occurred as was explained earlier.

The one or two Blacks per promotion period that were actually selected to be Sergeants were usually the ones who had the reputation for being (for real) "Yassuh, Boss," types, easily controlled folks who *would not* stand up to the "powers that be" in their troops' behalf, if disciplinary actions truly weren't called for. Some of the things we'd been written up and disciplined for would boggle even Willie Wonka's imagination, as offenses about as serious as a candy bar level slight or complaint would be grounds for disciplinary action. We've seen that a lot through our experiences on jobs that actually <u>PAY</u> something you can <u>live</u> on. What we Black Americans experience every time we manage to acquire a job like that is to be only harassed and harassed and harassed and harassed and ***harassed*** the whole time we're there.

First, the sick time policy changes. What previously was something the employees were able to do in reasonable freedom suddenly becomes, once a certain number of <u>us</u> get there, an occasion to write you up, label "an occurrence," be a reason to ultimately threaten your job, etc., etc. In the event you're thinking, "Well, *yeah*, if you abuse it." I'm not talking about abuse of it. Plus, there were Whites there who *regularly* sick out every other week—without complaint or job jeopardy whatsoever. We all know who and what abuse constitutes. But with those among their employees whom the higher ups are **determined** to retain there, instead of <u>those</u> people getting written up, given an "occurrence", etc., they just simply *rewrite the rules* concerning what constitutes a sick out that's a reason to let you go, and a sick out that's OK. With our department, if you had the same illness over and over again, it's alright. No, it's not grounds for telling you, "Well if you're *that* sickly, maybe you shouldn't work here." Oh, no—that was what the one(s) who sick out all the time had as their problem—that the company was dead set and determined to keep. We've <u>had</u> accidents and injuries beyond people's control that had them hospital-bound and everything, who were still written up and "given an occurrence". In other words, Doctor's excuse or not, legitimate injury or not—we literally did not have the right to get sick...OR injured without it risking your job if you'd caught a cold & sore throat and couldn't or didn't come in for a few days within that evaluation period.

Next, you find the telephone policies would change. I had worked at the mortgage banking department through Manpower Temporaries in Louisville (before I went to Atlanta). This was 1986. Cell phones weren't prevalent then, and you could still smoke indoors. While there, I noticed in true stereotypical fashion, the young and pretty White secretary able to sit at her desk, filing her nails, etc. and so on. I'd pass by cubicles and cubby holes with the business suit wearing White guys back there handling personal matters on the phone. One of the regular loan officers would *always* be standing up and staring at us from over his partition. One of the women supervising us kept complaining under her breath that he was looking at us to see what he could find "wrong" that we were supposedly doing, and then running to tell on us. The person supervising us was a pretty nice, cigarette smoking, rough voiced young White lady who told us that she was getting pretty tired of this guy's she-nanigans, saying, "I wish he'd mind his own fuckin' business." One of his complaints was about my co-worker who simply called her home on the office phone everyday at 3:00pm to check and make sure her son had gotten home from school okay. That was it. And I got feedback on the 'vine that he was complaining to our higher ups… "Well, SHE'S on the phone ALL DAY!" he was saying. Suddenly, for reasons unclear, she was no longer with us at the bank…let go, no doubt.

Because I knew we were seated at desks that contained, behind our partitions, the highly paid, well compensated other all-White loan officers (whom we regularly overheard turning down Black applicants), I had decided to talk openly about this guy who I could see keep standing up and peering at us over his partition. I knew the men on the other side would hear me, and then report what they'd heard to our bosses, in private.

When Mr. Complaints was standing up and leaning on the partitions looking at us while he was on the phone (his usual posture), I said to the lady at the next desk (and pretending to whisper), "Man, look at him over there staring at us. I wish I had a slingshot, I'm so tired of that guy popping up like a jack-in-the-box just *having* to look over here. What does he _want?_"

The next day, the assistant to the vice-president, a very approachable lady and who probably made $94,000 a year minimum, came to my desk. "Janet, is everything okay?" I looked at her, feigning slight puzzlement. "Uhh…yeah!"

"You sure?"

"Well…yeah!" And I kept looking at her in quizzical fashion.

"Because if there's anything you'd like to talk to me about don't hesitate!"

"Well, everything's okay."

"You sure?"

"Yes."

"Well, Janet, you know if there's anything you need to discuss with me, or that you want to talk about, feel free."

"No, everything's fine!"

The interaction went on like that for a minute. With her trying to probe me, and with me looking up at her in question-mark like manner. She finally left and I never said anything about anything. I did notice that afterwards I never saw his head overlooking that partition anymore.

Also, along with that complaint highlighted in the movie, "9 to 5," with Lily Tomlin, Jane Fonda and Dolly Parton, we _regularly_ watched ideas and new tech-niques that we would come up with in order to improve the job get taken from us, used by them, the credit given to some White male who copied (stole it, if you will), and we would get minus zero for our efforts. Each and every time we would turn in projects, do something required of us, etc., it would be nitpicked with, turned back over to us, the supervisor NEVER satisfied, always with things culminating in our having to stay over past quitting hours (typically unpaid for those hours), and after the company gets all it thinks it can get out of us, we're pushed out, forced out, maneuvered out, thrown out, basically "canned."

Then we get to suffer stress attacks, high blood pressure, strokes, etc. in having to work under these conditions.

In 1993 and '94, as more stations were under construction (primarily those going North into the wealthier parts of town), we were hearing about and having to attend meetings about how to increase ridership on the system. We heard on the 'vine again that certain voices from up North had been told by those denizens that they may be more inclined to ride the system if we had more White officers. There was evidence of that demand's having been made because MARTA began a massive hiring drive for the police department, but 98% of those being selected were Whites only. We saw highly qualified employees from other police departments who were Black being turned down for employment. We quickly saw they were trying to "lighten up" the force.

There was also an attitude among our Captains and Majors, whereby they seemed to have a real problem with even the thought that any of us may have been finding occasion to get off our feet some times. Oh, yes, there were breaks to be had, but even if they came out and saw us "just standing" patrol-wise, they would come up with some kind of task for us to accomplish, which I discovered was nothing they really wanted or were interested in. They just couldn't stand to see, for lack of better description, "Negroes standing around with nothing to do!" 'Scuse <u>me</u> for living! My reason for bringing this up is that this was one of the *many* for instances from the earlier described non-stop hassling of us. And the mood/feeling of hostility from these Captains and Majors was very pervasive. Well, with the massive hiring of these White officers…came suddenly and out of the blue, a climatized out door booth that was set up on the Five Points outdoor plaza for the officers to go inside of, complete with chair, air conditioning, heat, shelf-table, and vented windows. That made me mad. There was no **WAY** that would have been done for just US. As many times as WE had to freeze on snowy, sleet-filled, rainy days…and as long as we had to broil in the muggy Georgia summer sun, and ESPECIALLY with the way that they would have lost their minds if WE were *ever* caught sitting down unless it was to write a police report or we were in the car…yes…I was a mad ass. It pissed me off to that bad a degree when I saw <u>how</u> they were going to pamper and cater to these new White hires. If we had've suggested such, you guessed it, the response would be, "Be glad ya got a <u>job!</u>" Some bold souls in the past actually had requested such a protection from the elements, but it was always a moot point with the higher ups. NOW here was one. I didn't appreciate what they were flat out telling us with that move, at all. "YOU guys can go to <u>Hell</u>! Come, my White children, let us serve *you*!"

In 1994, one of our Malcolm X-type crusaders, Freddie W., arranged for us to have a meeting with the MARTA Board of Directors. The list of officers chosen to represent us was made up of about eight of us, and it was decided that I should be among the group, which left me feeling highly honored. We knew we had to do something about what was going on. Whites only, primarily being hired with one, or two Blacks here and there for tokenism purposes (and supposedly, to shut us up), and the fact that our department had no seniority for its officers. Seniority was something our police department heads had fought tooth and claw against to keep from coming about. You know who the senior officers were. And the head officials from way on high were not about to let *their* ranks become Blacker. Oh, and, uh, we didn't have a union. Several attempts had been made in the MARTA Police department's history to get one started, but the company had always found subversive ways to undo any progress for that. Freddie had tried again, that year in '94 to get us a union started, having even successfully arranged for a union representative from New York to come to us in Georgia. He had been made aware of what was going on with us in the police department here, and he told us that some trinkling of that information had reached all the way up to his home state in the Apple. He had a deep Italian Bronx accent, humoring to some of us as it was kind of cute. But there *was* going to have to be that so absentee item from among us officers when it came to the Big Cats, and that was Unity.

Nevertheless, Freddie and the other wise, intellectual, and dignified representatives chosen by our ranks went to see the Chief Executive Officers board member officials in 1994. Our complaints to them were that we, the senior officers, had been faithfully loyal and devoted to our department. We'd gone through, without complaint, dealing with all the "characters" we as officers are expected to, had literally "tamed" Five Points, crime was down in all sectors and locales (the precinct commanders kept crime statistics on the erasable boards, always updating and keeping track of how many robberies, assaults, and other serious offenses we'd had for certain periods, and the numbers of such had been greatly decreasing), had on *numerous* occasions risked our lives, had been shot at, etc., had done our duty. This was accomplished on *our* backs in absolute loyalty to the department. Now, that all the *work* was done, all these White officers were being hired in to enjoy the newly relaxed atmosphere and otherwise take advantage of the fruits of <u>our</u> labor. Since there was no recognized seniority, those of us senior officers who were working Day Watch (7:00am to 3:00pm), were watching ourselves get written up for things that amounted to next to nothing, and not only having that negative item put in our files, it also resulted in our being kicked off of Day Watch. Then they would move one of these newly hired White officers to the daytime slot from off Evening Watch (3:00pm to 11:00pm). This was being done to one after another, after another of us day watch (senior officers). You'd get written up, and then have it culminate with your being put on Evening Watch as well. It was obvious to everyone that this was deliberate in order to pamper some more to the Whites they hired…and, of course, with one or two Black officers here and there being brought to Day Watch in this fashion for the "covering of tracks" sake.

At this meeting I had pointed out the individual acts of heroism the senior officers had accomplished, i.e., single-handedly disarming gun-toting persons during the commission of a crime; jumping wayside (onto the dangerous train track way) all alone in the apprehension of <u>three</u> armed men and successfully effecting their arrests; chasing and apprehending armed, drug possessing persons—three or four at a time—and successfully busting up that bunch...winning these cases in court; innumerable car theft apprehensions of young car thieves, successfully administering CPR to heart attack victims, the list is ad infinitum. And **ALL** that these officers experienced in return for their heroics was to have the powers that be wait around corners, <u>inventing</u> if they had to, some kind of minor offense for them to be "guilty" of, written up, thrown on Evening Watch, leaned on to quit or be fired, etc., and the <u>only</u> acknowledgement of their efforts being a snidely stated, "Well, that's yer <u>job</u>!" Yeah, we know. But every time one of those new White hires used their key to let some little old lady into the john, THEY got a letter of commendation.

My dear reading public: **I EXAGGERATE <u>NOT</u>!!!** I'm telling you **<u>exactly</u>** what we were watching each other experience. **<u>NO</u>** thanks; **<u>NO</u>** appreciation; **<u>NO</u>** acknowledgement of our efforts. I'm telling you...WE DON'T <u>COUNT</u>. As was pointed out to you in my earlier history lesson about <u>why</u> and <u>how</u> these things came to be in the first place. WE were only to be **<u>used</u>** as far as what THEY, the ruling Whites, were able to get out of us...and then it was, "Get out." And they would enjoy the fruits of someone else's labor.

We pointed out to the Board members that these officers who had been loyal and no trouble to their supervisors and had faithfully served the public, were being unfairly and unjustly sacrificed, their personnel records blotched and ruined with write ups, being arbitrarily put on Evening Watch, and basically punished to accommodate these new folks. Apparently, in order to entice them aboard, they must have *had* to be promised that they wouldn't have to wait two life times before getting a chance at Day Watch, like the ones who'd been there forever had to. When we were hired, the seniors pointed out, it was, "You'd better be glad you've got a <u>job</u>!" whether you're working Christmas or not! And we had accepted that. It was an extremely odious point to be realized that these guys weren't going to be required to suffer like we'd had to.

At the end of the meeting and then afterwards, the Board members' reaction to us was comprised of one prime observation...they just didn't realize—they had no clue—they were just *flabbergasted*...at the level of and degree of <u>education</u> and **<u>INTELLIGENCE</u>** that they had been made suddenly aware that we MARTA police officers had. They just couldn't believe, we heard on the vine, that we were as smart and intellectual as they had just been exposed to. Which made us *all the <u>more</u>* aware that the police chiefs and his high ranking officials had been painting a <u>false</u> picture of us to the MARTA Board members and their Chairmen. <u>They</u> must have thought that we were dumb grunt gorillas, apparently, who *could not be* in leadership or higher levels of department heads in the police department. They just couldn't get over it, we heard.

AND the Board took action. "There's no seniority among their department? That's ridiculous! EVERY OTHER department recognizes Seniority...why not theirs?"

We heard that the Captains, Majors, and the Chief (all White) were rabidly, feverishly, and downright URGENTLY in the CEO of MARTA's face telling him that there ***could not be seniority***! And once again, this is stuff that was leaked out to us, with only trace amounts of information coming to us, therefore, I wish I knew just WHAT kind of argument they were making and in whose behalf they were pretending to make it for. If they were truthful to the CEO, it wouldn't have been pretense.

Nonetheless, the CEO and his Board (at least temporarily) *literally <u>forced</u>* the police department there at MARTA to recognize seniority. And lo—a phenomenon happened! Something that actually worked out in <u>our</u> favor over the others...we saw—all these **Black** officers...working <u>DAY WATCH!</u> All these BLACK folks...actually...being (hold your breath) **properly rewarded...compensated**...with nothing else, but just being able to enjoy the fruits of OUR <u>OWN</u> **LABOR**!!! The employees in the other departments, we observed, showed visible signs of breathing sighs of relief in joy...happiness for US. Believe me, <u>other</u> people observe what some people are either going through, or <u>have</u> to go through...and actually do a little suffering of their own in their behalf, even if it *is* primarily just feeling bad about what they see happening to them. There were more smiles when we passed by them, and some congratulatory statements made.

And on the flip side: All these White officers who'd been hired overnight and I guess had been made to believe they'd be on Day Watch in the same amount of time...THEY all ended up on EVENING WATCH! It was the most stirring and glaring case of the higher ups' attempts to twist things, racially and massively in <u>their</u> favor—being turned upside down and in OUR favor instead. Much of the time we don't get to experience visible and *timely* Divine Providence as what occurred that year.

Naturally, the Whites just hired were up in arms. I mean they were IN the Chief's office! Bleating, crying, complaining, threatening to quit—you name it. In those years whenever Whites couldn't get their way their rallying cry was, "This is UNCONSTITUTIONAL!" And we were hearing about how they were in the Chief's office crying, "This was unconstitutional!" "WHY?!" we asked each other. " 'Be glad ya got a job!' " Though we were aware that the Chief and his cronies would never rest until they found some kind of way to undo what had just been done, the forces from on even higher had things firmly in place. So, we senior officers basked in the breath of the fresh air of justice, truly being done.

CHAPTER EIGHT

THAT'S TOO MUCH LIKE "RIGHT"

THERE WAS AN INCIDENT of fare evasion at the Vine City MARTA station during that period where some of the officers were working plain clothes...the better to catch them pesky fare evaders, My Dear. During the attempted arrest of one of the persons who had walked in without paying, that person suddenly wheeled around on Officer Steve H. and shot him in the mid-section, just missing his heart. We did not have bullet proof vests required of us to be worn at the time. But after this incident, the department had us measured for and requisitioned bullet proof vests. Steve H. was the first MARTA police officer to be shot in the line of duty. LT. Downin conscripted my writing ability to assist her in coming up with a memorandum to the Chief for some kind of special recognition and possible medal for Steve due to this incident. LT. Downin had observed, and correctly so, that every time ANY of these White officers <u>ever</u> got hurt in the line of duty, she knew that accolades after accolades, awardings and rewardings, in fact...the <u>whole world </u>is given to *them* on a silver platter just for getting wounded. She did not want Steve to be neglected his proper due, as such. Well, no such additional recognition or rewards came his way, despite her best efforts. In fact, after about five weeks of being at work doing light duty in business casual clothes in the office, he was roughly and rudely approached by the higher ups, saying, "Aren't you better yet? You're goofing off! You're shamming! You're just taking off extra long!" And, no, they weren't joking. They meant it. The huge difference between Jessica Lynch and Shoshanna Johnson's treatment by the military, recently, is a perfect indicator of the vast difference in attitude toward those of us faithfully serving both the nation and the public. Jessica Lynch was practically handed the world, millions of dollars book and movie deal offers, eighty per cent disability rating, et.al. Shoshanna Johnson was practically told to kiss their ass and go to hell. Once again...predictable behavior from the root-driven source.

Steve was so taken aback and disgusted by their attitude toward him and his situation that soon afterwards, as Neal had previously, *he* also left MARTA and went to work at another police department. My mother had called me from Louisville to tell me that my brother, Edward, had fallen off a roof he was working on and broken about three or four of his ribs. At the hospital, some old White doctor had written in his doctor's excuse for work that Edward was to go back to work after *three days*!!! When I spoke with him on the phone he was in so much pain, he couldn't even talk, prone, on the telephone. His job, at Kroger, was not a sit down job. "Well, it'll be for 'light' duty," but that's not the point. It told me that there's still this attitude that, "Well, they're all still part ape, they're part bionic...they're still sub-human. So they can fall off buildings, break their bones, and go back to work in four or five hours!" The family sought a more sane doctor's opinion elsewhere, and he was given some weeks off to recover.

We had, to come aboard the MARTA force, a full-time security officer, making really good money at his security job. He kept it as he was hired on to work at MARTA. Both positions were full-time, so he made a good piece of change. The Chief took an instant hostility-filled dislike to Willie James, right away. It seems that not only was he making too much money for their comfort, but he also was practically RoboCop. He would arrest *ANYBODY*. We commonly said of him, "He'd arrest his momma!" In short, he hadn't learned, as was immediately made clear to all," that *some* folks, you look the other way with. Now that will **NEVER** be admitted to by ANY department heads ANYWHERE, but there are and were *ways* they let you know they'd support you in the arrests of and who they *wouldn't.* Willie, a very nice and big guy who sort of reminded me of Yogi Bear because of his size and nut-brown features, was a tireless worker...and I do mean *tireless*. We asked him, "How on earth do you manage two full-time jobs!?" He'd just shrug and say, "Well..." He was a supervisor at the rank of full-bird colonel on his security job. Even so, the Chief demanded that he quit that job if he wanted to keep the one at MARTA, supposedly because of possible conflict of interest. Just about everybody at MARTA had other jobs, although for the most part, part-time. But the fact that Willie was making so much money doing both, just flared the Chief's venom. So we knew Willie James was not going to make Sergeant or above, though he tried to qualify every time, they came up with their make-shift "tests."

One evening, Willie and his wife and young daughter were coming home from a concert at the Fox Theater. As he was driving past a projects-type apartment area he saw smoke pouring out of the windows and door of the place. A dog was at the door barking furiously. He stopped his car, got out, opened the door of the apartment—the dog *whooshed-sped* outta there! It was clear that dog, he said, was saying, "Get *me* out!!" Willie entered inside and saw a woman asleep on the couch. He woke her up, as she immediately began fighting him (she thought he was an intruder). "Ma'am, your house is on fire!" Apparently, the woman was slightly invalid, needing assistance out of the house, and then she told him, "My mother's still in there!" She was upstairs. Also, she was blind and needed crutches to get around.

After he put the woman in his car, he turned to go back inside. The smoke was so thick he had to put a handkerchief to his nose and mouth to breathe. When he located the elderly woman inside (who was 80yrs. old) and woke her up, <u>she</u> began fighting him, thinking him to be an intruder. When he told her the house was on fire and asked where her crutches were, she, of course, panicked. By then the smoke was so thick, there was no seeing anything. With her being blind, he told us, she would have *never* found her crutches because HE had a hell of a time finding them! When he located the crutches and helped her out, she was crying, moving as best as she could—but he got her out. By the time he reached his car to put her in there, they told him their grandson was at the top of the stairs. By then, flames were shooting out of the windows. He went back inside that building a <u>*third*</u> time and didn't locate the boy. As it turned out, he wasn't even home...he had gone out earlier to enjoy cookies at a friend's house.

The two women, while the fire department arrived and fought the fire, were in the back of Willie's car crying and thanking Jesus for forty-five minutes. This mean, Jean Valjean's relentless pursuer, had just risked his life and save two lives.

He was entered onto the FBI's quarterly hall of fame files for action and service above and beyond the call of duty. We got a copy of the listing with several photos simultaneously posted in that category of other officers and safety officials from around the country who'd made that listing. There was also a write up in the paper and coverage on the news.

As far as departmental awards...he was given by the Chief a blank white ribbon-medal. In other words, a ribbon to put on his uniform that had nothing but a blank white empty space on it. The Chief said it meant "bravery". That was the worst insult that could have happened. The White officer (who was *immediately* promoted to Sergeant) after supposedly "saving the life" of the guy who fell wayside all those years ago (in 1986) was given a ribbon with yellow and green border, a "V" in the center for "valor," landed TV commercials, etc. Yet, nobody wanted to emphasize out loud to each other that glaring difference, and just quietly went on about business as usual, as Willie was given his blank white ribbon.

In as far as the mentioning earlier about Sun Tzu's advice to "Know thy Enemy," that display of contempt from the Chief in our department is an indicator of, roughly, five prime points of the approach and nature of those Whites who choose a hostile, malicious, and downright, vicious attitude toward those of us who've "stayed in the oven too long."

You'll notice, I *hope*, that I said, "Those Whites who *choose to have*," such attitude. I do want to exclude from this group those who don't. Those five basic attitudes and feelings toward us are as follows:

1. They have a deep, driving, *need* to *have* to believe that excess melanin in the body causes one's brains to turn to <u>*slush*</u>...

2. They get an immense and *intense* pleasure out of watching US be humiliated. They get "high"...they literally get an <u>*orgasm*</u> out of humiliating us.

3. (This is where our illustrious police chief's actions come in...) They ALWAYS take it as a *personal <u>AFFRONT</u>* to themselves for one of us to get even a DOLLAR more than what THEY think we should have. It's as if we did something to them, if WE get, i.e., a *good* paying job: a *nice*, expensive car: a nice expensive home, etc. And rather than go on about their business and mind it, they <u>have</u> to reach out and try to take such away from us. Yes, I'm telling the truth. Every time one of the guys would get an expensive car, he was made to go take the drug test (they just *had* to figure that he *must* be doing drugs!) Bus operators had the same story. If, after working super duper overtime hours and being able to afford to get a Denali or Silverado truck, they'd go back to the garage where they were parked (largely populated by their bigoted co-workers or mechanics) after getting off work, and finding scratches in the paint, nails in the tires, etc.

4. They <u>don't</u> take it well when WE out do them in any task or achievement. Especially, if it's something that will get US recognition instead of THEM. So, as explained earlier, there's the <u>mandatory</u> negating of the importance of whatsoever task or accomplishment we've achieved.

5. They become rabidly and insanely vindictive if there's some kind of dirty deed they were in the process of doing to one of us...and they get thwarted, or otherwise stopped in the commission of it. And, therefore, if they don't get you one way...they work, overtime, to get you another. And if one of them actually gets "dealt with" or otherwise, punished for doing something or trying to do something negative to you...then begins their retaliation program against you. And it matters NOT if you're man, woman, boy, girl, or even toddler. They <u>have</u> to begin their program of reprisal us if they get stopped, thwarted or otherwise get in deep trouble over their wrong doing. It doesn't MATTER **how** *right* you are...it doesn't matter how WRONG <u>they</u> are. All they know is that one of theirs got in trouble over YOU. And YOU have to be punished. Frederick Douglas described this as the horse thief's blaming the HORSE for all his troubles and woes.

We just have to face the unpleasant facts, people—with a few refreshing exceptions—the WHOLE NATION is under a Ku Klux Pact. That's just the facts, Ma'am. And if we're going to intelligently deal with this unfortunate and unpleasant fact, the **FIRST** step in solving it is to get some downright admissions and <u>confessions,</u>

similar to the Truth and Reconciliation Commission in South Africa. I already know that these folks here are more than happy to admit to crimes and wrong doings...as long as they're all crimes that it's too late to do anything about! The things that are still <u>current</u>, though, like those hangings of young Black men in those Mississippi jails between 1987 and 1996 that they *keep* claiming are suicides; the shooting of young Tiyisha Miller by those four White Los Angeles police officers in 1997, the shooting of Kenneth Walker in Columbus, Georgia by that White deputy, Donald Glisson, that a grand jury is refusing to indict, the glaring reports about convicted White felons being given jobs over qualified Blacks whose records are clean, the list is ad infinitum.

Willie James, again, saved an elderly woman's life by successfully administering CPR to her when a nearby Atlanta police officer had failed to do it, arbitrarily declaring her to be "dead." Willie passed away a few years ago due to complications from diabetes.

In the meantime, that booth I had described earlier as "magically" appearing out of the blue at Five Points when the massive hiring of Whites had gone on, had since become forbidden for any officers to use, "except in the harshest weather or elements." You should have figured <u>that</u> was due to happen!

Later, the booth was removed entirely. The tests being administered for promotion to Sergeant and Lieutenant continued to be a fiasco, having to be administered over and over again. Once again, it was re-administered such as it was until the "desired" individuals passed the exams. And the choices of the promotees continued to be so dubious and incredible... "How did *that* dumb M.F. get chosen?" "How did *that* scary chicken shit get chosen?" and so on.

And, yes, the write ups and the pit-digging continued well under way at the behest of the commanders in charge.

"She's belly-achin'," you say. I'm sure I mentioned earlier that all our White counterparts had to do was show up for work, breathe, then go home. And, why, "That's the BEST officer in the field!" Their promotions all the way up the board were pretty much guaranteed, no matter HOW severely in need of some just plain *horse sense* they might have been. AND...no matter **HOW** badly they screwed up or had serious deficiencies and offenses in their files, they just couldn't seem to get in trouble enough to be let go. Unless they offended or pissed off somebody "upstairs" as we referred to upper management. Then, it was a case of having fallen so low that they couldn't cover up for them anymore. Then, the only consequences were to move them to an even easier, safer position than they had in the first place...and it was done in order to protect their pay. With us, though, most of the situations that management decided *had* to result in termination (yes, over even slight or unreasonable complaints or slip-ups) and because they knew their terms would never stand up in a court of law if the targeted individual chose to fight back) that individual would be given the option to resign rather than be fired. He or she would be told that in resigning, they could keep their P.O.S.T. certification, be able to collect their pension, be able to get hired at another police department, etc. If they allowed themselves to be terminated, then ALL would be lost. There were some unfortunate victims of this type of "let's get rid of him!" games whom <u>we</u> advised to <u>*let*</u> themselves be out-rightly terminated. Then, we told them, they'd be able to *get* the company in court. But, usually, that individual did not feel like going through all of that, and so they would resign. If the company figured they "*had*" the officer in an uncontestable situation (like being caught with feminine company/vice-versa, in an unauthorized "private" area of the station), then they would fire him/her outright. We'd seen <u>*plenty*</u> of Lieutenants, Captains, and persons of those high ranks caught dead on in those very situations, yet it did not result in their being terminated. If the company couldn't cover up for them, they would simply be demoted to the next lower rank, and then fall-backs like, "Well-*years* here, training *there*, special stipulations the *other* place," and their <u>*salary*</u> would be protected and kept right where it was so that they wouldn't lose their pay. Once again, you understand, because of the time and the hassle it would take, not to mention the fact that most people just wanted to keep on working and earning their respectable salaries, these things were *verbally* complained about, but no real action would be taken any further by us regular officers.

We had a certifiably insane precinct commander who was the bane and the thorn in the side of ALL who worked at MARTA, in other departments as well as the police department. This individual, no matter HOW much he was complained about by EVERYONE there, would just not be distanced from the company because he did <u>*everything*</u> the upper eschelon wanted him to do. We would have other department employees who would come from having to deal with him and then say to us officers, "Y'know, I just want to look in his car trunk so I can see the Klan robes for myself!" But he was the bane of White officers *as much* as he was to us Black officers. When you talked with him one on one in ordinary situations, he was a hell of a nice guy. It's just that when reason and sanity were called for in what to do and how to do it...well, let's just say Patrick Star and Homer Simpson show some degree of Stephen Hawking-type intelligence in comparison.

EVERYWHERE this joker worked, whether it was the Detective's division of the police department, precinct commander, or officer in charge of special projects, various individuals would literally <u>flee</u> that area he was in because they were being driven close to becoming "postal"—(sorry, Postal employees). The reason for his working so many different departments was due to upper management's moving him around to both protect him and to finally give in to the near rabid demands of the employees he was placed over to "**DO SOMETHING ABOUT THAT MAN.**" <u>EVERY WAY</u> there was to cover for him, have him lay low, or otherwise retain him at the department, was resorted to by the Chief and his cronies.

One particularly nasty time period of his being a pain in the side of the *thorn*, itself, I think at least two of White officers, along with one or two Blacks practically *stormed* the Chief's office, almost frantic. "<u>DO </u>something about him...get rid of him...we can't stand it anymore!!!"

So, what the Chief did was to take seventeen of the newly hired White officers and three Black kiss-ass officers...twenty officers in all. They were going to do a poll of these twenty officers, asking them what they thought about Captain Nero. The plan was to have these twenty officers whom they figured would do exactly what they figured was desired of them...to give Nero a positive over all score and poll—and then to have the upper eschelon confront the rest of us officers and department employees with it. "Well, _twenty_ officers were polled, and <u>they</u> gave Nero a positive rating!" Well, the plan backfired because ALL TWENTY of those officers said that Nero was an "Incompetent Jackass." We heard that Nero's feelings were hurt, and that almost in tears he said to the Chiefs and his group, "I just do what _you all_ <u>tell</u> me to do!" And I could believe that. Every kind of asinine, dumb, retardate excuse to fall back on to screw us any and every way _possible_ was resorted to by the department heads in either getting rid of us, or giving us suspension days. And Nero was the instrument through whom much of it was dispensed.

If we needed Elevator Repair to come and repair our escalators as well as elevators, much of the time (as they were authorized by their company to do) they would come in their own car or truck. They would park (obviously) where needed along the street curb or pull onto the sidewalk for quick access to their repair tools and hydraulic machines, which is exactly where the Elevator company trucks would park routinely as well. **There** would be Nero to write them a ticket and order their car towed, **_knowing full and bloody damn well_** that THAT was Elevator Repair! Doing the job that WE CALLED THEM, BLOODY MURDER TO DO!!! I figured I'd better give you an example of what I'm talking about when I tell you, this was just plain insanity on the part of him and on the part of Management that <u>refused</u> to do anything about him. When the head repairman told us about how Nero (using all the threat of Police powers) bullied him away from his repair truck to tow it for being parked where he could conveniently repair the elevator/escalator, we could only try to apologize. The head repairman, though obviously astounded, was surprisingly calm. I guess he knew something we didn't when he was going to have to report back to his own redneck owned company about what just happened, and the sudden unreasonable reactions to his parking in the places Elevator Repair was used to parking in. Needless to say, that policy got modified real quick.

We also came to be grated upon by an old ex-hippie who was also now part of the Ku Klux pack, Sgt. Klak. When both he and Nero came to be put over our precinct at Five Points, two officers immediately transferred out. One of our calmer, wiser officers who was among the two that left said, "I can take Nero. I can take Klak. But I can't take Nero AND Klak!" To say that Klak wasn't too bright, himself, let's just say that as Patrick the starfish and Homer Simpson look like MENSA members in the highest stead compared to Nero, Klak made Nero's brain actually appear to fully function...and Beh-Beh—_that's_ **impossible.**

One Sunday morn, while I was on mobile patrol in the vehicle at Hamilton E. Holmes MARTA station (it used to be Hightower station), I drove over to the next station to take a quick leak. Because that station is so big, there are two cars on patrol there, so I knew there would be coverage. Plus, it was 8:30am and no other soul was out and around yet. The reason for going to the next station was because the only restrooms at H.E. Holmes had no locks on the door, it was in the bus loop where the other drivers had to relieve themselves, and it was just one open stall in the male and female facilities. In other words, for me—with all the police equipment that has to be fought through to go to the bathroom—I didn't want to be in an awkward situation should the door suddenly swing open un-knocked upon—which *did* frequently happen.

My reason for explaining all this to you…? Because, as I was coming out of Westlake station back to the car, who was there but Sgt. Klak. Yes, he wrote me up for being off my beat. Yes, he did get Capt. Nero involved. They both had me sit my unrepresented, lone Black butt in their squad car and Nero proceeded to talk to me as if I had just tried to deliberately run over somebody with the car. I interrupted their chiding and said, "You know, I could see it if I slapped a kid, or pepper sprayed a hand cuffed subject just for spite. All I did was go to the damn bathroom!" They go, "But you should've called out for permission to go." I retort, "I'm 43 years old, I'm not a five year old, going 'Daddy, can I wee-wee—Mommy can I go potty?'"

Well, as I mentioned, I was unrepresented and they wanted me to take either a service point deduction (which takes about a year to earn), or an unpaid suspension day. I knew I wasn't going to go for any loss of what it took a year to get. I also didn't fight it the way I probably could have…because even with these two power geniuses, I just truly didn't believe they were really going to give me a day in the street over something as asinine and beyond belief as going to the bathroom without asking. Well, guess what, folks… And they leaned on me and leaned on me to take the point. They kept claiming it was for *me*… "Oh, keep your money…save your money, Janet, take the point!" Of course, it was *them* trying to save the *department* money because they'd have to pay somebody overtime to work in my place.

Yes, I got a day in the street…over that. Because I *didn't* call out first. For all you defenders out there of them and the system…"Well, Garnett, ya *shoulda* called out like they wanted," let me point out to you, since I'm pretty sure of WHO **you** defenders *are*…if that had been **YOU** that happened to; and **YOU** were given a day in the street over that—I know that I know that I know; and YOU know that you know that you know—that **YOU** would have had <u>FIVE</u> lawsuits going all at once and simultaneously. **THEY** would have known that too…thus, it no doubt, wouldn't have been done to <u>you</u>. Welcome to the world, folks, of the cheek turning, enemy loving <u>saps.</u> THIS is what you get when you try that kind of tactic with dangerous and insane wild animals. All you're doing is giving them a knife and then stretching out your throat. They <u>can't</u> *appreciate* a kind, and cheek turning, enemy-loving attitude. They don't speak that language. The only reason Dr. King was *finally* given the respect and cooperation he got from on-high, was because the Panthers, the Muslims, angry young Blacks out there knifing Whites in the back on the streets arose simultaneously. Before they made <u>their</u> presence known, though, Martin Luther King, Jr. was the "worst kind of Communist, this-that and the other" there was. But when those "groups" arose, much less patient, MUCH less tolerant—**THEN** it was, "OH! OH! Thank-thank-thank **<u>GOD</u>** for Dr. King! Thank **GOD** for Dr. King! Now—what do you want now, Dr. King!?" But as long as we keep being patient goody-two shoes, well—WHY should they be fair and equitable with you? Who are you??

I was told (on the sly) about other officers caught at that station "off their beat" by Klak, but he did nothing to them. That was because they had the reputation of being tough, no nonsense, no taking that kind of crap type of persons. And, they were respected. Not so with little, no trouble causing, no trouble making lil' ol' me. I was told also on the sly that Nero was overheard in the Chief's office talking about what happened to me, and that he was sounding very regretful. "I had to do up one of my good officers!" But the tone of it, I was told, was more akin to, "I had to touch up one a' my good niggers!" It was useless for me to tell Klak and Nero (as I vehemently did) that I could understand such harsh treatment if I had gone there in the middle of the day, or something, lolly-gagging around for 20 or 30 minutes, a car got stolen, etc. Then I could understand. If I was somebody they genuinely did not like, due to being a pain in the rectum, a__hole, trouble causing complainer, etc., then possibly so. But by now, my solidly healed reputation well in place, I had NONE of that negativity on my slate. So, it was primarily a case of contempt. Klak even sabotaged my appeal meeting that I was scheduled to have with the Chief's board to get my day back. He hid the memo under some papers in my in-box, so that I was unaware of it. Nero (how about that!) stepped in and got me up there. But, all the board saw was that loop hole—ya didn't call out, so I was not given the day back. How could I have been so non-combative about such, you ask? Well, the atmosphere had become so negative under those two running the precinct that I figured it would be worth it to be away from them that particular day. At the job on the day I was out, with people asking where I was, and then seeing in the beat assignment book this red "D" next to my name (for Disciplinary action) one of our solid, wise young men asked Klak what happened. "She was off her beat." When they learned it was Westlake, that I was at H.E. Holmes, and I was in the car, he said, "She probably just went to the bathroom!" "But she didn't call out..." The young, wise officer waved him off, cut him off, and walked off from him in disgust. And they were paying somebody twice and a half what it would have taken to pay me for a regular day at work.

You know, it's a sad, but necessary observation one can make at this point. There are basically two kinds of people in this world. The first type is the kind of person who doesn't kick a little dog, because that would be a terrible thing to do. It would be horrible, monstrous, and because they have a soul and a sense of decency, they don't kick the dog. Then, you have the second type of person whom where the ONLY reason they don't kick the dog is because the dog is a fully grown pit bull, a rotweiller, or some other breed of dog whose jaws can bite through a *parking meter*. And, thus...that's the ONLY reason they don't kick the dog. Police officers of the world have a job because of the second personality type that runs around the world.

When it comes to those kinds of people who, due to particular *bents* in their personality go around injuring and endangering people, those kinds of people *aren't* stopped by asking, petitioning, begging, negotiating, etc. Like pearls with swine, the swine just trample the pearls under foot, then turn around to rend you. The only thing that works with that type is use of force. Raw power. Defenders of the weak and helpless can't do their job against violent, uncaring, heartless individuals *without* Force. For those individuals who actually take great delight in being violent and abusive with others...it's called being a bully.

Just as with individuals and roving bands of hooligans, so it is with larger forces and nations. When one group of people wind up in power over another group—and that first group begins to make it a regular habit of stomping on that other group's basic human and civil rights...they don't stop because you ask them. They stop only when it begins to cost them too much to continue. In other words, it has to become either detrimental to their wallets—or detrimental to their *health* to continue! It's because the ones in control *don't listen to anything else*! Folks, the **only** reason Rodney King got justice was because Black people got *angry*—and started pulling White people out of their cars and started beating the hell out of *them*. I mean I truly hate that had to happen...but you see with your own two peepers the results of our staying calm, cool and just "bowin' our heads in prah-h-y-y-a-a-h." Just an, "Aw, shoot!" attitude from the people in charge. How many police shootings of unarmed Blacks have we been seeing occur throughout this country? And how many, "Not Guilty," verdicts have you been seeing? It's literally taken the word of other police officers, the ones of us who truly *are* there to protect and serve, and who want justice done, to get some kind of governmental repercussion to occur.

Tyisha Miller was having a seizure in her car. She was 19 years old. Four downright NAZI's with the LAPD showed up, shot her window out, claimed she had a gun, and shot her twenty-seven times, with four shots going in her head. The neighborhood folks ALL claimed they saw those officers toss a "throw away" into her car, because the "gun" turned out to be a cell phone. "Throw away" is the term used by people in the know for a handy-dandy spare gun carried by certain crooked cops for the purpose of tossing by the dead body of a person unjustly shot by them. When the gun was recovered, it didn't even work. The judges and jury just arbitrarily decided the people were all lying, and (as always) found the officers, "Not Guilty." So then her family secured the services of the late, great Johnny Cochran. During that trial, one officer with a conscience attested to the fact that HE observed those four White officers high five each other after shooting her to death. This was covered on "60 Minutes," television program. And when the girl's grieving family arrived on the scene, that same officer overheard them making "horrible, horrendous degree racial slurs" about them. All they got was fired. I mean, did ANY jail time come their way AT ALL??? WHY aren't these four guys UNDER THE JAIL??? I mean, it's already obvious that the powers that be don't give two dead flies about the victim...that's obvious. But we've seen some police officers get in a hell of a **LOT** of trouble over outright, and down right criminals that they've unjustly mistreated. This was an innocent girl who was sick in her car. And THIS isn't enough to warrant prison time???

Folks, if any of us actually *have* to kill someone...even if it *is* truly justified...

well, we're going to have a little trouble sleeping that night. These guys were _happy_. Congratulating each other over a successful kill.

Do you all recall the 1980 police shooting of Eloise Bumpers in Chicago? Ms. Bumpers was **EIGHTY-YEARS-OLD**. Six deputy sheriffs (all White) claimed she "had a knife," and thus that's why they shot her to death. Realize, folks, there is NO WAY there would NOT have been horrible outrage if Ms. Bumpers was an eighty-year-old White lady. "You mean you six, big, full grown guys couldn't handle an EIGHTY YEAR OLD <u>LADY</u>???"

These six <u>MEN</u> were allowed to describe this <u>eighty-year-old</u>, in bad health <u>woman</u> as if she had the strength of Samson, the speed of Carl Lewis, and the agility of Mary Lou Retton. And they were found, "Not Guilty."

And the whole reason why things have deteriorated to the point where unarmed Black men, women, young people, etc. are not only being shot, but being shot a _**psychopathic**_ number of times and over wallets, combs, cell phones and pagers, is because the justice system over here WILL NOT PUNISH THEM, ACCORDINGLY. I mean, since it's YOU...once again, <u>SO</u>??? And it's because we're so consistently patient and long suffering in silence. Power only respects Power. And power is _stringently_ kept <u>out</u> of our hands. Being financially well off, or having access to some good amount of money is a form of power. And if you'll notice, ANYTHING income producing is carefully and methodically kept out of our hands.

One disturbing thing I noticed some years even before I started work with the Police department, was that whenever we had a legitimate Black business, if that business began to make <u>too much</u> **money**...**SOMETHING** was going to happen to get it shut down. This was especially so if we found a way to finance it, ourselves. I noticed that if we were financed with White money or Jewish money, it would be allowed to stay—sometimes. But <u>anything</u> that <u>WE</u> owned, once large amounts of money began to flow into the coiffures...there was a pattern of some regular excuses resorted to from the government sources that suddenly found reason to shut them down. 1: They come up with some mysterious four people from somewhere who are supposed to have gotten sick or hurt from your product, and thus, you have to be shut down. No, not able to see what was the problem, see if it was a particular situation with those supposed individuals, not be able to do like White owned businesses and even make disclaimers. No, YOU have to be shut down. 2: Some "I" or some "T" wasn't properly crossed or dotted, so you have to be <u>shut down</u>. 3: Somebody's got a complaint about you or how you did business. No, it can't be worked out, negotiated out, or properly looked into to see the nature of the complaint. As far as the governing authority is concerned, that complainant's right, you're wrong, YOU have to be shut down. 4: You're accused of some kind of vague illegality, or some kind of improperly attended to government documents, wrongly signed paper, et.al. <u>You're</u> going to be shut down.

The ONLY enterprise they leave alone, yet pretending to _war_ against it all the way, is the illegal drug business. THAT, they'll let you do—for a time. And you <u>have</u> to look at the final result in ALL of these things. So that YOU can end up with <u>noth-</u>

ing. No ownership of anything. Piecemeal goods, large electronic and digital goods, automobiles, and ESPECIALLY **LAND** and *REAL ESTATE*...if you don't literally walk as if on egg shells, things are deliberately designed to break up if it begins to go or grow in your favor. It's because <u>power</u> is carefully and methodically kept OUT of <u>our</u> hands. This way, you'll be easy to control, you'll be willing to work for lower amounts of pay, you won't be of any financial power and influence to keep certain "things" from happening to you...you name it.

What I'm describing here is the exact same situation the Jews during the Roman Empire period were going through. They were not allowed to be in a self-determinate state of financial or lucrative power, either. The fact that they have power now is due to the fighting and direct conflict they put up over two thousand years ago, and that they fought for nearly that whole two thousand year time table until the 20th Century. The fight was NOT over being given equal treatment with the Romans. It was for the right to <u>have</u> and <u>own</u>, and <u>reap the benefits</u> from their own businesses.

The Jews fought from the days of Christ, to the fortress at Masada, through the Crusades and Inquisition periods, to Middle-ages Europe, et.al. During the 1400's in Russia through Poland, their government officials carried out activities called, "Pogroms." That was literally, "Jew-hunting season," in those lands. And they would literally hunt down and kill Jews, just like Fox-Hunting Season in England and Duck Hunting Season in the U.S. But the Jews persevered, stayed unified and banded together, kept their monies among each other, thus becoming a much needed financial source for the steadily declining European middle and upper class who suddenly found the Jews to be lucrative group to borrow monies from. When the European nobles didn't want to pay them back, though, they would resort to some other excuse for mass extermination. We know what the later half of the 1940's period brought as far as continued frowning upon Jewish financial independence. But, that war was won, and they owned motion picture studios, some banks, hospitals, television stations, etc. And the primary advantage of their having won the war in this respect is that they don't have to worry about games being played with them and with their finances. You know you've won when you're free to do as you bloody well please (obviously, within legal parameters), have what you want, own what you want, etc., and not have to be bothered with some joker somewhere coming up with one hundred and one different excuses to take them away from you.

And, thus, that's what's meant by <u>power</u>. When young White males come into the work world, they're immediately started out with jobs that pay between $60,000 to $110,000 a year. <u>WE</u> don't get those jobs. No matter how many college degrees, technical institute certificates, diplomas, summa cum laude, advanced educational levels we have...WE **DON'T <u>GET</u>** THOSE JOBS. But they're grooming and tailoring their Whites to get on Boards, seats, and chairmanships. When a young Jewish boy reaches the age of fourteen, he has his Bar Mitzvah. That's when the young man's male relatives all come to his place of ceremony with *large* sums of money. I don't mean $500 or anything like that. I'm talking about $20,000, $50,000, etc. It's for him to start his own business. And my fellow Leopards, take a lesson from this: that young Jewish man is *expected to SUCCEED*. Failure is NOT an option. He's supposed to take that money and become successful. If the young man is starting to have problems or difficulties with his business then the older businessmen will come to assist him. Now if this enterprising, young Jewish boy turns out to be a lemon in the successful accomplishment of business, the older businessmen will take necessary steps to keep that kid from failing or falling. Would that WE had such unity. OUR young men end up where? Either dead or in prison. THAT is NO *accident.* And it's because power has been strictly and methodically kept OUT of OUR hands.

The end result of all this? You can be shot to death by the forces that are *supposed* to protect you. So? Nobody gives a damn. ANY and EVERYBODY is able to kill you, rob you, cheat you out of your goods, and you can hardly find protective sources to defend you. Your schools are NOT designed to teach, but to warehouse, only. Those enterprising groups that took on building schools or taking them over to redesign them in your behalf are roundly stopped—some "I" or "T" not properly dotted or crossed. Your businesses that you try to power and get successful are not allowed to succeed beyond a certain point. You're mocked and insulted at every turn. ALL of society's woes and problems are blamed on YOU and laid at YOUR doorstep, as if YOU'RE the ones flying or floating drugs into your neighborhoods, and other dangerous substances and objects.

The forces that be--traveling to other countries tell the foreign peoples, "Don't let Black Americans into your country, 'cause they'll bring drugs and they'll mess up your economy. And if you have a terrific welfare system they're gonna try to get on it, 'cause they don't wanna work!" Likewise, when they come to visit this country, they're surrounded and told about how we're to blame for all this nation's troubles, so when we pass by foreign visitors on the street—we're wondering WHY they're looking at us as if we just killed their parents or something. The ones of them who've been *over here for awhile,* and who've had a chance to see for themselves just who's doing what to whom...they're a little bit nicer to us.

In every stage, with our being powerless and particularly, voiceless, we are consistently left out and unconsidered when it comes to the great spectrum of things. Like inclusion.

CHAPTER NINE

IN THE YEAR NINETEEN NINETY-SIX

IN THE PREVIOUS YEAR TO THE ABOVE, Atlanta was chosen to host the Olympic Games. All of the cheering and congratulating that came about as a result of knowing that all that money was going to come to the city was spearheaded by Andrew Young and his council members, as was seen on TV. And the Olympic officials and heads of committees went right to work in making available proper licensing for the selling of Olympic related items. We're talking about real money. So, I don't have to tell you the hundreds of millions the city was due to enjoy...*we* weren't going to see that kind of money. Oh, we'd get to make a few beds, wait a few tables, answer a few phones, guard a few buildings. But the real money was staying in the "usual" hands.

Olympic pin fever hit everyone also. People were talking about various people spending hundreds of dollars on certain kinds of Olympic pins, particularly the ones with mistakes on them. The most popularly sought after pins were of our MARTA buses, the Varsity Onion Ring one, police badge pins in miniature. The visitors from China were offering a hundred dollars for MARTA Olympic-related polo style shirts, and we heard about bus drivers in UnderGround Atlanta taking their polo shirts off and giving it to the visitors, and just calmly driving the bus in their tank tops! Stories like that abounded. We got law enforcement employees from other top cities like New York, Texas, etc. who came to work with us, and we were on twelve hour shifts. I got a very pleasant and great sense of humored Phillipino U.S. Treasury Customs agent working with me. We traded lots of stories about some overseas locales we'd visited or been stationed at. I worked Vine City station, which had a connecting walkway from the station to the Georgia Dome where several of the events were to be held. And, Darlin', you ain't seen security like you saw for that event. You'd think Osama and his Mama had've threatened to do in THOSE places where the events were to be held! We police officers couldn't even go into the Dome! We thought that was a tad odd. Ticket holders for the events among the general public could get in; ordinary folks *just* hired for security work there, fresh off the street, were given their authorization badges and allowed in to those super secret, blocked off locations. Yet we actual law enforcement personnel, who have to go through strict and the most *stringent* screening, training, and background checks *couldn't* get in??? Okay.

A thing that kept occurring during these events were problems and disputes concerning the tickets. They were supposed to mean free entry into the MARTA stations since that was the main transportation method all were encouraged to use for the Games. However, the free entry became effective for the main events, while some ticket holders were attending the pre-events, which was not covered. So, for the first three days, we *kept* having disputes with persons entering the system with tickets and expecting free entry.

Because we officers were aware of this fact being addressed on the *very tiny* print, and *knowing* the problems it was going to cause, (especially, with our not needing *that* to be in addition to the things that can happen everyday, anyway).

We just played dumb and allowed everybody with an Olympic ticket to enter free of charge, throughout. Well, orders then came from "on high" to start making the people with the tickets pay a fare, because "free entry" was not in effect yet. Now, I can shorten this and possibly make some people mad/self-conscious, or what have you, and just say that every time somebody White decided to stay there and contest it to the point of our having no choice but to make an arrest—we were told (from "on high" again) to back off and allow free entry again. Or I could go into a long, drawn out, detailed explanation of the thing, and how one thing lead to another, and lead to another, etc., etc. But, what the end result was…every time some hysterical White dame got ready to break into tears, or some, "I'm God," attituded White male decided to threaten to call the papers, we were told to allow free entry again. This happened day after day.

Now, we weren't that concerned about whether they called the papers, went into hysterical crying fits, or whatever. That kind of thing happens all the time from persons about to be arrested. It nearly wasn't even the fact that the upper management kept making these changes to accommodate Whites only. Because THAT kind of thing happened with constant regularity to the point of where it was almost not noticed. What DID annoy us was the constant change of orders we kept getting. "We're looking like a bunch of dumbasses!" the various officers complained. We looked like WE didn't know what WE were doing. One rule one minute/another rule the next minute. We knew we HAD to be getting talked about... "They don't know what the HELL they're doin'!" If left to us, though, we were glad to let them all in free, anyway. But we had to follow orders too.

Mr. Clinton, the President of the U.S. then, was having no end of problems due to his perceived fairness to ALL. That's right, I did say, "perceived." All he did was appear to include EVERYBODY in the Democratic process, instead of just paying attention to rich White males only. And he was being exacted a heavy toll from everywhere...be it from the ultra-right talk radio circuit, Ken Star, an attorney who probably was not guiltless, himself, of the very thing he was supposed to be prosecuting the President for...and a thing that ALL of his detractors proved to actually be guilty of, from news stories, to editorial press. His only friends appeared to be us –Black folks.

I do recall that when Mr. Clinton first took office in 1992 and he gave his inaugural speech...I felt for the very **first** time like I exist! For the very *first* time in my existence in these United States...as if from all the way on high—the man in charge looked *all the way down from up there*...and saw me. And then said, "Oh! There you are! Well let's see what we can do about your problems!" In other words... Representation...the way it's SUPPOSED to work. The reason leaders are in office is to REPRESENT you. When you don't have a voice to be heard, and everything is done around you as if you don't exist, and even to your detriment, every time...that's called being under "occupation."

But the President's speech was all-inclusive—of EVERYBODY and ALL! The local Black militant talk show host, Ralph from Ben Hill in the 640 AM dial was also saying after the speech, "I feel funny, Man. I don't know what to say. I feel like...I feel like...an AMERICAN! I – I don't know what to say, Man. I've never felt this way before!"

Naturally, (and I already knew) he was going to have problems. And they'd been non-stop from Day One. Travel-gate, Haircut-gate, White-Watergate, Hilary, called the Hildebeast by Flush Scumbaugh (all because she tried to help enact something or some program that was going to make health care more available to the poor and UNREPRESENTED), one thing after another, after another. Mr. Clinton, during one of his *many* townhall meetings in talking to the Blacks in his audience, said sadly, "I see what you all have to go through now. No matter how good a job you do, no matter how faithfully you accomplish your tasks...it's **never** appreciated...it's **never** thanked...not even acknowledged. Rather, people just wait and wait until they can find something to jab you with. They look for something to blame you for or hold against you. I see now what you all have to deal with."

The degree of stupidity involved in accusing and trying to burn somebody for what one is not guiltless of him/herself is an indicator of HOW desperate some powers are to "make an example" of someone. And everyone of those detractors of his who blew out of proportion that Monica thing—to the point of *impeachment*—all got their just desserts in being unable to return to the elected and appointed offices they had held for an eternity—'cause they'd enjoyed a little candy under some dresses besides their wives, too. And *knew* they did, that's what gets me!

Looking at what we have *now*, (in 2006) all I'll say is that when he and *his* are responsible for there finally being a mushroom cloud standing over where this nation once did, the current president's supporters (the survivors among them, anyway) will be stumbling around *still* talking about "what a fine job he did," "what a great leader he was," AND **still** blaming Bill Clinton.

In the meantime, the leadership here at MARTA was beginning to chip away at the Board's holding the police department's seniority standing. We soon began to hear the word that seniority would soon be out the door, and we would begin rotating shifts every six months. However, other forces apparently persisted too, and we managed to hang onto, a little longer, our seniority status due to our badge numbers. Mine was 194, while others with numbers from 30 on were assured a guaranteed spot on the watch they chose. We basically had the system in place so that the now newly hired officers (after the earlier years' debacle) knew they would have to patiently await more officers being brought aboard to be bumped up into a more senior bracket.

One astounding Black lady who had been earlier hired aboard with us (in fact, not too much longer after me) was Andrella G. She was a strong, physically fit specimen who worked for a time for Sgt. Punkin Puss, and she too suffered the same kind of 1's and 2's evaluation crap like the rest of us Black women under him, before the department allowed us to work where we wanted.

One thing that occurred that showed the caliber of the type of person you have to work with was as follows: Punkin Puss had arrested somebody up on the North line and Andrella, newly hired and assigned to the car, was the transporting officer. I, as the more senior officer there, was put with her to "show her the ropes" after she was released from her Field Training Officer (F.T.O.)

Well, since I'd been so badly trained and unused in certain necessary areas, when it was time for me to show her how to get to pre-trial detention...I had *NO* idea how to get there. I knew where it was, but just couldn't tell her what street(s) to go down. "Now Say With <u>ME</u>, Class! Can you say—'Duck and Cover'!?" I cannot emphasize enough...*how* embarrassing! I mean we drove and drove... *assuredly* verifying the, "She's a Fuck-up," status I had around me at the time. We (or I) *couldn't* say to the Sarge over radio, "Hey, how do we get to pre-trial?" It would have been a **sure** indicator something was wrong. But poor Andrella was getting visibly frustrated with driving around and around fruitlessly, and rightly so, with me there who was supposed to tell her how to get there. I mean, it was *awful*.

I was expecting *any* and <u>*everything*</u> to result from that little escapade. I was just envisioning her later chatting with our co-workers, verifying God knows what about me, etc., etc. But she silently held her cool. She did a *beautiful* job covering for me when the Sergeant radioed us asking what the delay was, and so on. I was

IN THE YEAR NINETEEN NINETY-SIX

choking up, I didn't know *what* to say to her, really feeling that "hanging one's head" sensation and so on. I couldn't even look in her direction.

After that deal was finally, mercifully, over I was expecting (as was earlier stated) to see those unmistakable, tell-tale expressions and smirks on the faces of the other officers around, fully expecting her to have "told the tale." She never said a word about it, apparently. I didn't observe any hushed or sudden starts, and hidden laughter...nothing. I have to mention also that coming from previous military active duty, I guess it's safe to say that we all pretty much admire physically fit, super strong, athletic-types of individuals. It's because the military (particularly Army and Marine types) does emphasize strength and physical ability and prowess. If you were on the "average" side, like me, and was "just adequate" in passing one's physical training tests, leading and training the troops by example and all, when you observed the "Ubermensche and Uberfraulines" sail through all physical obstacles with ease, you have a tendency to stand back in some awe and admiration. And whenever these Ubermenshe and Uberwomensche would deign to even speak to me, let alone be my friend and actually want my company, I found myself feeling that near "primitive" level of gratitude in being so complimented and accepted by them. Well, it was that way with Andrella. To me she was "big", but that's probably because I'm really short, and she was muscular and "built" as we say. A real female Adonis that one like me would feel compelled to stand back in awe and admiration.

I was one hundred per cent convinced that she'd never want me to cross her shadow anymore, let alone say, "Hi" to. But, whenever we met, we'd talk in the staff room, sharing life's stories and heartfelt information about things, gripe about the way we observed some things to be going...in other words...she genuinely seemed to enjoy and accept my company. Yes, folks, I felt extremely flattered. And she never said a word about the debacle that had occurred with me in the car during that period. I never heard a word about it from any feedback from anywhere *else* either. I never, ever forgot that incident because of her nobleness about it, even though the soreness of the incident lingered more in my brain than I guess (or hoped) in hers.

One night about 2:30am while on Morning Watch on the Eastline (in about 1999) Andrella was in the car on patrol. She saw a crowd gathered outside this home and thick black smoke was billowing out of the windows. She stopped the squad car, got out and radioed that there was a fire at this location. The crowd members saw and pressed upon her. "*Please*, Ms. Officer! There's an elderly couple trapped up there!"

Andrella jumped on top of the air conditioning vent outside the building, climbed up on to the roof, and crawled inside the smoke-filled window. She located the elderly man, and put him out on the roof, where he fell but was caught by the crowd. The smoke was so thick when she went back in that she couldn't find the elderly woman, so she used voice contact. Andrella had to crawl on the floor to get to the woman. She located her and got her out. The crowd cheered her and applauded, and the fire department arrived. Andrella had to be given oxygen. But...she went back to work that same night. I feel like saying at this point, "Yes, I'm glad *you* enjoyed the TV movie made about her too!"

At the Georgia State Capital they were having an awards ceremony and luncheon with congressmen, council members, etc. present. Andrella was one of the awardees. When the councilman stood and read out to the assembled VIP's the details of Andrella's heroics, the entire room of members arose and gave her a long standing ovation. We officers who'd heard about it, including some of our sympathetic commanders whispered to each other, "Would **you** have gone in there?" "Would <u>you</u> have gone in there?" The mood and tone was that we knew it would have been the thing to do, but we were in such hushed tones because, as we said, "I don't know!" I said, "Well, I could've tried to go in and do *something*, but then there would have been <u>three</u> bodies in there!"

The response from <u>our</u> command leadership...? Just the usual, sad response and reaction from people who <u>*don't*</u> want to be put in a position to where they're going to <u>have</u> to promote someone from the "I don't wan'em group." The "vine" news again was that the Chief was privately seething. By that time though, nobody's actions from on high came as a surprise to any of us. It took a long, *long* time, but Andrella was <u>finally</u> promoted to Sergeant. Million dollar book deals??? Accolades and offers from the film industry??? Yes, well, moving right along, we had a young man who shot three people at Five Points and was on the loose. When the MARTA train had come into the Station containing two young men involved in a fight and I was the officer who had to intercept and break it up. One of the young men had a gun, which it turned out, he had taken from the man he was fighting. The young man who had the gun, originally, was the same young man who had shot the three people some weeks previously. So that was my capture and the case was brought to conclusion. Everyone thought my name would be in the paper...but only on page 3 of the Metro section was one short paragraph about it saying, "Police apprehended..." And that was that. As my sister said about it, "Well, what did you expect? YOU ain't Angie Dickinson!"

CHAPTER TEN

NOTES ABOUT SO-CALLED BACK UP OFFICERS

AS IS A COMMONLY KNOWN FACT FOR ALL POLICE OFFICERS, our jobs can entail great fun and some perks, a general hearty demeanor and swell times with the members of the general public we serve. And I love serving the public. I love having that power and that means at my disposal to radio up and call up whatsoever public service agency or additional available organization in place for the purpose of assisting or saving the health, welfare and lives of the people out there that we're hired to be of help to. We're not just there to arrest people. People, in general, can have all sorts of situations, problems, concerns, fears, loves, hates, gripes, or a just plain hunger to be heard and listened to. There have been and probably are more potentially *horrible* situations that have been successfully diffused, and unbeknownst to anyone nearby, from just *listening* to someone and letting them gripe and blow off steam. I've had a few come back to me who'd later told me that they *were*, in fact, about ready to go do some shooting or other violent damage to someone who'd really pissed them off. Instead of over-reacting and jerking the cuffs out, I just calmly listened to them explain the nature of their grievance, totally, hear what they felt like they wanted to do to that someone, and then calmly respond. I'd tell them, patiently, that they really needed to find another way to voice their complaint, like through MARTA's phone complaint line, if it was against an employee, or they could find and report the problem to a department head/supervisor. If that didn't work, they could come to us and we'd take the complaint for them. I'd sometimes explain about Magistrate Court when it had to do with a monetary gripe, you name it. The main thing from this whole interaction was that I, an authority figure…was *actually* <u>*listening*</u> to them. Actually, sometimes all these folks need to do is *talk*…talk out their frustrations, make known their complaints to a listening ear. LT. Downin and CPL. Reed patiently listened to <u>me</u> make my gripeful complaints about the way I'd been done from my first year(s) at MARTA. I was allowed to blow off steam…though one does need to know when…'nuff said.

I was 31 years old when I started at MARTA's police department. Many of the other officers there were much younger, still in their 20's. Plus, there were some protocols I'd learned from the military and how to present a united front. However, with the reputation I'd been saddled with from my early days there, it was negative enough in just going day to day with minimal problems. God forbid that you actually make a real mistake. And God ESPECIALLY forbid that you bump heads with some squad members there who already have decided that they don't like you…for whatever reason they'd been encouraged to have. So, my bad rep was further aggravated by some things that occurred with my fellow co-workers that, in my opinion, just couldn't be tolerated. Well, screw 'em. I'm a mess, anyway to 'em, I figured. I might as well not let myself get walked on by *them too.*

Two good and faithful friends I actually managed to make during that period, Pat and Pam, were very instrumental in helping me to calm down, take it a little easier, and not work **so-o-o-o** hard like I was, since it wasn't doing me any good, anyway. I'd say Pam was the more steady officer than Pat, whom a lot of us called, "Crazy Pat." I'd say they took real good care of me and showed me how to relax. I *was* working myself really ragged at the time, trying to please superiors who were just not going to be pleased…even if I saved MARTA from a nuclear mushroom terror, single-handedly.

Pam's take on how I handled things (and with the high degree of successes I was having in bringing most of our trouble calls to a peaceful conclusion) was that since I was older and had a certain degree of maturity, I also had, she said, a certain amount of wisdom.

As was also mentioned earlier, the veterans at the department, along with our academy instructors acknowledged the fact that, yes it can get scary out here. They told us if anybody tells you they aren't scared, they're either lying or crazy. Due to the fact that we are the "thin blue line," we're armed with escalating degrees of weapons according to need. For every positive and downright wonderful interaction we have for the most part with the public…there are those situations we sometimes fall in where you can earn your entire year's salary in just a couple of seconds. And folks, your back-up is no joke. Similar to the armed forces of the world, the thing that has to be concentrated upon is wielding all kinds of people, kindred, different backgrounds, and yes—*attitudes* into one solid, unified field of force against negative elements out there.

I've gone on some dangerous, bad calls backed up and very well so, by persons who, if they *weren't* in the Klan, then the Muslims aren't out here selling Final Calls and bean pies. But those truly racist m.f.'s out there, who had, "I don't like niggers," oozing out of their pores truly risked their life getting to me and backing me up against some dangerous, knuckle-head turds, jumping wayside without notifying Central Control, putting their foot over the dangerous third rail (where the live, dangerous electricity powering the train is) to jump up over to the side of the platform where I was to assist me.

On the other hand, I've had those fellow Black folks I'd be on speaking terms with, and who were supposed to be my friend, fail to back me up, as well. We had a few such persons (fairly speaking, across the spectrum) who were notorious for being noticeably absentee during such "hot" calls involving fights, guns, knives, domestic disputes, disorderly while intoxicated individuals, etc. They would always arrive only *after* they heard the other units responding that they were on the scene. Then, they would come either running up, or sauntering up to the scene.

Of course, as you've heard about that "blue wall of silence," we, for the most part, would complain bitterly to *each other* about so and so who didn't and regularly failed to show up when needed at a bad call (and we *knew* they were in the vicinity). But as far as reporting them to the "big wigs," we would generally keep our cool. There were some incidences, though, where the coward would fail to show or back us and it nearly cost us our life, let alone our health. And that would be when the left alone officer would report in writing what happened to the command structure. THIS would be something they finally couldn't cover for, particularly if the complaining officer was vehement about it. It was one thing to cheat and try to beat us out of seniority, proper recognition for bravery, etc. But even <u>they</u> knew they couldn't cover for someone when it nearly cost someone else their <u>*life*</u>. If something is about to happen, to the point of getting hurt, we *better* get hurt <u>together,</u> instead of you leaving me or not showing up when I need you.

I was once placed on a task by LT. Downin that I found at first inexplicable. It was at H.E. Holmes station (called Hightower then), and she had me to go into the ladies' restroom and perform radio checks. Then she had me stand at various points in the station lower level while she performed more radio checks with me telling her whether I could copy her at different areas. I finally put two and two together. When I satisfactorily told her I could copy her fine at all levels, my conclusion was confirmed. LT. Downin gave some disciplinary suspension days without pay to a particular female officer who had just continued to go too far in failing to back us up, and failing to get to us in time—while being at the very station she was dispatched to. The radio check test the Lieutenant was having me to assist her in running was due to this particular officer's using the excuse that she couldn't hear her radio in various parts of the station. That was my Lieutenant...she ran the check, herself, to give the benefit of the doubt before just <u>*having*</u> to do *something* to this individual.

My buddy, Crazy Pat, was the officer that the other one had failed to back up for this particular "last straw" situation the Lieutenant got involved in. Pat handled nearly <u>all</u> her calls quickly and mostly herself. She was expertly able to diffuse nearly anything before it *needed* to be put over the airwaves. So, when SHE called out that she needed another unit (which is the next thing to the most serious need for back up call we've got) everyone knew it was no joke. I was headed toward Five Points from Vine City, roughly two to three miles from Hightower (in the car) and when I heard Pat's call, I wheeled around almost on two wheels, sped past Ashby, approaching Westlake and I just missed hitting by inches a black Buick Regal, which would have caused me to be able to go no further.

We'd been advised that even if on the way to back up an officer, if you hit somebody's vehicle with your squad car you *have* to stop. Even if there are clearly no injuries, if you leave that scene (and with MARTA being involved), it's a sure bet that people see dollar signs involved. And when you come back to the scene, there will be dozens of "bodies" everywhere, the vehicle you feather-tapped will be upside down, ambulances will be all over the place, and yes, they'll all say you did it!

However, I railed past that, got to Hightower in about six minutes (I was timed) and thankfully, everything got successfully diffused by her after all. As soon as the units called out that they were cleared of the call, Officer Whatsername came sauntering out from (don't know where) and to our location. The question began to be asked, "How does Janet get to Hightower all the way from Vine City in six minutes, and it takes Whatsername all day long (ten minutes, which IS all day long when we're talking about an incident of this nature) to get to Pat's location—and she's been at that station the whole time!?"

When the Lieutenant was giving Whatsername the disciplinary days she told her, "You better be worried about whether or not Pat decides to kick your ass too!" However, the only reason something was happening about this in the first place was because LT. Downin took the step to do something about it. Pat wouldn't have complained to upper management about it.

However, another bad situation we had was when Pat and I had this big, drunk, roughly 28 year old who decided to take a fighting stance with us, pull his shirt off, and become dangerously violent. The male back up officer we had was a lean, dark tall Black officer (we'll call him Harrods). Though he had a fierce face and some maturity, and had an, "I dare you to "f" with me!" aire about him, <u>he</u> was also notorious for not giving adequate (or any back up) at all when needed. I knew we were going to need all the help we could get. I also <u>*knew*</u> we weren't going to get it from Harrods. Things were getting so badly out of hand, with this being one of those guys who had no weapon on him, just relying on his two dukes (and remember I had said that this was the type that usually took between five to seven of us to get subdued), that even one of the Sergeants who was recovering from bone splinters in his hand and was on light duty had come down there with us. I had pulled out my baton and was braced. Suddenly, the conflict was on, with the light duty sergeant, myself, the Klan member who, as earlier described had jumped wayside to get to us, Pat...and Harrods who was just standing back, looking. We desperately needed ALL hands to help subdue this guy. But that's all we did…subdue him. Yes, I cranged on his legs with the baton in prescribed manner (though I was quickly halted by the Sergeant), received a nice kick to the mid-section so that I carried a large dusty shoe print in my middle, and the best everybody was able to do was to manage to get the cuffs on him from the front, rather than the prescribed "behind the back" requirements. When we all got upstairs, the other sergeant up there (who we all nick-named the Marlboro Man, because he looked and had a demeanor just like him) who had other units who had caught the train in and driven to the station to meet us there for additional assistance. Sgt. Marlboro said in his gruff, cigarette-cracked voice, "I want that man handcuffed in the back." The other male units there decided among themselves, and two stalwart officers slowly took their gun belts off, got their cuffs out, left their weapons outside, and went into the holding cell with our violent guy to remove the cuffs from his front and get them to the back. They were successful and apparently the guy didn't give them much trouble.

However, I along with Pat, were livid about the non-back up received from Harrods. Officer Klan was in a precarious situation, jumping wayside (he truly could have been electrocuted), Sgt. Holt (from light duty) was injured and had no business having to risk further injury to himself to help us, but that's him—he wasn't going to leave us hanging…we NEEDED Harrods. And he was standing by unmoving. That was the one time that we lowly officers (Pat and I) angrily complained to the Lieutenant (another male one on duty) and Sgt. Zach, who had also made it to Five Points to help on this call. The Lieutenant on duty calmly said, "Well you can write it up, if you want. We'll process it on through." Well at that point we suddenly stopped and backed down. We weren't prepared to carry our complaint that far. We both went, "Wel-l-l-l…." and trailed off. But Sgt. Zach (after meeting in private with the other officers and leadership) and discussing his feelings about it came back to us. He knew the deal…that it would take _substantially_ much for us to ever want to write a fellow officer up, even under that circumstance. Both Pat and I alike quickly left off of being angry for very long about things. Sgt. Zach stuck his head back in the Lieutenant's office where we were still seated and still blowing off steam when he learned that we didn't want to pursue it.

Sgt. Zach told us in his own inimitable way, "I'm giving you two a direct order. Write him up." Being the years ago it was, he had probably said, "I want you to write his ass up. This has to quit happening." Well Harrods was a drinking buddy of one of the other long-reigning lieutenants and from what we heard, nothing of a substantial nature was done to him. We could live with it. What choice did we have? We weren't going to write him up, anyway.

Two other White officers who failed to provide back up in a dangerous situation were _seemingly_ successfully disciplined. One of them was, in fact, fired. He was on the same train headed into Hightower on one car, and an officer who was on another car with a wild bunch of out of control juveniles called out that he needed another unit to assist him because the group was beginning to start fighting, despite an officer being on that train car. The officer with disorderly juveniles could see through the train window the other officer on board in the next car. Trying to cover for the White officer who wasn't responding, the officer in trouble called on the talk-around channel, Channel 2. He called and called the other officer, and then came on the main channel and yelled out, "Hey, man you better get over here and help me!" The White officer, when the train arrived onto the platform, stepped off the car, *turned his radio off*, and left. That made B.W. mad. He complained substantially to the higher ups, and the non-responding officer was fired.

Then, one of our White sergeants pulled a similar boner at that same station one night. The call was involving a gun, a person who was shot at the station, and the sergeant claimed he couldn't find anything. It was when a patron at the station *found and turned in the gun*, himself, that the sergeant had a lot of questions to answer. Well, management covered up for him in that they removed his stripes, but put him in a cushy daytime assignment handling police and parking lot equipment while driving the van all day. And things were also affixed into place where he wouldn't lose any of his salary. The sergeant who had been in charge of this detail, Sgt. Gaither, was an older Black sergeant who always looked *sharp*. In fact, militarily sharp. He drove a Goldwing motor cycle, ALWAYS looked crisp and together--he looked **good**. The other officers said of him that when television news crews and live coverage was made over something that happened on the MARTA system, and it involved police, they hoped and prayed that Gaither would be the one captured on TV and/or interviewed, because he always looked so good, it would give the viewing world a positive image of us officers there. Sgt. Gaither was deep voiced and very well liked by us all. He was fair and NEVER went out of his way to burn anybody. The only time we saw him get pretty agitated would be when a lieutenant or above would go behind him and change either the work schedule or our beat assignments without telling him. "And I'll be working on the old schedule, calling out the wrong beat assignments. And see, that makes me look like I ain't got MY shit together!" he would say. I also saw him get annoyed when he and I were both given a "bus in trouble" call—that is, it was a "disorderly person" aboard the female driver's bus— and she stopped it out on the road and refused to budge any further until a police officer(s) got to her location. A clear indication of something reasonably serious. Sgt. Gaither and I were both in separate cars but we got to the bus driver's location at the same time, emergency blue lights going.

When we boarded the bus we found out that the "trouble call" involved a female passenger with a baby stroller—and she supposedly refused to fold it down, as was required. The passenger told us the stroller didn't break down, and that's why she wasn't doing it. The other passengers aboard, visibly annoyed at being late for their destinations, kept saying, "It's not in <u>our</u> way!" "We told her to go on!" "I'm late for work!" We convinced the driver to continue on to Hightower station (she was just a little ways away from it anyhow) and we cleared the call. The Sergeant said to me when returning to our cars, "I'm pissed off, Garnett! I'm pissed off! We could have had an accident on the way out here! And over something like <u>that</u>!" Although he was very right, still, when a call (especially a potential "trouble call") is success-fully cleared, with ALL parties leaving in-tact and unharmed, I for one, am <u>always</u> relieved.

Even so, Sgt. Gaither was the one who was over these special equipment and parking lot projects during the day. So when the Sergeant who was demoted was "punished" HE was placed on that daytime assignment, and Sgt. Gaither—more senior than him or anybody there—was put in that Sergeant's old slot...on Evening Watch, 3:00pm to 11:00pm walking a beat, riding the trains. Some "punishment" for the Sergeant who screwed up, huh?

CHAPTER ELEVEN

THE RODNEY KING DEBACLE

WHEN I WAS STILL A YOUNG ADULT (having just turned 18), there was an incident that was covered on the news in Louisville. A White man was shown going before a judge for prosecution. What happened was he was a spectator/attendee at a Ku Klux Klan rally. This White man went and got in his car, started it up—and drove head on and dead in to the group of Ku Kluxers as they made their hateful speeches and so on. When asked by the judge why he did it he said, "Because I just couldn't stand to hear anymore of the horrible things they were saying about all those Blacks, Jews, and others." My mom, who was also watching the report suddenly said, "The NAACP ought to take up a collection for his defense and bail him out!"

Those seemingly few Whites who don't jump on the Bandwagon with their fellows, and go out of their way to expose something or do something that's beneficial for US are priceless in their exposure of things supposed to be hidden. That is due to the fact that <u>whatever</u> WE say or attempt to bring to exposure is **ALWAYS** ignored, disregarded, and just plain accused of being false news. To date, I don't know of ONE Black woman in these United States who has **EVER** been successful at bringing a White attacker or offender to trial and prosecution. We can <u>always</u> expect one of four excuses, but the outcome is always the same:

1. They can't find who did it—(they're not trying to, either)
2. There's not enough evidence to convict
3. If you're pointing to him/her and vehemently saying, "That's the one who did it!" you get accused of doing it to *yourself.*
4. If you've got unmistakable proof, witnesses, video tape, etc. of the offense and offender and DEMAND something be done, the powers that be just plain and simply <u>don't act</u>. Nothing is done.

My sister was struck by a hit and run driver (a White guy), knocking her down with his maroon car, not stopping, and speeding off. SEVERAL witnesses came to her aide, gave her their addresses, phone no.'s and names, and promised to be available when the police called for their testimony. We couldn't **GET** Louisville Police department to do anything. So I just went up to the offices <u>everyday</u> until they finally sent someone to the home that they traced the guy's license number to. This woman who was home alone when they came vehemently stated that on that particular day, "My husband was in/at such and such place!" I could tell by the tone and declaration she had that apparently she truly believed he *was* at the place she thought him to be in. The fact that the place he *was* in fact at, rather than the place she thought him to be told me that apparently, he must have been enjoying some "hanky-panky" behind her back. Needless to say; I continued up there daily, the excuses and final tone of theirs wavering back and forth.

When I wouldn't be dissuaded, I got a call from a Louisville Police sergeant who told me, almost tongue-in-cheek, that since the car had an Indiana license plate, it was going to have to be handled in Indiana. When I telephone Indiana Police and relayed that information to them the officer on the line said, "He's (the Louisville Sergeant) crazy! NO, you don't have to prosecute <u>here</u>!" And I knew it. When I told my sister about the conversation she sighed and said, "Just forget it. He's probably run over two or three other people by now!" And nothing was ever done. The only consolation I have is that *maybe* this may have put a slight and a damper on the trust in his marriage...if his wife is not a ditz!

But that's the general result of <u>*any*</u> kind of offense committed against us by Whites...they cover for each other to the bitter end. No matter HOW wrong they are and how RIGHT we are. And if one of theirs actually *does* get in trouble over something they've done to us...then the retaliation game goes on against the Black individual they got in trouble over harming. It's a blatant case of the horse thief blaming and punishing the *horse* when he gets in trouble for horse theft, as Frederick Douglas pointed out. And it matters not if the butt of their retaliation is man, woman, boy, girl or even toddler...they *HAVE* to engage in their program of reprisal against their Black victim.

In my noticing of that, and in keeping with Sun Tzu's advice, I observed a particular fact in how to fight or prevent such. When the group of *them* targets one of us and starts to smell blood and they ALL surround you from all angles (whether this be them ALL talking about you terribly in the press, ruining your reputation, clamoring for your arrest for some bullshit reason, whatever), they don't let up or stop until you're either dead or "destroyed." There's only one thing that stops them. IF you can manage to reach out and severely injure or kill (so to speak) at least ONE of them—they **ALL** back off. That is the earmark of a coward. They were ALL piling on at once—with glee. Same as with a lynch mob. There have been White sheriffs in the nation's sordid past history who successfully defended their Black prisoner from a lynch mob by calmly walking out to the crowd, drawing his gun and then *killing* the leader of the mob. And the mob would disperse. To pile onto and enjoy victimizing a lone, defenseless individual is the action of a bunch of cowards...face it. And when persons committing cowardly acts are faced with a downright **_brutalizing_** punishment that is just as merciless and severe as the crime the mob was going to commit against you, they're not only stopped dead in their tracks, they back off and forget about trying it (at least to *you*) again. They'll *want* to very, very badly. But for the most part, they'll keep their claws to themselves from then on.

Since the powers that are representative of those running the show have control of the court systems as well as every other system in place, it should come as no surprise to anyone that offenses committed by members of the governing group are usually *VERY* leniently dealt with. For the non-represented group, when being yanked up for the same or comparatively minor offense, punishment after punishment is heaped upon that group member to the point where it reaches *medieval* proportions. The drug war is the most glaring, damaging and unnecessary thing we've got going in this country to date. I mean...they DON'T WANT TO STOP IT!!! Drug use, that is. Plus, there already IS *defacto* legalization of drugs for Whites, anyway. They're free to smoke all the dope, sniff all the coke they want...and they don't have to worry about being sentenced to eternity in prison the way our people are.

There are hundreds of thousands of *harmless* people currently serving **RIDICULOUSLY** long prison sentences...behind some stuff that *can't even get IN* here without government assistance—in "looking the other way," when they come in to this country. Too many forces are making *FAR TOO MUCH MONEY* off of this. And if you want to play games and *pretend* to be desirous of stopping illegal drugs from coming into this country, AT LEAST **stop** destroying all these promising young lives (some being Honor students) with imprisoning them behind the mere word of some turd who would lie on his own mother to get a break. And for the length of *time* they're being jailed for. The whole reason, again, for this lop-sided inconsistency is power and who has it. This government of ours **KNOWS** better than to jail young White kids for these harshly lengthy drug sentences...or for any sentences, period, barring murder. Because they know that if they imprison Whites with the same total disregard and wreckless abandon as we get jailed, i.e., 24 years to life, 15 years to life, three consecutive life terms over NO physical evidence...just the accusation of "conspiracy"—THEY will turn this WHOLE COUNTRY into a Twin Towers building. Overnight! Without conscience. Without hesitation. And WITHOUT DELAY! So the U.S. Government forces don't *dare* pull that kind of foolishness with them. As far as the consistency analysis, whenever some law enforcement officer sees a Black skin with *any* kind of cocaine substance, even if it be powder...they almost always classify it as "Crack." "It's CRACK." "Crack cocaine." So that the harsher, harshest, lengthiest sentence will just arbitrarily be given to *them*. The whole and true facts are that it's because we keep taking it. THEY, the Whites, don't take it.

Dick Gregory had observed years ago that no one had shown a more *passionate DISRESPECT* for non-violence than our American government. As long as the American Indian, he stated, behaved himself and didn't make any noise, he was forgotten about, neglected, left to diseases, alcoholism, suicide, poverty in the extreme—you name it—all up there on the Reservation. It was only when he made some noise in 1971 with leaders like Russell Means and Leonard Peltier, that President Carter (the last human being before Bill Clinton) in the White House began to enact some kind of programs of small restitutional compensations for them. It wasn't a whole lot, but it got them noticed. You remember I had already mentioned the attitude toward Dr. King before Malcolm X, Stokely Carmichael, and H. Rap Brown with his, "Burn, Baby, Burn!" cries alerted them that maybe they should be grateful for someone like Dr. King, who wanted to use a milder approach.

So now we come to the incident with Mr. Rodney King and the way that the debacle with him changed the face of some police departments.

Yes, the original jury could find "nothing wrong" with what they had just witnessed on video tape. The police were just doing their job...keeping *them* (i.e., <u>us</u>) under control. As much insult of the intelligence of the largely Black jury members who found O.J. Simpson "Not Guilty," it appears no one remembers the way the all-White jury members in the first Rodney King trial asked the judge to define the word, "Beat" for them.

And, this is where I, as an officer and also as a Black American citizen, want to express my heartfelt thanks and appreciation to that conscientious citizen who video taped and then turned in to the news the shocking scene he caught. He tried, first, to interest the police department in it, but they didn't give a rat's patoot. Thank you, George, for going farther and giving that tape to the news for the world to see.

When nothing was found wrong, and the four were all acquitted, the normal outcome for all things that happen to citizens Black, and the Black community—finally exasperated, did what they did,, it was the subject of news programs, worldwide. My fellow Black folks...don't LET yourselves be taken in by a large portion of White America's claims that as far as they were concerned, the Blacks were rioting, "Just because they WANTED to!" Don't be taken in by that statement. I'm telling you. WHITES are much *more* astounded, in truth, that it took you *this* long to respond like you did. Trust me, good people, they **KNOW** you're being wronged, and wronged *horribly* every waking day of the week in these United States. They <u>know</u> better than WE do that **they** would have revolted and torn the country to pieces in a matter of moments if just a *fraction* of what's been done to us were done to <u>them</u>. A few honest White callers called in to Larry King Live on CNN during that second trial period going on, saying, "Larry, all it would take would be one in four WHITE males to be incarcerated. That's

ALL IT WOULD TAKE! And there would be a revolt and revolution here that would make the Civil War and Revolutionary War combined look like a tea and crumpet picnic outing."

One of my Sergeants at MARTA told me about a White drinking buddy he had in the military reserves unit he serves in. They're both Majors in the Reserves. And he told me that this White drinking partner he has would say things to him like, "You know, I don't know WHY you all don't just start shooting White people...I would!" But for all appearance sake in public, Whites will forever, it seems, want to stay on that river in Egypt, "Da Nile." And never admit, publicly, to ANY wrong doing, whatsoever. Oh, they'll freely admit to wrongs done in the nation's history—stuff it's too late to do anything about.

I've noticed this trend of our judicial system of today to start dragging out and re-trying cases of lynchings and murder that happened nearly 90 years ago, practically—the most recent being 50 years ago, where most of the persons involved are either dead or about ready to die. Ladies and gentlemen of the jury...THERE ARE <u>TOO MANY</u> wrongs that are CURRENT, right NOW that you should be trying...those twenty-six hangings in those Mississippi jails of young Black males that have occurred between 1987 and 1996 that the officials arbitrarily listed as "suicides," the Tyisha Miller shooting by the four White officers I spoke of earlier, the questionable hangings right here in Louisville on Cane Run Road at the Big A shopping center in the late 1970's...again being listed as "suicides," although it was impossible for those persons to get all the way up to where they were without some kind of a crane. It was when some racial wrongs were about to be righted in the city during the time, and there were several White reprisals going on in retaliation. There's also the Kenneth Walker shooting in cold-blood by a White Columbus, Georgia sheriff's deputy, Donald Glisson. Glisson first said that Walker was behaving in a threatening manner, so he put two bullets in his head. After a year of patient fighting by the NAACP legal officials, the tape of the incident was finally released. It showed a calm, subdued Kenneth Walker, one of five innocent subjects roughly pulled over in their white SUV, being rough housed out by police, and then Deputy Glisson aiming his gun and putting two shots in Walker's head. When that tape came out, Glisson then changed his story and said the gun accidentally went off—twice. Authorities there in Columbus are STILL failing/refusing to prosecute the officer. These are some of the many ills and wrongs still in place, among *many* more, that can be re-opened and prosecuted, their being *much* more recent.

During the second trial phase of the Rodney King trial we police officers throughout the nation (we heard even in Canada) were on high alert and had to work 10 hour shifts. People in the 'hood for the most part though, were very cool and very supportive of us regular officers who they knew served them so well. And then—there were the camcorders...everywhere! It seemed various citizens and other persons were following us around with their camcorders trained on us! We had been briefed by command about our demeanor and what to say and not to say to any media and press that might question us. It was quite a time! I had one group of visitors stop me on the plaza at Five Points wanting me to pretend to beat them with my baton while they filmed. Obviously, I couldn't oblige.

The police departments throughout the nation also changed the type of police baton we used. We went from the long, black stick to the ASP baton—a metal collapsible one. It was meant to both diffuse a situation and be a weapon, if necessary, for our protection. With this type of baton being collapsible, when you took it out, it was small, short and had a gray handle. This would be much more unlikely to cause an already excited subject to become more agitated if we were pulling out this big, black stick. If the ASP baton was suddenly needed for action, you'd flick it and out the metal stick weapon would come, in sections.

When the jury came back with "Guilty" verdicts this time, we heard about how, later on, belligerent White supporters of the police came up with collection monies for Sgt. Stacy Koon for when he came out of doing his jail time. I hear that because of his fellow Whites sticking by his side so he wouldn't be "hurt" for his part in a racial crime, they've made him, to date, worth six million dollars.

On the local WSB radio AM in Atlanta at the time, there was still on that station a liberal talk show host named Mike Malloy. He was a pleasure to listen to as he didn't run down Bill Clinton all the time or talk about Hilary as if she were going to doom civilization because of caring about the powerless and the voiceless. On the night before the second verdict I had gotten a chance to call in to talk to him. The unfortunate Reginald Denney incident had also occurred. The same Whites who were praising and protecting the four policemen's actions suddenly had eyes to see and ears to hear. They were crying for charges against Reginald Denney's attackers for, "Attempted Murder!" "Torture!" I had pointed out that difference to Mike, but he chided me for that comparison, saying what Police did and citizens did under these two different circumstances shouldn't be compared. Nonetheless, he gave me a *lot* of time to make my point. I told him that as a police officer, myself, we'd all been made to look bad by these guys' actions. I pointed out that even the F.B.I. officials, who had no love for Black people, themselves, stated that what we were witnessing on that video tape was a hate crime. And also, reflecting on how much like an animal the officers kept describing Rodney King... "He was like a bull..."/ "...a Bear", and so on, I said that if Rodney King *had* have been an actual animal...a bull, a bear, a dog, cat, horse, sheep, pig, or what have you...and being beaten like that, can you imagine the OUTRAGE that would *truly* grip the heart of America?

However, *before* that tape, nearly ALL of Black and Hispanics' complaints were disregarded unless there was unhidden evidence to back it up. Remember the audio tape that another conscientious White citizen made of that Texaco Gas Company executive talking about "Black jelly beans being stuck at the bottom," when it came to company promotions? Another invaluable source to back up claims of the "glass ceiling" thing. The whole benefit of these captured filmed and taped evidence is to get an undeniable confession or admission from the perpetrators' own mouth about what they are truly doing to both keep things the way they are, and to turn back the clock.

The one real victory we can consider ourselves accomplished of will be when OUR WORD will be respected and considered, <u>without</u> having to wait for somebody Caucasian to verify or back it up. When our complaint can be seriously taken and investigated, to truly see if it warrants just being arbitrarily thrown out or not, that will be another breath of fresh air in just that accomplishment, itself.

CHAPTER TWELVE

THE OKLAHOMA CITY BOMBING INCIDENT

THERE IS A WORLD OF INFORMATION observant people can gather from even small occurrences, let alone big ones. When that tragedy in Oklahoma occurred in April of 1999 and the first trinkling reports coming in were that it was suspected that the perpetrators were Middle Eastern, you remember the clamoring calls and cries. "Well we ought'a BOMB Arabia!" "We ought'a BOMB Libya!" "We need to **bomb** over there!" "**BOMB! BOMB! BOMB!!!**"

As soon as the report came out that the perpetrator was American—and White...all of that **stopped**. Dead on in its tracks. NO call to bomb the Michigan Militia, <u>no</u> calls to "Bomb Michigan!" ALL of those cries for retaliation <u>stopped</u>. Instead, the calls coming in to the Right Wing radio talk shows were, "Uh, well, we understand their frustration." "Well, what <u>DID</u> happen at Waco?" etc...

For **ALL** of the unwarranted, unnecessary and downright *dirty* attacks on Mr. Clinton from ALL sides except ours, if these same knucklebrains (who also NEVER even say, "Thank you" to Rev. Jesse Jackson every time he brings American hostages back home) would stop and *THINK*, they'd have seen the successes there were in dealing with the terrorisms that occurred during his administration. The blind

Egyptian cleric, who was fingered by CIA forces as being behind the first bombings of the Trade building in New York, was *apprehended* afterwards in 1993, put on trial in the States, convicted and is now in prison. Mr. Clinton appeared on television after the Oklahoma City bombings and after consoling and reassuring the affected families, he said that justice would be swift and "Certain." McVey and his associates were captured, brought to justice, imprisoned, and McVey was executed. During his administration.

And as his detractors continued to shoot themselves in the foot, Mr. Clinton desperately wanted to go and get Osama and his bunch...but the cries from Flush Scumbaugh to the ex-burglar who tried to steal your Constitution during Watergate...G. Gordon Liddy, ALL were hollering about, "He's just trying to 'wag the dog'!" And the Congress, which is supposed to OK these acts allowed *themselves* to be taken in by the negative mood of the nation and only allowed that mistaken bombing of the African clinics. I know that after the ship has sunk <u>everybody</u> knows how she might have been saved, but just as Mr. Osama and his Mama finally did the deed in 2001, one September of the eleven...he *may* have been *neutralized* before he had a chance to do it IF YOU'D HAVE GOTTEN **OFF** THAT MAN'S **BACK**/ shut **up** your attacks and accusations/and let him do THEN in 1996 what he felt was going to have to be done.

Plus, don't think common sense or even *consistency* worries these detractors. BECAUSE THESE <u>SAME</u> DETRACTORS...WHO JABBED AND STABBED AT MR. CLINTON WHEN HE WANTED TO GO AND GET OSAMA AND HIS MAMA <u>THEN</u>...**WERE <u>SOON</u> IN 2001 WANTING TO CRUCIFY HIM STILL FOR NOT GOING AFTER OSAMA'S GROUP** IN 1996...**AGAIN, <u>WHICH HE WAS TRYING TO DO.</u>**

For these people NOW in 2006 who are wandering around aimlessly, hopelessly, jobless, some now homeless, retirement money-less (thanks to ENRON, et.al) I'm thinking of Bill Maher of the former, "Politically Incorrect," show that he lost employment with due to his criticisms of the administration responsible for all of the above and more. He, along with Congresswoman Barbara Lee and some others, received very grievous death threats when they weren't in favor of invading Iraq. Now that facts have proven them and those others to have been very correct, Mr. Maher said, from his new HBO run series, "I wonder how many of those people who called in all those death threats are planning to offer any apologies, and take back those u-u-u-g-g-l-y statements and descriptions of me and mine!" For you same detractors (I take it who don't have loved ones in Iraq right now) who are still trying to justify the invasion, remember it was over their supposing to have WMD's over there. Little North Korea with their bouffant hair-do wearing, "I wanna be Elvis" crazy dictator, Kim Jong IL, has been standing there, both hands out in a "wave it to me" gesture saying, "Yeah, WE got WMD's! <u>WE</u> got 'em! Come on with it!" But just like with Timothy McVey's group, the Michigan Militia, the U.S. is tolerating all that with the patience of Job. My heart truly goes out to the American soldiers AND the hundreds of thousands of killed and wounded Iraqis during this debacle.

NO human being on this planet has any business talking about the sins of other nation's rulers (when they really haven't been talking about invading YOU), and using what <u>they</u> did as an excuse to do what you want to find justification to do. You're not over there to benefit <u>them</u>. You're over there because they've got something YOU WANT. Initially, when the <u>first</u> Gulf War was fought, once everyone *admitted* that it was because of oil more so than these news reports that turned out to be false of Iraqi soldiers taking Kuwaiti babies out of their incubators and onto the floor, the whole thing was about NOT letting oil prices, thus gasoline prices, <u>shoot through the roof.</u> Which is what administration forces *<u>promised</u>* would happen if the Arabs and Hussein were to be in charge of those prices. But <u>who do you see those oil and gas prices shooting through the roof under</u>??? Hussein's gone. America's in charge. And America's Big Businessmen, with their bottomless pit greed levels, can't seem to stick it to us all enough. After all, they've got their four hundred prophets of Baal and talk show circuits who have but one primary message only... "The poor have too <u>much</u> money and the rich <u>don't have enough!</u>"

Quick scenario Some foreign power from somewhere shows up at our American shores. They talk to us American citizens; "Your president is a b-a-a-d man! He stole your election (Shut up and let me finish). He's ruining your economy, isn't he? Tell you what...<u>we'll</u> invade and remove him from power! We'll put in somebody who'll...*take care* of you! <u>We'll</u> bring freedom and fairness to all your citizens! How does that sound?" It's called "oily"—"slimy" is more like it. The foreign power goes to work, arbitrarily bombing everything and everybody in sight. And their love, care and concern about the American citizens is observed being carried out by these foreigners spending <u>all their time</u> at the Federal Reserve Bank, Fort Knox, the Silicon Valleys and other places of potentially wealth containing interest. I won't go into describing further outrages, I'll just pose one fact of our response. You don't think that from every rooftop, from every Church, from every house, even American Muslim mosques,

from every synagogue, every man hole cover, etc., there *wouldn't* be hard, horrendous fighting, shooting and angry cries from all American citizens working feverishly to get those suckers OUT...? Even the kindly, positivity teaching, patient and loving Robert Schuller of the Crystal Cathedral, with his 95 year old self, would be out in the street with a bandana tied around <u>his</u> head tossing Molotov cocktails everywhere yelling, "GET OUT OF MY COU-HUNTRY, YOU **BASTARDS**!!!"

I said earlier that my heart goes out to both our soldiers AND the Iraqi citizens suffering through this escapade. The soldiers have no choice. And it's not their place to complain or choose where they go or what they do. The whole thing is about "orders." They go and do what they're *ordered* to do. So the arms and tools can't really be held responsible for what the brain at Central Headquarters is compelling them to do. Likewise, the Iraqi citizens under attack can't be blamed for resorting to what they are in their own defense, and trying to drive the invaders out of their country... whether you call them "patriots" on our end, or "insurgents" on theirs. There was no exit strategy that was properly thought through before U.S. forces went.

Getting back to McVey and his Militia members, keep in mind, those of you who can find a way to justify ANYTHING this country does, EXCEPT give equal representation to all of its citizens, those guys were suspected of sending Anthrax in the mail to governmental and politicians' offices. There was, just briefly, a news spot covering how the Militia members cheered when THEY heard about the Twin Towers going down. Being the news junkie that I am, I manage to catch stuff that the news programs only report one time. Yet and still, even these facts aren't enough to seem to cause the American populace to rise up in righteous anger and indignation, calling for these groups' end. Hmm—wonder why?

In observing the earlier described vast differences in the reactions of the main American populace when it was learned who had in fact done what, I discovered a fact that I suppose I hadn't really *felt* previous to that. White people are—*free*! I mean, truly, truly—and absolutely free! I discovered that fact like I did at no other time in these United States, until that difference in reaction to the offenses, no matter how terrible or no matter how minor. You know and I know too what the reaction would have been had any Black American group or Nation of Islam, or whatsoever *other* group in place had've even been suspected of something like that. The "yee-haws" from gleeful White people finally having a license, it would seem, to go on the hunt for Blacks again with their shotguns and so on, as they did in the good ole' bad days would resound North, South, East and West. Had those Enron, World Com, and other executives who'd done what they did been us...the jails would have been filled with the executives, their families, their relatives, their friends...they'd have emptied out the *drug dealers* to make room for all of them.

But the fact that all that their fellow Caucasians do is quietly, patiently tolerated and allowed to exist...only going after them if enough of their own fellows get hurt really showed me something. I personally believe that everyone of these pharmaceuticals, drug companies, doctors and hospitals, etc. ought to be charged and sentenced for having the actual, outright *cures* for some of these diseases out here—and are deliberately holding them *back* so they can keep making more money only *treating* the disease, causing people to have to keep buying more product. I would **love** to get my hands on these jokers in charge who don't give a damn about human beings, human life or human suffering...but just give that damn about lining their own pockets. As I had also previously mentioned, there *is* legalization of illegal drugs for most wealthy Whites. I mean, they openly talk about and freely get hold of and use everything from Mauwi Wowy, to cocaine, their ecstasy...even with it being technically illegal. When and if they get caught, it *does not* result in their getting lengthy prison terms. The ones of them that aren't super wealthy *may* get a *little* time (2 to 3 years) only if guns might have been involved. THEY do NOT get sentenced to eternity in prison.

Plenty of us have been told by in-store security guards that they have seen their fellow security guards observe Whites shoplifting items...and they looked the other way. Yeah—when WE enter a store, we're followed and followed, and watched, etc. Some enterprising young Black hooligans who decided to be up to no good, and in knowing what the deal was concerning this nation's attitude toward us, would arrange for White group members under their employ, to go into stores with him. Knowing the security guards, store detectives, etc. would ALL be watching <u>him</u>, the Whites in his employ would *clean that store out*. Then they'd divvy up the spoils later. Some groups made very good takes out of this racket. Some, like Dick Gregory who said he did such when he was a teenaged youngster, found it not to be so lucrative. When the Blacks of his era would shoplift it would be for hats, shoes, coats, etc. The Whites, he said, kept taking things Black folks had no use for—like skis!

What I'm saying is that White people in America are—<u>FREE</u>. Because they can do ANYTHING THEY WANT TO DO...and just short of murder and theft *from and to each other*, there <u>will not</u> be that mood or tone to where the guilty parties must practically pay with their <u>*souls*</u>. Timothy McVey's group, inspired by such writings as the "Turner Diaries," resulting in such things as blowing up a whole federal building...hundreds of lives lost...and yet, that group of his is still allowed to exist. They're not being run over, taken control of and knocked out of existence the way the Panthers were of the 1960's. And THEY truly did form in the south for the purpose of self-defense against out of control police forces and other out right criminals that were deliberately and unlawfully victimizing Black lives...free of prosecution. No, the powers that be determined that THEY had to go...NOT the Klans and the rouge bigotry groups.

O.J. Simpson's situation caused that mood and tone among our Caucasian counterparts, not so much because of his being accused of killing Nicole and Ron Goldman. The *real* reason there was so much trepidation about his situation was because <u>*the system worked*</u> in his behalf. The system (here) was <u>never designed to work FOR US</u>! But everything his money could buy...from technical evidence to getting the principals (like Mark Fuhrman) to admit that they would and did plant evidence on certain unpopular individuals for phony prosecutions, the impressive lawyer team...it worked! And it wasn't supposed to work for <u>*him*</u>!

In the meantime, any and everything WE would like to do...no matter HOW MUCH within legal parameters...if it looks to be definitely lucrative—beyond a certain dollar point...it's going to be blocked, written out of legal "right to do," fought against, spied on, lied on, taken to court, you name it...IF **WE** are the ones able to financially foot the bill for the origination of it. Whatever we do that involves White money or Jewish money (like with Oprah or with Bill Cosby, etc.) and it begins to flourish...THAT might be allowed to stay in operation. Yet and still, certain things will be done to let you know *who's* really in <u>charge</u>. Because, when someone *else* is footing the bill...YOU are STILL under their say-so and sway.

Look at what happened to Arsenio Hall when he decided to act just a little *too* independently and have Minister Farrakhan on his show. As popular and Number One reigning as he was...because *someone else* was in charge of the financing/funding and ultimate <u>decision making</u> position...HE ended up out the door. They let him know, "Boy—YOU ain't in charge of a @#$%^&*%* thing here! **WE** are!" If someone is going to drill you or nail you based on who you like and support for leadership...not only is that not being <u>free</u>—it's also a further indicator of being under occupation. Suppose you Black Americans were to approach the Jewish community and tell them you don't like one of their Rabbis...presumably, because he'd shown some racist, anti-Black sentimentality. And, therefore, you don't think HE ought to be followed or adhered to. What do you think their response would be? The Jewish persons there wouldn't be able to hardly choke their words out, they'd be so astonished with outrage... "Uh...we...don't **HAVE** to consult <u>**YOU**</u> about WHO we follow and serve!" That's because they enjoy the <u>FREEDOM</u> *without consequences* to do so! This lack of <u>freedom</u> for *our* part is prevalent throughout the length, breadth, fiber and fabric of the whole country—in every nook and crevice...every office and every station: On the job: we're not free to get sick and take off work: we're not free to use the telephone (unless you sneak and do it—thank God for cell phones nowadays, huh?). At stores and shopping centers: we're not free to shop in peace...we're followed and followed and followed, whether you show clear signs of honesty or not. At restaurants: (Yours, truly has experienced this numerous times) we have to be wary of "things going on" in the back kitchen like attempting to serve <u>us</u> something that needed to be thrown out days ago, the order deliberately being prepared wrongly (in order for you to get the message that *you're* not welcome there), liberties taken with meal preparation protocol, like mayonnaise spread upon your lobster tail/certain mixed drinks like White Russian being prepared with chocolate ice cream/certain items guaranteed to come with your order deliberately being left off...yes—White waiters, White food preparers. Certain neighborhoods: we're not free to move there in peace before "KKK" and "Get Out Nigger," signs are spray painted on your intended house. And then, if you point to a definite suspect that you know did it...you get accused of doing it to yourself. And again, law enforcement, "Can't find who did it." College Spring Break: young, Black college students are not free to visit some cities that they'd like to flock to without being "contained" by police. They're literally not free to walk, drive or move without some suddenly created ordinance restricting movement. With freedom of speech: Whoopi Goldberg was not free to say what she said, even in jest, about the Bush's without reprisal from her Slim Fast sponsors firing her. Congresswoman Cynthia McKinney of Georgia was ganged up on by all White Republican voters going into her district in DeKalb County from their own districts and voting as Democrats to insure that she got voted out when she made her critical observation about "What Bush knew or didn't know." Although, *several* White male constituents, senators and congressmen said *exactly the same thing*, and asking the <u>same</u> condemning questions...SHE didn't have the <u>*RIGHT*</u> to say it, without getting hammered from them all for it. Oprah Winfrey said what she said about the Beef industry, criticizing it for its unhealthy properties. As LONG as health groups, vegetarian groups, animal rights groups, and especially the great Jack LaLane have been <u>stringently</u> relentless in their criticism of the beef industry...as soon as OPRAH said something about them...SHE had to be <u>sued.</u> Because, <u>she</u> didn't have the <u>RIGHT</u> to say it.

Mark Fuhrman <u>lied</u> to a jury about what he claimed he never said about Blacks, only to have in fact said it and worse...HE gets his own radio talk show after what appears NO reprisals for it from the legal system. The nations' _then_ whipping boy, Bill Clinton, was jacked up and readied to be impeached about not being truthful before a court jury about Whatsername...and (thankfully) he pulled through that. Lil Kim says, "Uh-uh," to a jury (that's it) concerning something that turned out to be not the case...SHE gets a year in prison/a $50,000 fine, and three years probation. Which was <u>harsh</u>. And I believe uncalled for. If G. Gordon Liddy, the ex-burglar who broke into the Watergate Hotel and Mark Fuhrman who says he wants all Blacks put in a ship, sailed out to sea and the ship set on fire...and _LIE_ to a jury about not saying such...can both get their own radio talk shows in kind...WHY was such done to Lil Kim over some mess about a boyfriend? Because, we're not <u>free</u>.

We're not free to make mistakes: a father in the 'hood in Atlanta was cooking on the stove when he heard gun shots go off outside his home. He rushed out to make sure there was no dangerous dude or whatever outside, immediately in response. Because of the excitement and suddenness, he'd forgotten and left the food cooking on the stove. A fire broke out, killing his nine year old son. He was arrested and charged for that accident. A White family, on the other hand, in Georgia, routinely lit about a thousand (nearly) candles all over their house, an accidental fire broke out there, injuring one of their children...no charges. Both occurrences happened in the same eight month period.

"20/20", the television news story show had a story on some years ago about two different occurrences whereby mothers who were breast-feeding their babies suddenly discovered they were malnourished...and both babies died. One was an older White mother, looking very confused and sad about losing her baby. The other was a very young Black girl who had lost her baby similarly and was visibly crying over it. HER, the authorities wanted to lock up. "Well, she should have known," they said. But no such talk was going on for the White mother, and who was much older and also should have <u>definitely</u> known. The babies did not appear from their photographs to be suffering malnourishment, at all. It was a news piece coverage of the accidental and unintentional result of what most families and mothers would never expect to be the case. The young Black mother interviewed talked about how fat and healthy her baby appeared to be. It was just totally unexpected and unintentional on both their parts. But again, they wanted to arrest the Black girl.

Remember the "wardrobe malfunction" of Janet Jackson from Justin Timberlake's unhooking her strap? ALL EYES WERE ON <u>JANET</u>...barely mentioning Justin's actions that caused it to occur. It would verify the fact and accusation from us that ALL ACTIONS for blame automatically fall to US, no matter WHAT. To emphasize my point, and if you've been paying attention to the statement of the origins of root causes for things, think about what the responses (from White America, anyway) would be had that been Wesley Snipes and Gwyneth Paltrow. Or Taye Diggs and Meg Ryan. I'm <u>telling</u> you—NOT A <u>THING</u> would have been said to Paltrow or Ryan. ALL EYES FOR BLAME would have been on TAYE DIGGS or WESLEY SNIPES... "A-A-A-A-A-A-H-H-H-H-H!!!! Look at that Black **MONSTER** undressing our Little Bo Peep!" And I assure you they would have worked themselves up, and worked themselves up some more...in the press, in the news, in the papers and on talk radio...until out right criminal CHARGES would have been brought against Taye Diggs or Wesley Snipes. I'm tellin' ya. Mark my word. ALL EYES ARE TRAINED and ORIENTED into BLAMING US for _ANYTHING._ Punishments, jail terms, prison sentences, fines, repercussions against us for things that don't even have enough evidence to warrant charges, or something comparatively miniscule in nature, reach _unreasonable_ degrees of severity, outright medieval and draconian in nature from the justice system here—not because you or the offending party are *re-ally* a danger or a menace to society. It's done for one reason...because they _can_...and there's nobody to stop them or cost them for such unreasonably harsh response when it comes to YOU and me. It's because the systems here are *so used* to doing this, and you keep taking it.

PLENTY of forces, organizations, and groups here already _KNOW_ these facts and do try to help. It's just that our own supposed leadership consists mainly of a bunch of toothless panthers...and the powers that be know that all they have to put up with is having that leadership showing up and *gumming them* to death.

CHAPTER THIRTEEN

AUDIO OBSERVATIONS

I WAS REACHING THE AGE where my tastes and preferences were beginning to go to listening to talk radio, as opposed to all the music and jamming most other folks like to listen to. There is a man on WSB radio 750 AM, one Neal Boortz. I first discovered him on 640 AM, WGST in Atlanta, and <u>he</u> would be saying some things that would cause me to really seethe, and at the same time, he would say some things that I was truly, <u>greatly</u> surprised to hear an upper class, pretty wealthy White male actually confess. It was the year some enterprising television movie makers were going to do a sequel or something to that effect for "Gone With the Wind." Neal, who was still at 640AM, was talking about it in his usual, "Oh what are they bothering with THIS for?" tone, and he said, "I've never liked 'Gone With the Wind,' I've never liked that story. Margaret Mitchell never wrote anything else…she probably *stole* it from her maid!" That was the first time I chose to call in to his show. I'd never done such before (except trying to guess and win prizes on our WAKY 790AM radio music station in Louisville), and I had to make sure of what I was going to say when I got on. I wasn't prepared for the lo-o-o-n-g wait I was going to have to be called on next to talk to him.

I had been told by the Black Georgia natives that Margaret Mitchell's maid was the aunt of an eighteen year old Black girl who was going to school at Booker T. Washington High in those post-antebellum years. The girl wrote a story for her school assignment, "Gone With the Wind." When her aunt saw it, she proudly took it to Margaret Mitchell to show it off to her. Margaret met with the young girl and *purchased* the story from her for $25.00—a lot of money then. Then she signed her own name to it and the rest is, well yeah, you know the rest.

That was exactly what I told Neal Boortz when I got to talk to him, telling him that I was surprised to hear *him*—a White guy actually admit that. Don't you know, not another call came through that morning from <u>anyone</u> about that up-coming TV movie...and it had been the "talk" of the Georgia south all through the time they were making preparation and shooting it.

Another thing about Neal was his being instrumental in the helping of Ralph From Ben Hill get his show on that station. Neal does a *lot*...and I do mean a <u>*LOT*</u> of race-baiting-type talk. He's <u>*always*</u> highly insulting about welfare mothers, Black politicians who he says "will always play the guilt race card when they get in trouble..." he's a no holds barred, very angering, rough talking individual who made a name and fame for himself in doing just that. I've heard about death threats he's gotten, although I'm reasonably sure that those kinds of truly serious ones aren't coming from <u>us.</u> We don't give death threats to people you would *think* we'd waste no time giving them to. Neal manages to piss off a lot of his significant other-type listeners. Neal Boortz is also another American citizen who is allowed to carry a concealed weapon on his person most places that many of us aren't authorized to do. I was told about some crumb who, apparently, sent him pictures of his children going to and coming from school in an attempt to threaten him and his—really ugly. I was told he removed them from that school.

C. Ralph Miles used to call his show almost daily and stump him with his own sense of banter and wit. Ralph, with Neal's help, was taken onboard WGST radio on the evening circuit, calling himself by his show name, "Ralph From Ben Hill." Ben Hill, in case you're not aware, is one of the area subdivisions around Atlanta and East Point, just like Mechanicsville, Oakland City, and so on. Ralph, just as sometimes racially divisive as Neal, would NOT let his listeners call in and talk badly about Neal. And Neal wouldn't let <u>his</u> listeners call in and insult Ralph... "Ralph's my Buddie!" he would say. Neal also wouldn't let his callers talk about Rev. Hosea Williams. Rev. Williams would call up Neal and call him a "White" this and a "White" that...but Neal was crazy about him.

Some years later Ralph was replaced (I suppose fired) and the station brought in one Sean Hannity to go on the aire in his place. As soon as Hannity walked in the door—he was started out at a salary three times what they were paying Ralph, who had been a radio fixture there on WGST for nearly eight years. Sean Hannity when hired by Ralph's station, was an unknown, working for no salary at some Alabama radio station somewhere. When his bubble began to get big, he turns around and starts talking about the "e-e-e-v-i-l-s" of "preferential racial treatment," but only when it was a case of the structure making some half-hearted effort, at best, in paying back some damages and evening up the scores and hirings of some of us. Yet, he apparently had no complaint when <u>he</u> was the recipient of preferential treatment when he walked in the door at WGST, and started out at what he was in pay—*just* for being inside of that skin of his. And then, he had to hang around both Ralph AND Cos Carson to learn how to do that job. They had mentioned that Sean just couldn't figure out *how* they were able to do all that they did, have the kind of banter, and be able to work all the stuff that they did. But they schooled him, and he was reasonably amiable with them...until he got on his feet. Then it became the usual situation of pushing the Blacks out of the way, hand in the face-style, didn't want anything more to do with them, behaved flaky, acted like he didn't know who they were, etc. My only view on such is that IF you're going to make your way on talking about "preferential treatment," knowing full well that even as you speak, it's STILL going on for Whites giving to Whites only, then either start talking about THAT evil as well, or shut your "riding on a gravy train for downing the usual victims" mouth. Because all you're doing is talking out of both sides of your mouth.

Then, in the early 1990's we got an all-Black radio talk show station, 1340 AM WIGO which was an absolutely heavenly breath of fresh air...the talk being of a *positive* nature concerning us Black Americans and Blacks throughout the world. World problems were also definitely addressed, but it wasn't the constant, non-stop bombardment of everything negative concerning us and our situations, and the 100% always right White consensus of things from their end. Ron Sailor, who was a newscaster on Channel 11 television, was the brains behind WIGO's new talk show format.

It was when Harold Lee on that station began to make a solid, no way to get around it, definite justification for slavery reparations, that was when WIGO was suddenly taken over, the old crew nixed, and music came back to it, the powers that be saying that they hadn't received monies due them for the station. Ron Sailor made a brave effort to keep it, as the fence surrounding the station had been kicked in and the airwaves suddenly went silent when this intruder apparently disconnected it. Some community volunteers, including one of our MARTA officers who also enjoyed listening to that station, stood vigil over the opening of the fence to keep anymore damage from being done to the control tower airwave circuits.

If, indeed, it was a case of monies due the station owners, it's only a matter of questionable timing to me, in that it was when slavery reparations, the hot topic of the time period, was looking like it was undeniably going to be justified by what was being said by the WIGO team. The right-wing radio station hosts were saying, "Well the slaves are all dead now. Who's gonna collect?" And other such statements were made by them, as though if any slaves were still around we could pay them then! But keep in mind, when the slaves were alive and *here* and able to collect, just like with the American Indian, the U.S. government had absolutely <u>no</u> intention, whatsoever, of honoring its end of the bargain concerning the 40 acres and mule. Today, it would be some land, homes, and a car equivalent.

But we don't have to go back to 1865 and before. We can just go back a mere forty or fifty years in this nation's history and come to the present...and too much in the way of damages will be due us...in stolen inventions alone that we weren't paid for or acknowledged for inventing...and the untold _billions_ in wealth enjoyed by the thieves of our efforts while we wasted away in poverty and obscurity...let alone murders and lynchings of us that were never punished...as well as being taxed for public services such as fire department and police services...which when we would have fires at our homes, the fire department would show up, just sit on their trucks and watch it burn. Or police services, which when called for emergencies _might_ arrive some time next week, and other non-responses to our needs. We've got plenty of damages and offenses regularly being committed against us right now...never mind from 1619 A.D. until 1865 A.D.

In, roughly, 2000 A.D., we got WAOK 1380 AM, which went from all Gospel music all day to talk show format, and this was a new resurrection for talk radio geared toward us. Thus, another child was born on the Atlanta talk radio circuit for our listening pleasure. Obviously, I was being placed on mobile patrol duty an _awful_ lot! I never asked for the car, but it appeared I was always assigned in it. It _was_ considered a more desirable beat assignment, especially during the cold winter months. When I would be returning to work from my off days, I would be told in hushed tones about some minor complaints about my getting the car all the time. Pam would tell me it was because I was trustworthy enough in it to where the commanders would know that I wouldn't be off my beat area, and that I would always respond to _everything_ that was put out on radio if it was anywhere near my beat area. I had been working so hard, previously to these brighter, more positive days that it just didn't seem like such hard work for me now to respond to any and everything before the station units would have to catch a train to it.

LT. Downin began to order me to stop taking on _everything_ to do. She said, "Look you go to everything. You slow down. Let some of these other units have to go handle some calls." Of course, what she was saying was that _some_ of the other units—she wanted them to do some _work_—which they weren't having to do with ME on patrol. Also, SHE told me that one other reason I was assigned to the car all the time was that if she did put "so and so" in the car, they would be all over creation in it, taking full advantage and full leeway of having access to those wheels...so that every kind of personal business would be getting tended to instead of station and parking lot patrols. Such could be a common thing among the mobile units. It was just a matter of ensuring that one could get to their calls in a timely manner and pray to God one didn't have an accident where you weren't supposed to be while on the way to a call!

Chapter Fourteen

FURTHER MARCHING ORDERS

THE POLICE DEPARTMENT AT MARTA went through more re-organizational structuring. This time, the Chief decided to get rid of all Captain's ranks and the promotion would be from Lieutenant to Major. We all ascertained that it was because the department had an inordinately large number of White lieutenants, but was now becoming increasingly full of Black sergeants, as the hiring attempts of more White officers was diminishing due to there just not being enough of them trying to come aboard. Also, the ones the department did too quickly hire, they had to immediately fire when certain "pasts" came up in their records and to the command structure's notice. There were certain unfunny and not very humorous, downright <u>dumb-assed</u> and stupid little "games" being played on Police radio during this time period too. Somebody had a joke department "laugh box," that they kept keying the radio mike and playing over the airwaves. Apparently, this same individual would hold the police radio over a commode and flush it, so the sound of it would play over the airwaves too. It was really only bad if we were around the general public and that nonsense would play out within their earshot. All this corresponded with the attempted massive hiring of some of these questionable types of individuals.

Well, a good thing about this strange kind of promotion system was that LT. Downin now became Major Downin. When she began at MARTA during the bad old years of good ol' boys all over the place, she was a rarity who <u>would not be held back</u>, played with or insulted. She also stayed in the rules and regulations books and learned them to the letter, so that anything they tried to do to her was not able to fly. She would also cut loose on any racial insults, overtly or covertly implied by the ever-growing in frustration good ol' boys who outranked her and would try every way they could to stick their foot out and trip her. I had heard that one evening one of the downright "crackers," the very epitome of the stereo-typical description—tobacco-chewing, pick-up truck driving, 'neck, had come right out and insulted her—racially. I was told that Corporal Downin at that time nutted up and had to be held back, other officers getting between her and him, while she nearly screamed at him, "DON'T YOU **EVER** TALK TO ME LIKE THAT AGAIN!!! WHO DO YOU THINK YOU ARE??" And that she made him almost afraid for his hide. He spoke later on to Black sergeants like they were dogs...almost puppies, with them standing there, their head hung down, and he, at the rank of Captain, just enjoyed deriding them. But to Ms. Downin, he was as meek, humble and respectful as a manservant before Queen Elizabeth.

She, nearly alone, was promoted through the ranks, staying up there with the current sergeants, lieutenants, and now with Captain's status gone, a Major. And, dig this, SHE was about the ONLY human being at MARTA that could handle working for Captain (soon to be Major) Nero. He would put tasks in her hand, then actually leave her alone to fulfill them. Being a true judge of nature, she had him figured out and knew how to handle him. Plus, it was so lovely to have someone on OUR side in a powerful position now. That was how I looked at it. Yet, it was not a total bed of roses or an absolute "friend-to-friend" situation between everybody on my rank and with Major Downin. There were some folks that she did, indeed, have no choice but to have to correct. However, she would do all she could to save that individual's job before *having* to do something of a negative nature to them.

The other sergeants and few Black lieutenants who had attained that rank, essentially gave upper management unmistakable hints that *they* would be easy to control, in other words, to be used as the means, arms and legs to do the dirty work to certain upstart officers they may have their eyes pinned on for "dealing with."

One particular day while on patrol on the Five Points platform, myself, and two other officer friends of mine observed about four young guys smoking one of those Philly Blunts inside the station. For those not in the know, this was what the young people would split open and fill with marijuana, then close the blunt back up, with nobody supposedly able to tell that they're smoking such. The indoor ban on smoking had been well into effect for years by then. We're thinking, "Stupid little young punks!" and take our positions: when the train pulled into the station and people board, one of us will go through and block one side of the exit doors around our suspect(s), the other of us will block the other side (the train doors open to both sides at once at Five Points), in case of attempted flight.

Sure enough, the four guys, when they saw all these uniforms approaching their direction began to go into/out of/back into the train doors again and again (the train doors only stay open for so many seconds), but we were positioned to crowd/move them back toward where WE wanted them, and they ended up all cornered by us while we searched and questioned them. What do you know...they had four guns on them, 156 hits of cocaine hidden in one of those .35 cent Lays potato chip bags, and quite a bit of folding currency on them. Quite a successful arrest. It was only because Sgt. Holt was the sergeant on duty that day that we all got a letter of commendation for that hugely successful arrest. They came along quietly, nobody got hurt/there were no foot chases. Several of us had made quite a few hugely successful arrests and captures of dangerous or wanted suspects—often...and never heard anymore about it as far as, "Good Job," in writing or letter of commendation. If anyone just *might* step out and hint that *maybe* the department would like to commend or put a positive note in our file (because they sure weren't slow in putting something negative in there), we would always be hit back in smarmy fashion from the Chief with, "Well, that's yer _job_!" Yeah, we know that's our *job*! But when we've literally risked our life single-handedly disarming an armed subject, or successfully chased down and captured someone who had contraband on them, or turned out to be "wanted," it doesn't dampen anyone's working atmosphere to have such, at least, acknowledged. I told you about how even things that really *weren't* all that big a deal for our Caucasian counterparts were played up and played up until the forces in charge were practically ready to make them a Gen. Schwarzkopf equivalent.

And if those Caucasian counterparts of ours was *ever* hit with that attitude of, "Well that's yer _j-o-o-b_!" I'm quite sure _they_ would have a more colorful and more effective way of dealing with such a "waving off" attitude. I <u>know</u> they would. Once again, they don't *take* it. They've been ready to sue the system, take MARTA to court, make a _HUGE_ stink in the papers when arrested for crimes and offenses they've truly been caught red-handed at doing. And they get by with it.

I wouldn't doubt at all that probably most police departments, as well as department stores, grocery stores, etc. *regularly* look the other way when our Caucasian counterparts actively engage in shoplifting, fare-evasion, urinating in elevators or in public...they're left alone. Because they'll raise so much sand and trouble over being caught and dealt with. I can give you further examples in addition to the ones already described, previously, in the earlier chapters. We go to great lengths and great troubles to catch and arrest offenders guilty of vandalizing property, deliberately making false alarms, breaking equipment in a drunken craze, attempting to fight law enforcement officers, you name it. If the offenders happen to be White, and when taken to court to be ready to have the case addressed, we find out that all charges had been dismissed, or charges persuaded to be dropped by officials from on high.

Some of these offenders are good friends with the judges ruling their case and they find some hidden, obscure loophole or technicality that is NEVER addressed or even known about...and it's used to dismiss charges. There have been definite and solid cases of outright drug dealing and drug use going on in their wealthy, higher classed apartment complexes that dedicated officers have _begged_ their superiors to allow them to go into and bust...always with the response being that sheepish-toned, "Nah, nah, nah!" from the superiors. Unless it's some poor old drunk that we take in because he would not leave the property, or was too sick to be able to leave, the powers that be seldom backed us up on arresting Whites who broke the law with apparent impunity.

When MARTA command officials visited New York's subway system officials (way before 9-11) for their input on successfully dealing with crime in their area of concern, we were put to a new task. "Quality of Life," ticket-writing. In New York, if someone was caught eating or drinking on their trains, their officers were required to write them a ticket for such. Then they would have to appear in court behind such. When that requirement came to MARTA police officers, some dove in with gusto and our Environmental Court was filled up with "Big Mac Attack," tickets that some citizens paid, and some fought. I never heard about these tickets being written any further North than the downtown area. Instinctively, we KNEW what the deal would be if they wrote those tickets in the wealthy (White) Buckhead areas.

In 1996, MARTA got its version of a SWAT team chosen from specially selected officers who were physically fit, could shoot very high scores on the firing range, and were "bad-asses." They were called, "SORT"—Special Operations and Tactics. They came into being in time for the Olympics. After the Olympics, they were used to work undercover and catch fare-evaders. Once again, though, they <u>never</u> worked farther North than downtown. They primarily worked the inner-city downtown area, the far west lines (where <u>we</u> all lived) and some parts of the east lines that were also NOT racially mixed. When all my White readers who *may have* inadvertently gotten mixed up in the tickets or arrests (and if you do indeed exist...trust me, I would *much rather be wrong* on these observations than correct...but I'm recounting to you some <u>routine</u> actions that have and still do occur), and want to angrily shake their fist in defiance about being immune to these sweeps...you know, and you KNOW that you know, that <u>all your charges </u>were **dropped.** And that's if it made it <u>THAT</u> far, as far as to court.

When I began to get older, beginning to hit my early 40's in age, and it began to be a little trickier chasing and wrestling with people, I consulted my mentor(s) to see what their view would be of my transferring off the downtown and west line and going to work up North, since they don't want you to do anything to anyone up there. They told me with finality that it probably wouldn't work out for me. "Janet, you're an aggressive officer," they told me. "If you go up there, number one, you're going to see all those White folks driving into the bus loop and dropping all their friends off..." The bus loops were the "paid" inner area of the stations for buses only. Personal vehicles were absolutely verboten—unless you were a bus driver coming to work and someone was going to quickly drive that car out of there...or if you were a bus or rail supervisor. We had a very unfortunate incident right out of my graduation class of some smart-assed White rookie who had no respect for the Rail supervisor's position. Apparently, he was just another "nigger" to him, and he roughly ordered to Black rail supervisor to move his car out of the bus loop, kicking it while he told him. As it was standard that rail supervisors could and did regularly do such, he was a bit incredulous about his attitude. This officer *just* started and didn't listen when told that the Bus and Rail supervisors parked in there all the time. This guy finally threw the rail supervisor over his car, cuffed and arrested him. It was, primarily, disrespect for him and for his position. Yes, we know that his Caucasian counterpart being of the same age and bearing, MARTA business suit upon his person, would not have been treated in such way. And if he had—no officer would surely retain his job after that. But this guy did, even though the Rail supervisor was correct. I'm bringing that incident up, primarily, to highlight *how* it is against MARTA rules, otherwise, to drive a car into the bus loop if you're a *patron*, and need to pay to come onto the system.

Well, not only did the wealthy "significant *others*" of the Buckhead and further north areas *regularly* walk into the fare-gates without paying, they also regularly drove into the bus loop, dropped off their friends and drove off, leaving that friend to freely walk up or take the elevator up to the trains and ride free of charge. ALL OF THESE THINGS ARE SUPPOSED TO CULMINATE IN THE PLACING OF <u>ALL</u> THOSE PERSONS UNDER ARREST! So to get back to the advice I was given concerning my looking at possibly transferring up there to work, I was told that <u>when</u> I started stopping those cars and those people from driving in there...and WHEN I started making them actually PAY to get onto the system, the results would be as follows: WHEN those angry, pissed off Whites start their Letter Writing Campaign against me in complaints to the Chief: and WHEN I get written up and jacked up for doing my job...which I'm *supposed to do*: "And when they **FIRE** you...<u>they</u> will be *right back* to driving in the bus loop, letting their friends out, walking in the fare-gates, etc.

"So, Janet, it will be a frustrating time for you if you go to work back up there. Some of us have already been through it. We ran out there to the bus loops up there, yelling and waving our arms, making them leave. They started their phone call/letter writing to the Chief...*PISSED OFF* about what had happened, and I was told to leave them alone. I went to the Chief (or to the commander in charge of the precinct who'd ordered them to cease their law enforcing activities on that behalf), I told him, 'That' not fair! We sure do arrest people in town for that!' The Chief or commander would quietly, almost meekly say, 'Yeah. I <u>*know*</u> it's not fair...' And then they'd be at a loss for words to put it any further. So, if I were *you*, Garnett, I would stay my ass right where you are. Because you're in for a frustrating time if you transfer up there!"

We had traffic checkers and customer surveyor representatives who would talk to me in private about the differences in working the North lines as opposed to the South and other lines (where <u>we</u> lived). And again, due to the subject nature of it, they would talk in very low tones. "It makes me so mad. I'll be standing there at the Brookhaven/Medical Center/or other station way up North, and just watch *those* people walk in all day long without paying. Nothing is said to them." The checkers and surveyors were posted to talk to customers, interview a few of them, and see what could be done to increase ridership.

We would talk about such things at our numerous police get togethers in staff and board rooms with the Chief and his big wigs to discuss ideas about how to increase ridership. Since the big idea about, "if more White officers were at MARTA..." turned out to be a lot of bunk, there were other avenues they were approaching. The main problem in some of our humble opinions was that MARTA was failing to properly take care of the regular ridership that daily carried the system through as far as fares, parking, purchasing of monthly and weekly rail cards, etc. They were going for the folks who basically stayed a million miles away from the system, and that was the suburbanite residents. Since MARTA is an authority and not a state governed system, it has to have the permission of the residents of some suburbs and outer cities before it can build and go further into them. Of course, the main rallying cry these suburbanites had was that they were afraid of "Crime," coming their way. That was always the catch phrase. We, of course, felt that they meant something else…N'words. But that was tactfully avoided and we continued to play along like it was a matter of assuaging new territories of their fears of "c-r-r-i-i-m-m-e!"

When it eventually became clear that these outer suburbanite residents were going to take a helicopter before they took MARTA, and still wanting to do *something* about the ever burgeoning traffic problems plaguing the city daily, these outer places eventually got their <u>own</u> bus systems in co-op with MARTA in stopping at and utilizing some of their stations for pick up/drop off points. I got onboard both the Cobb County Transit and the Gwinnett County buses just to see what it looked like onboard. Well, my, my—they had cup holders and such on their buses. So much for Quality of Life requirements, etc. But these folks <u>were not riding MARTA</u>…period. That's all there was to it. Period.

For a certain amount of time too, when we were getting told what it would take for more suburbanites to ride the system, they said if they could have an officer aboard *every* train, they *might* be willing to ride the system. So, for some time, we officers were *agonized* with having to stand and ride a train for eight hours of our shift if so unfortunately assigned. It was *miserable.* Then, because of so many sick outs and complaints, they shortened it to four hours on a train. If you were caught off a train, it could mean disciplinary days off or just plain firings. We had a few firings during that period.

The lieutenant structure and even the majors and chief *tried* to convince the Asst. General Managers and CEO's of MARTA that all our crime statistics showed that most of any incidents of criminal activity occurred in the *stations*, NOT aboard the trains. But this did no good. It was always a matter of bowing down to the **PERCEPTIONS** of where and what the "crimes" may be. *Those* people said, "Trains," by dingies, and we're gonna ride the *trains*!" Yet, the upper command structure could see what a heavy and exacting toll it was playing on the officers to have to ride these trains non-stop for hours at a time. No, ridership did <u>not</u> increase.

Another thing that occurred in the early to mid '90's was the city's and the system's desire to address the problems of truant juveniles cutting school all day long. The youngsters would be hanging out on the system or loitering the streets, etc. Some civic minded officers would take them up and/or attempt to talk to them, lecture them, attempt to get them interested in some kind of "life" for themselves. But getting our youngsters to school, faithfully, was a struggle that appeared to be a losing one. Still, you had those "colorful" and inventive officers who were the epitome of Barney Fife's sincere, yet comical, attempts to lecture wayward youngsters with doing the right thing. They'd literally take these truants into staff rooms, sit them down and walk back and forth among the row of our captive listening (obviously disinterested) young people, giving them their speech and spiel. You'd have to literally imagine Don Knotts' Emmy award winning performances (he really did win about five or six Emmy's in a row for his Barney Fife portrayal on "The Andy Griffith Show") as he would self-assuredly stroll up and down his row of youngsters, and telling them, "Now, boys...you know-w-w you shouldn't be skipping cla-a-a-s-s!" etc., etc. You'd have the very picture of these sincere officers' attempts to encourage these truants onto the right path. We other officers in the staff room with that officer (you'd NEVER leave an officer by himself with <u>any</u> suspect of <u>anything</u>—even a youngster, unless that suspect is cuffed to a bench...and we're talking about a whole room of teenaged juveniles) would just sit and listen to this individual's attempts to win these kids over. We would glance at each other and just give a "Bless his heart" look at him or her for their efforts to inspire these youths.

I thought the possible reason for these youngsters' disinterest in their classes might be that their history lessons might be on the same par with ours when we 1950's baby boomers were in school...being taught that every, but everything was European/European in origin and accomplishment. Thus, that could be a likely reason for not wanting to sit through that junk. Yet, when we would recover lost school textbooks, I did glance through one or more of their World History books and lo and behold, there *was* the ancient, old African kingdoms of Mali, Songhai, Timbuktu, King Mansa Musa, the Benin Empire, and so on. To my great delight, I thought, "Wow! They <u>are</u> teaching our ancient African history!" Then the great let down with, "Well, what could be the problem that they don't want to go to school and *learn*???" I'll confess, yours truly took up the attempted lecture circuit, Barney Fife style, herself here and there. And the thing is, the young people we had in there with us, wayward as they were, *would* quietly listen. Their stance and posture *wasn't* the bored, leaned back, cocky, gum chewing, delinquent image one would have of a societal "problem child." They would be watching us with those big innocent eyes, leaned out toward us, quiet as church mice as we told them what they could expect in life without education, or being able to read, write, spell, add and subtract, etc. They'd almost have you thinking you were getting somewhere with them. After talking with them and releasing them to their parents or just plain letting them go...those *same young people* would be right back in custody day after day...some getting in trouble for tangible misdemeanors, and so on. *S-i-i-i-g-g-h-h!*

There *were* those smart-assed, smart-mouthed, disrespectful sass boxes—they were sent promptly to Juvenile Detention, too. That was in the days before Juvenile Detention became so full of young people that they were having to release, dismiss, or even just not bother to get them on some crimes like car theft. They had to make room for murderers and assault and batterers, etc. Just signs of the times.

One very important note to all us American (and possibly other nationality) human beings when it comes to dealing with police or other authority figures: Your **mouth** will get you in more trouble, more discomfort, *more* inconvenience than an actual, tangible, definitive criminal act will. WE are in the position (given the authority by the citizens and the State) to, if necessary, even take the life of another—it just better be with true justification, although we haven't seen that work very well with Black and Hispanic Americans, I'll admit. Therefore, if we get called to a location, and someone has to be talked to or dealt with, it's that person's attitude and approach that determines what degrees and levels of tools at our disposal (I'm talking about letter of the law, legal time parameters, and agency access) that we employ. Thus, if you wanna be an asshole, it's up to us how much time you have to wait for a decision, or be inconvenienced waiting for a warrant, or have to sit in the holding cell while paper work is being searched up, or have to wait while police radio does the "wanted check"-- it depends on how big a pain in the rectum you want to be. We have a popular slang term that we used among ourselves, called "P.O.P." It stands for "piss off the police." Some jokers who deliberately cough on us if they're sick, spit at us, tell us about how our Mama is a "goddamn, street-walkin' whore," etc., in actuality, *those* little ditties, we can handle. It's those smart-attitude, smug, "you can't do anything to me" types that really get our goat. The folks that think they're immune and the "world revolves around them," in outlook, I found **I** really couldn't stomach. But you still have to maintain that calm, professional approach in attitude, yourself, if you want to be in the right when you go to court behind these turkeys.

Admittedly, the same does definitely go for police officers, too, when it comes to knowing *how* to talk to people. One very definite fact about some kinds of our kindred law enforcement people out there...we *KNOW* who the ones are that are forever getting into conflicts (usually, unnecessarily) with people they feel they have to stop. In the days when *most* of us were a lot more careful about when and if to pull our guns on people, there were any number of cop to perp (perp is a usual term we use as a shortened version of "perpetrator") fist fights. The laws and rules were that if a suspect is not armed with a gun, knife, or some other illegal or dangerous object, you were NOT authorized, neither could you justifiably pull your gun on him or her. A baton would and could be allowed, and then you were only supposed to go for forearms, thick of thighs, calves, hand, or some part of the body that would not result in serious injury. Absolutely NO aiming for heads, stomachs, groins, and definitely no *jabbing* of the end of the baton into someone (such as what was seen—and excused—when it was done to that overweight Black man who died after his struggle with police outside a White Castle restaurant that was aired on television in 2003).

There were those police officers (men and women) who were *very* capable of dealing, one on one, with individual perps who decided to put up a fight or a struggle. And there were those gas-bag types that would typically blow things out of proportion because of *his own* negative attitudes toward certain races, etc., who would ALWAYS get into fights...and usually lose. However, and I do believe, commendably, they <u>still</u> left their hands <u>off</u> their guns...even though they were getting their "ass stomped." And as often *would* happen, it would be citizen by-standers, *very* often of the same race that very officer being creamed couldn't stomach, that rushed and pushed down and held that very perp who was stomping the officer...and actually saving the officer's (preferred colored) skin. These problems all due to the "tongue."

We've taken into custody *wonderful* personality type individuals...the kind who were *s-o-o-o* angelically sweet, that we would actually be going into almost stomach pains trying to find a way for them to be as <u>leniently</u> dealt with as possible. Of course, if we couldn't, we just couldn't. But if we *could*...believe you me, we would do it. We have a deal called, "Copy of Charges," whereby that individual does not have to be placed in handcuffs, interrupted from his/her normal daily routine, jeopardizing their jobs, etc., and if it appears they can be trusted, we can schedule them an appointment to appear in court before a judge in about two weeks—for their convenience. Yes, we have options like that at our disposal. You primarily, though, used it for people who have a little bit more to lose if they don't come through or show. They can be issued orders for immediate arrest if they fail to show.

When we would go to court there were some particular judges that everybody hoped to get, and some that people would agonizingly groan, "Oh, NO-O-O-O-O!!!" if we got. Judge Mickle could have a fully loaded entire section of subjects on trial for City of Atlanta court cases (some twenty to forty persons at times) emptied out and completed in less than thirty minutes. We'd breathe sighs of relief if his was the name and courtroom our arrestees were going before. A typical appearance before Judge Mickle would go as follows: upon the person's being found "guilty" and generally for something relatively minor, Judge Mickle's spiel would be, "$75 fine or five days in jail-pay your fine on the way out-don't wanna see ya back here-next case..." or if a serious crime, "Case is bound over-next case"...or if the defendant wanted to plead "not guilty" or argue his case (which he/she usually did not do a very good job of), the judge would patiently, though expediently hear the complaint after the arresting officer's side, then proceed with the defendant being found "guilty" anyway or the case bound over...which meant being scheduled for Fulton County Superior Court at a later date.

The other judges were sometimes temperamental, some were slow in getting the cases through (they'd still be trying 2:00pm cases at 4:30pm), and others sometimes *always* appeared to be on the defendant's side. There was an incident (in fact there were a *few* incidences) where it was MARTA police officers that successfully intercepted and stopped sudden lunging attacks on judges by crazed-out defendants standing trial. Sgt. C. Hill, our first guiding officer at Five Points when our class of 1988 came aboard, who retired as Lieutenant Hill, was one of those officers. He and another MARTA officer tackled and stopped a defendant who suddenly sprang for the attack on a female judge he nutted up on in court some time before we came to work there. It was due to this heroic venture on the part of MARTA police that whenever we brought defendants to that particular judge's courtroom that no antics would be pulled to get "certain privileged folks" off the hook. For the department's and for public perception's sake, we HAD to be assured our cases were winnable in court.

For our juvenile truancy problem, in 1992 MARTA police and City of Atlanta Police decided to go into a co-op effort together and try an experimental program of eradication of it. The Captains (we still had them at the time) of MARTA and the Commanders at Atlanta PD coordinated roundup/transportation *en mass* of ALL JUVENILES on or in City of Atlanta, as well as MARTA premises who did not have written or otherwise verifiable authorization to be out of school. The efforts were also coordinated with the local David T. Howell gym/meeting center to hold all the kids we knew we were going to end up with. The vans were readied, police cars and special buses readied, ALL police officers, system wide geared and readied...and off we were unleashed—upon unsuspecting, school-cutting, mischief-causing little knuckleheads.

If only I could impart to you readers just an inkling of the thrill and joy that surged through my heart at this program of no holds barred unleashing of all us officers upon these kids and PUTTING THEM BACK IN **SCHOOL**!!! I felt a new feeling rush through me...one that was a brand new level of rarity of feeling I hadn't felt before. It was similar to the brand new, *new* feeling I had of actually being *noticed* as an individual who <u>exists</u> here in these United States when Bill Clinton gave his inaugural speech at his first election. At <u>this</u> instance when we police officers were given full authorization to swoop down upon the heads of ALL THESE TRUANTS...and *force* them back into school...I felt a refreshing and brand new sense of ___*hope*___. That was what I felt. Hope. For OUR young people.

The results and public response was enormous and elated. All the adults, regular employed patrons, senior citizens, et.al., were outrightly cheering us as we swept past them, yanking up young people and youngsters after 10:30am who were still on the station premises. We'd enter onto a train, spy some obvious kids, it would be 11:00am, go grab them, tell them, "Come with me!" And Five Points staff and precinct rooms, previously cleared through with newly created open space, would fill up. We'd be hauling and pushing these kids ten, fifteen, sometimes twenty at a time into the rooms. Some young person would look in their direction, start to laugh and jeer, I'd approach him/her with five kids in my tow, ask "What 'er <u>you</u> laughin' at?" A sudden and confused look would come over their previously derisive features. I'd say, "How old are you?" "Fifteen." I'd grab their arm and pull them along saying, "<u>YOU</u> come too!" And then the kids he/she was laughing at would in turn start laughing and deriding at them next. It was wonderful.

Additional results that we noticed during this swoop-up period was that police radio was s-o-o-o-o *quiet* during the day time hours. There were practically NO calls coming in of nearly any kind of nature, save the two or three here or there of intoxicated individual or fare dispute aboard a bus. Otherwise, "Juveniles loitering in station," "Juveniles harassing customers," "Suspicious juveniles in parking lot moving in between cars," were nil.

It was s-o-o-o positive and the public response so great that when the program was over and we were going back to normal routine, I for one, begged Cpt. Rogers, our precinct commander at the time, to let us continue...pointing out all the wonderful feedback and results we were enjoying. Cpt. Rogers (later, Major Rogers) apparently had a heck of a lot of clout with big boys, and even though the program was officially over, our area (and some cooperating other agencies outside MARTA) kept pockets of it going, here and there, which I was glad to over extend myself within.

Then, in 1994, the department established the Community Police Program/ Juvenile Youth Patrol. This was made up of a volunteer squad of police officers who's duty it was to take over the extensive paper work involved with processing all of the juveniles we had for truancy, and to extend their duties further into community concerns. They were going to maintain regular parental contact for the juveniles, attend community meetings where police and public concerns were established and otherwise engage in extra-curricular activities. That was one reason why I didn't join this squad. Not only were they going to have somewhat irregular hours, but to be required during my off duty part of the day to engage in work related matters...I don't think so. When I'm off, I like to be OFF. But they ended up with quite an illustrious list of volunteers for that squad. We nicknamed them the "Kiddie Patrol." All in all, the years for me going along at MARTA were becoming quite a career expanding experience. I would spend a total of fourteen years with the department until the year 2002 when they began to offer police officers "Early Retirement."

That was based on the very valid viewpoint of...could you realistically envision someone in their fifties, then their mid-fifties, *still* getting in fights and foot chases? But what it really had to do with was the fact that we were beginning to top out in our salaries. And as we've all seen and experienced in this nation's history...BIG BUSINESS runs this country. They don't _CARE_ about your years of faithful, loyal service. ALL THEY SEE is *dollars, dollars,* **DOLLARS**. That's ALL. And if they find they're paying you too much, no matter _how_ worthy and deserving you are or your work is...YOU have to **GO**! All they know is that they can hire two and a half more people on just your salary, alone, if they get rid of you. And that's all that matters to them. Plus, we were all very, very aware of this fact AND their attitude toward us and our salaries, so we were willing to let them offer us a deal.

It was a highly desirable offer to me. As of the age of 43 when the offers for early retirement were coming through in the early part of 2001, I was beginning to find my patience levels that I had in my early 30's starting to wane. I found myself becoming increasingly impatient with a lot of young mouthed sass coming my way. I'd told people that I never thought I would sound like my "folks"...but here I was catching myself too often declaring to our wayward youths, "When I was *your age--!*"

Chapter Fifteen

SEPTEMBER ELEVENTH

IN JANUARY OF 2001, my sister called me from Louisville to tell me that Mom had been diagnosed as having Cancer. I immediately broke down upon hearing the news. I made arrangements to go home the next week for a period of time not known. Major Downin had gotten married (to the very rail supervisor, it turned out, who had been so disrespected by my White classmate those years earlier), so she was (and is) Major Johnson. And SHE was our new precinct commander. Yippee! Also, Klak was gone and in his place a well-meaning new Sgt. Boldoe, who's now Lt. Boldoe. It must have been a matter of Divine Providence that we had this new leadership at Five Points. If Klak and Nero had've still been in charge they would have feigned concern and sympathy, but I would have still had to deal with further emotional discomforts of wondering what was being done with my pay and my sick-time/emergency leave status.

My sister, Jamie, had remarked that SO many people were dying of Cancer in our region of the city of Louisville that she felt a "60 Minutes" news story or some kind of show like that ought to be notified. In the Louisville, Kentucky West End (where <u>we</u> primarily lived) there had been all kinds of air polluting, odorous, sky darkening factories, and other such refinery and sewage system plants built.

The well-documented incidences of "Environmental Racism," where smog and sickness inducing chemical plants would be built and installed in poorer and usually Minority sections of cities...ours was no exception.

There was also the very unfortunate occurrence of sorry medical coverage for non-wealth imbued persons in our area even if they did have Medicare or Medicaid coverage. Mom's doctor was an elderly Caucasian gentleman who had continuously told her that, oh, she was probably suffering osteoporosis/oh, she was probably just suffering bad heartburn, etc., etc. They say that when a parent, particularly your mother, is in pain and discomfort—they usually won't say anything about it...not wanting you to worry about them. And that was when they actually admit something hurts...you know it must be pretty bad if it's not something they can brush aside and endure, and get back to business. And every time I would call Mom, she was unable to play off the pains in her mid-section she was having.

My sister's phone rang at 3:00am in January, 2001. It was Mom. She was in so much pain she was in tears. Jamie rushed to the house, got Mom to the Emergency Room of the hospital, where after making arrangements to go back to Dr. Old Dude's clinic, she decided to have a "talk" with them. She deliberately by-passed Dr. Dude and spoke with the more competent and younger Black doctor there. Since Old Dude was Mom's doctor, it was a matter of protocol that the other doctor(s) not step in to each other's patients' business. But Jamie made it perfectly clear to them in her diplomatic, professional way that she WAS going to go Postal in there if HE (the younger doctor) didn't look at Mom and see what was really wrong with her. He finally obliged Jamie, examined Mom, himself, and found out the "news." Jamie was so mad that she and my brother were truly wanting to throw Dr. Old Dude out of a window or something. She said, "You all let my mother stay in _pain_, all this time. If we could have found out sooner..." But it was too late. She would only live another three months, her passing coming April 21, 2001 at 9:50pm in the Louisville hospice. She was 61.

As unhappy as I was too, yet knowing Mom...she probably _didn't_ want to know that was what her pains were due to. She probably wanted to believe that it was "just" this or "just" that, as Dr. Old Dude was telling her. As it turned out, my sister's husband's mother, years earlier, had gone to the _same_ doctor when she came down sick—and finally died of Cancer, herself, in her early 60's. Dr. Old Dude just threw a bunch of pills at her and sent her home too.

When I got back to work at MARTA, there had been a collection taken up for me, along with flowers and a card, as was our custom for such events as this. And time marched on up to the day of days here in the states of that year.

On the morning of September 11, 2001 I was attending one of our mandatory regular training classes that roll around every so often. Our group was up at Dunwoody MARTA station (far, FAR up North) and we were going through the typical "emergency scenarios" about what to do in the event of an overturned train, dangerous chemical spills, crazy gun toting patrons, etc. Our break time came at about 9:15am that morning. When I started milling back well within the time period we were told to return I noticed that the class members who'd gotten back from break earlier weren't sitting inside the classroom itself anymore, but outside in the main area of the precinct. The Lieutenant was giving that group some beat assignments. I thought, well, they must be getting us ready to go to our scenario practice drill or something. The Lieutenant was continuing with, "The two twin towers of New York City have just been bombed and another plane has just been slammed into the Pentagon..." I thought, "My, they're coming up with some colorful emergency scenarios for us!" He was continuing with other reports of either suspected air or terror attacks and I was thinking how graphic the simulated incidences were they were wanting us to train by.

Soon, though, I noticed that the class atmosphere was not of a mood of officers in training. There appeared to be a bit more serious tone to them. I was silent for a minute as the Lieutenant began giving beat assignments to various precinct's officers. Again, it wasn't the mood or tone of training beat assignments, but actual ones. I looked over with a questioning look at one of my training classmates. I asked, "What...is this our training assignments?" He said, "No. This is really happening. They just flew two planes into the New York Trade Center. We're getting' sent back down to our precincts."

You know, when sudden terrible and dire events happen and people are recounting what they were doing and what their response was when it happened, how many ways do we hear that they said, "What!?" Or, "I was speechless!" Or something to that effect? Well, I too, just quietly said, "What?" "Yeah," was the response. "And another one flew into the Pentagon!" And reports of a third something (at that time) was still rolling in. Suddenly, someone burst out of the training room yelling, "Y'all come in here—look!" We had a TV in the class room that was for the showing of training videos on, but someone had it turned to the local news channels. We all crowded around and saw the video footage of smoke pouring out of the Twin Towers of New York and then the whole thing coming down, the news casters then hurriedly going over to coverage at the Pentagon.

Yes, shock. Yes, a deadening, mind-numbing flooding of emotional limbo. With report after report coming in, I just stood frozen at the television thinking, truly, that it was Judgment Day—the end of the world. Attacks on America, itself. Couldn't happen. Not in _my_ lifetime! And of course, when you think it's The End you start thinking with great regret about all the things you'd intended to do, and didn't get a chance to. I knew I couldn't stay there staring at that footage for long, although plenty of people were. We had been given our beat assignments to report to, immediately. Training, naturally, was postponed.

A buzz of speculations, anticipations, accusations about the whys and wherefores were all spoken in hushed tones on the trains while on the way to our beat assignments. I can barely remember just what was said. I was still in that empty limbo land of mild shock. And I was also thinking that, at least, Mom wasn't here to experience these terrors occurring in the world and now right here. It was not known _when_ we were going to be released to go home. But we could expect, the precinct lieutenant said, to be there for at least ten hours.

The Lieutenant on duty at Five Points told us that when the Chief called him up from Headquarters to tell him the Twin Towers had just been bombed and were now collapsed and destroyed, *he too*, thought it was just some kind of playing around talk. In Atlanta we have a twin towers too, called the Georgia State Twin Towers. From the Five Points precinct window those twin towers are in clear view. So Lieutenant Chris L. thought the Chief was screwing around with him when he told him the news because he thought he was talking about *those* twin towers, and he laughed. There was a dead silence on the other end of the phone. The Chief said, "I don't find that *funny*, Lieutenant!" "Yeah, right, Chief. What are you gonna tell me next—that the Pentagon's been destroyed too!?" Yes, that was what he said! From the other end of the phone he heard the Chief literally choking in trying to get his words out as he angrily said, "Uh, where is your precinct commander!? *Where* is your major!? I wanna talk to him *right now*!!!" And Lieutenant Chris was saying, "So, I dunno if I'm gonna be <u>Sergeant</u> L. now or even just *<u>Officer</u>* L!" Thankfully for him, he still retained his lieutenant rank and is now, himself, a major and precinct commander too.

For a full *five* minutes of time span here in these United States, White people who had previously wanted nothing to do with poor, down and out, downtown regulars among the Black populace at Five Points, were going out of their way to be generous and actually *nice* to them! We were having our homeless, shabbily dressed Five Points regulars coming to us and telling us that some well dressed, business suit wearing White man had just bought him a full McDonald's meal; others of the desperately poor were going around waving dollar bills in the air, saying, "This White man just up and gave me five dollars!" That was happening a lot during that period and to my understanding, other parts of the country. My guess is, thinking they were going to die any possible moment, they wanted to be sure to go before God with *some* kind of atonal act carried out for somebody Black! We regular workers throughout the coming months noticed that there were *scarce* numbers of Whites visible on the system, or apparently going to work. I said to one of the Black revenue agents at MARTA, "Where are all our White customers? I don't see hardly *any* of them! You and I are here, aren't we!?" He responded, "You and I are here because we *have* to be! Apparently, *they* have a choice!"

And, Great Day in the Morning...Arabs or people of that Middle Eastern heritage were feeling the brunt of what we Black Americans had been the recipients of for decades—even centuries. I don't applaud it. It's very sad. Plus, the reasoning in going out of the way to single them out wouldn't deter a determined Terrorist. In seeing that everyone with a turban or an accent with brown skin was being halted and questioned, a determined Terrorist would just conscript or trick an elderly platinum haired White lady into carrying his device of destruction. That was something several analytical minds were attempting to get across to angry and upset Americans and officials in charge of government security agencies who were demanding profiling of all "<u>A</u>-rabs!"

As far as the speculated reasons for these attacks (as far as folks here were concerned), the accusations by the far right-wing radio listeners was this lame, sorry, abstract charge of "They hate freedom! They're jealous because we're well-to-do, and *they* are in dictatorial poverties..." and so on. Well, folks, to *me*...it had all the earmarks of the same thing as when these young bone thugs' "deals" go bad...which some wise minds say that, tragically, is the <u>best</u> example WE have to compare to world events.

You see, folks, when somebody rich, ruthless and powerful gets screwed when it comes to their *money*...they react just like this. When it comes to the "drug deal gone bad" type of thing in the 'hood, and when the drive-by occurs with gun fire or Molotov cocktails thrown through windows...they're not concerned about the two year old toddler who's going to die. They don't care about your blind, crippled, invalid grandmother who's also not going to get out. They're after **YOU**. And they don't <u>care</u> how they get you. They just want <u>you</u> to pay for the screwing of with them. They want *your* hide...*<u>your</u>* skull for the fracturing of. Because they're mad at *YOU*!!!

Likewise, when mob members want one of their own or somebody associated with them "taken care of" for betraying or screwing with them...they do like to concentrate on making that member's demise as unpleasant as can be arranged. But NOTHING, I repeat **NOTHING** will get you dead faster or surer than messing with somebody rich and powerful's **money**!

So this contention that a lot of poor people "over there" got their poor little hands and heads together, and with scarce funds, monies or means, got these PLANES arranged, piloted, trained and PAID for (with *what?*) and then sent out over here to blow up these buildings just because, "Boo-hoo-hoo—you're rich and I'm poor...*you* got a Lexus and I have to walk! *Sniff! Sniff!* I'm gonna blow you up!" GET REAL! FACE FACTS! THAT'S the kind of *pettiness* that WE put up with <u>here</u> from the power group...always acting like it's the end of civilization, itself, if they— the owners of ALL the cookie factories in the world see *us* with one broken off piece of a half a cookie. My fellow Black Americans *know* of what I speak. If we get a nice or reasonably expensive car, as was covered earlier, our supervisors <u>will</u> attempt to lay charges or claims against us... "Must be doin' *<u>drugs</u>*!" We **know** we've put up with such. A good number of Black folks in America who've played their cards right, saved their hard earned money, and found a way to not get "taken" when purchasing a new and expensive car, just save themselves the hassle and *don't <u>dare</u>* drive that car to work. The higher ups <u>WILL</u> make a Federal case out of it. That's what YOU do with people who aren't of your own and who get "nice stuff"! Those people over there have <u>been</u> having their buildings detonated and bombed, terrorist acts permeating left and right, day and night, nearly every other day. The acts have been primarily occurring at the hands of regimes formed and financed by our government here, and those people are well aware of it. Yet, for decades, they've put up with it. What makes you think that <u>now</u> they're going to suddenly take this action? No, folks, this was done by somebody who felt they were screwed in a business deal...they're <u>money</u> f'- -ked with. And that somebody came back and struck at the financial headquarters and nerve center of these United States. You'd better remember that the very one,

Osama, whom the government is saying was behind it all, has his family members who are _business partners_ with the Bush family. Like it or not, that's a fact...the Bin Laden Group--construction work, for the most part.

Whatever occurred or went down, as plenty of tellers in the know have stated, there had been _various warnings_ of impending attack upon the U.S. from "his group." However, let's keep in mind that when this thing initially occurred, Al-Qaeda said to George, Jr., "If you will just provide _proof_ to us that Osama did in fact do this, as you say, WE will turn him over to you, ourselves!" And George, Jr.'s response was, "I don't have to prove a damn thing to y'all!" Then the catch phrase was and is, "Al-Qaeda, Al-Qaeda, Al-Qaeda!" So now Al-Qaeda and the "Moo-slim Fundamentalists" are the new "Commies" in town.

Very soon (what else was new) we were hearing about the uneven distribution of the donations coming from all over the world for the victims of "9-Eleven", to where the people (whom do you think) who were making boo coo "jillions" were apparently getting the brunt of the donations given to _them_. The reasoning, we were told, was that they made more, had _more_ to lose as far as salary...so they had to be compensated accordingly. The contributors (who ran all across the board, race, creed and color-wise) I can pretty much guarantee did NOT donate with the intent in mind that only the well-paid would get the brunt of their funds. It was to help them ALL –not just the well paid. We've heard about the minimum wage earners who died in there whose families have not received a dime to this day. But then, that's an indicator of who's in charge of that decision-making process of "who gets what"...and as ALWAYS, <u>WE'RE</u> left out. I know some noise was made about that. When the news profiles were going out about some compensated families, they made sure to have that young, pretty, Black lady's face on all their shows. Hers was the only one we saw on those news stories among the other faces at that time.

Then, there was the case with the emergency rescue units whose photos were taken while going through their rescuing of the victims. Remember that picture that was taken of the three White firefighters, and a statue commemorating that stance of theirs was going to be built in sculpture? And the sculptors were planning to make one of the fire fighters Black, one White, and the other Hispanic in order to give a panoramic representation of all the city's emergency rescue personnel. Remember the flak made by the firefighters captured in the picture? They wanted _that picture_ reproduced in sculpture—of the White guys, no other representatives. During one of the many "Dateline" and other such news shows going on during this period, the photographers who were rushing and scrambling to get as many pictures as they could of rescue and search operations as possible were telling of the problems they were having from the personnel who kept chasing them away. No, they weren't positioned where they would be in the way...they were a good distance away from the firefighters and policemen. But the photographer crews were telling of how very often when they were attempting to take pictures, they were rudely and crudely ordered to get away from there, or "No" don't take any pictures. So the photographers had to resort to photos being taken on the sly, with their specially set up cameras where they appear to be hanging nonchalantly around the neck, but are actually well into photographing or video filming. Therefore, apparently, only a few—with only *some* kinds of emergency personnel in photos—got through. Uhm, do you think the same forces wanting only the captured photo would want that photo, only, being sculpted if there were three Black firefighters in it, instead of an across the board representation? Uh, let me answer that for you—**HELL** no!!!

Back to the police department duties during this September 11th period. Oh, my God...the head shaking incidences of our mainly frightened Caucasian riders who were seeing a "terrorist" under *every* plant and behind *every* telephone pole! We got so many calls, needlessly, I daresay, of *their* wanting us to investigate and absolutely *jack up* every olive skinned, dark haired innocent rider...some were even Hispanics mistaken for "Arabs" who the scared-to-death main groups wanted questioned and questioned and questioned. At every turn. Though, there was nothing to question them for. Some regular, though Brown skinned, riders who'd been working all night and were tired and nodding off on the trains were fingered and pointed out by unseen callers who were "Uncomfortable!" and wanted them stopped, and so on. Of course, with these calls coming in though police radio and filtered through Command, we had no choice but to have to bother all of these people who we could tell didn't need to be bothered.

One thing, in this police business, once you've been in it for a while you grow a second pair of eyes. You can sort of look at a particular subject and just tell*l* that this individual needs to be "watched." Of course, that would never stand up in a court of law, but you get to where you can look at the group of the "stereo-typical Black males" who are beebopping along and yet you just know... "Aww, their not bothering anything, or about to be up to no good." And about 99.9% of the time we're correct. And then you can look at *another* even smaller group of persons or whatever...and there will be something about them that just tells you, the officer, that you need to keep your eyes on them. As I mentioned, these are instincts and hunches that you just take on in your profession. And since you don't convict or harass anyone (at least you're not supposed to) based on such hunches, that's the reason for just "eye-ing" them until or unless they actually do something that warrants your approach. In about one hundred percent of these hysterically pointed out cases and reports on our passengers during this period, NONE of the stoppees were *"terrorists!"*

In hindsight and in fairness to overly held detainees wheresoever they may be...if you haven't brought or even *found* actual _charges_ against these folks then you need to release them. I know saving face is more important to you authorities (some of you) than saving further agonies and discomfort of your supposed *suspects*, but war or no war/ peace or no peace, there's a time limit to everything. WE police officers in the battle against wrongs committed against fellow citizens have to be wary of overly detaining someone without *SOME* kind of charges being brought against them. Why and how do you think you can justify holding _forever_ some folks who happened to be in the wrong place at the wrong time and got swooped up with the rest of the folks who, by <u>now</u> have been found to be guiltless. In your holding and holding people over days, weeks, months, and now going on _YEARS_, then if there wasn't a conflict being held against you, along with somebody in charge who just may be the brunt of a personal vendetta, then there certainly WILL be one brought by these folks and theirs, eventually. Mark my word. As was so wisely put by one of the listeners to WAOK, in quoting a soothsaying philosopher... "He who makes peace impossible will make war _inevitable._" Folks, to the people in charge of these secret, private prisons in and on behalf of the U.S. overseas, just outside of the interests of law here, AND to those in charge of Guantanamo Bay, Cuba...let these people _out_ if you're not finding anything on them by _now_. At some point, unless they just tell you what you want to hear in order to be cut a break, it should be obvious that you're not going to find any charges on them. Why do I put it so emphatically? Because, dear readers, _if you don't think YOU'RE going to be next_...you'd better take a lesson from the history books about such actions and practices. YOU WON'T LIKE BEING DETAINED FOREVER AND FOR **NOTHING.** Arab, White, Hispanic, or what have you. Black folks have **been** getting detained and forever for nothing. And we always seem to come out smiling, "Hah, hah, hah!" as if everything's cool. And because power doesn't respect non-violence or a calm, cool, forgiving attitude...that's precisely WHY such keeps happening to us, even when the authorities in charge KNOW we're not guilty! But with YOU, I doubt that all the rest of you will be taking it as well as we have...World War Three—HELLO! And because your government knows that and intends to protect itself, once the prisons, jails, and closed down military facilities converted into additional prison space become filled with enough malcontents among you and me...an _accident_ will happen; whereby hundreds of thousands, if not nearly _millions_ will be instantly obliterated.

We've been having leaders decades before Malcolm X—even _decades_ before Elijah Muhammad, who've _been_ warning us that the day _would come_ when the same thing that was done to the Jews in Germany would be done to us right here in the U.S. And just as when the first inkling of such leaked out among the Jews there, they said, "Aw, look...this is _Germany_...that can't happen here!" –so will you and other fellow American citizens be saying, "Aw, look, this is AMERICA—that can't happen here!" All that's needed is some excuse for the massive round up of whole neighborhoods to be "transferred" somewhere. You'd better keep an eye out for how much touting the powers that be are going to do with this supposed, "bird flu break out." The biologists and scientists in the know had stated that the same numbers of either death or illness that are purported to be so "out of control" are the same as Asiatic and some city-states in Africa normally experience. And you'd better pay attention to all the wiser and educated heads out there who've had this same foresight back in the early **1980's**. Because, they were able to predict the Enron and World Com-type debacles that have taken place...KNOWING that such would be tolerated and allowed to expand and go on _simply because of WHO_ was behind it (or rather who wasn't), along with the Savings and Loan scandals; "Oh, that's alright. We'll just increase the taxes on the lower classes and THEY can pay for what our rich White males are being allowed to abscond with!" And when there's nothing left for man, woman, boy or girl to feed themselves with—right here in the good ol' U.S., and I am talking about you formerly *wealthy* socialites...when **you** find yourselves with <u>nothing</u>, and I do mean absolutely **NOTHING** to survive on—you are going to be in a position where <u>you</u> are going to have to turn to <u>us</u> Black folks to learn *how* to survive on **nothing**! You're going to have to turn to your very victims to learn *how* to take a handful of beans, and add *a little <u>more</u>* water to it, to make it stretch to feed a few *<u>more</u>* hungry mouths. Smarter, wiser and more educated persons than me, and in high positions have *<u>been</u>* predicting such. And such <u>*ALWAYS*</u> starts by despising and casting off the smallest and the *least of these* in <u>every</u> society. Yet, as the holy book of the very people you guys are *so scared of* right now aptly puts it, when these signs and evidences of grievances are sure to come, God gives <u>*plenty*</u> of warning that such is on the way. Yet, as always...the sinners and offenders NEVER learn or repent!

Chapter Sixteen

THOUGHTFUL CONCLUSIONS IN PERSPECTIVE

AS THE YEARS PROGRESSED and more "incidences" and "occurrences" of racial animosity, none of it called for, continued as reported in the news, I began to find myself becoming a bit heated in my attitude. We had an Ashanti queen from Ghana visit the United States some years before the September 11th situation, and when she came through, I think it was Kennedy Airport, she was stopped, her luggage searched out in the open, and basically disrespected according to her office and status. _WHENEVER_ a visiting dignitary, from no matter where, comes through ANY airport in the world, it is a matter of political protocol in how they are to be treated. With the United States, even with countries and nations that are not on the friendliest terms with us, they are _still_ properly treated and with respect for their dignity. Do you think Princess Di would have been jacked up the way this Ashanti ruler was? Huh, huh, yeah _right_! Even with downright _enemy_ nations, if they have a dignitary or statesman coming through the American airports, they are still not made to stand there while all their things are gone through. And with persons of politically high rank that our secret service and other confidentially protective agencies are almost **certain** may have questionable devices in their possession they, still again, will quietly and confidentially go through their things, incognito, behind the scenes or in private baggage claim areas to keep from insulting the dignitary, even though it is a matter of national concern for the nation's protection.

No, this Black queen was made to stand there while this White baggage agent went through every one of her bags and belongings, the other baggage agents looking away in some embarrassment and shame, and nobody bothering to correct him for this while she was put through this outrage. Folks, this was done—FOR NO OTHER REASON...**BUT** to insult and harass *them*. In fact, in African airports they have a travelers' advisory posted along the walls, saying, "If you are going to the United States, expect to be harassed and insulted," because apparently, this kind of thing happened all the time.

For you folks whose response is, "Well, if ya don't like it, why don't cha leave? Just don't come through here!" and other such statements indicating no intent to change or correct such actions, would'ja just keep one thing in mind...? Even if you **don't** respect _us_ enough to not look like dumb baboons to the rest of the world, would you at least respect the <u>way</u> you're making the United States appear to all concerned? You're causing all others, even the ones you _think_ you're fond of, to come away with a sentiment of, "What kind of _cave people_ are these?" As my grandmother once said to me, people sometimes don't like you, NOT because of how you treat _them_, but because of how they see you treat *someone else*. You g<u>e</u>t respect by <u>showing</u> respect. Even if you truly don't like someone else for whatever reason, *how* you conduct yourself despite your feelings when around them, will tell people you *have* to deal with <u>what</u> kind of tactics and actions they need to use whenever *they're* around you. If you <u>HAVE</u> to behave like an escapee from the "Angry Red Planet" toward *some* people for no other reason than because of <u>who</u> they are...and you <u>have</u> to experience the jollies you get from your diseased little moment in needlessly harassing them...other peoples are going to take a lesson from it and respond to _you_, accordingly. Grandmother also said, "You don't do to <u>one</u> what you don't do to <u>all</u>." She had a lot of wise sayings like that. And as I'm sure I don't have to state, as you've seen other peoples shrink away from you in disgust, similar to the way they did with the Apartheid regime, you've only ended up with and encouraged among each other the _same_ contempt and disdain for *them* as you have toward _us_. Yes, certain kinds of treatment of certain kinds of people, just as unwanted weeds...<u>grows</u> and spreads. You've seen this exact same sentiment towards others flare up among our "majority" group here, especially with the United Nations, which just so happened to coincide with their placing Kofi Anan as its head. It's been, primarily, the United States that from Day One, has had a negative approach and attitude toward him. There have been any number of presidents and leaders (barring the Hussains and Fidel) whom this country has not been fond of, but their statements, such as, "He's a sideshow!" were not said of them as they were of Mr. Anan by U.S. senators and congressmen. And as the contemptuous and condescending attitude toward more and more others in the world grows—all from starting at seedling level with your one (Black People), now two (Hispanics...*illegal immigrants*, as they're called), now

ALL (Asians, Muslims, people on welfare, the poor and homeless, most foreign visitors not from Europe, Middle Easterners, Indo-Europeans i.e., Greeks/Turks, now the Spaniards and the French, Koreans, let's not leave out Haitians, South Americans, you name it) and you begin to treat them all accordingly...folks, *these* are some of the things that's causing the <u>terrorism</u> in the world today. You're finding out the hard way that the <u>rest</u> of the world *does* <u>*not*</u> have the same patience level and tolerance level that we Black Americans do. *<u>THEY'RE</u>* telling you, "Look, Buddy, you're not gonna go <u>spittin'</u> in <u>MY</u> face over and over again, and think <u>I'M</u> gonna lay down and take it like a whipped dog!" And as I've said earlier and very unfortunately, this government of ours *does <u>NOT</u>* respect patience, tolerance or a forgiving heart. That, and that ONLY is the reason why any charges at all were brought against Lindy England and her immediate supervisors for those prison pictures they took of themselves with those Iraqi captives. The U.S. government knew they'd better do <u>something</u> to them. I remember seeing on the news that charges and actual "guilty" verdicts were successfully brought against the prison guards there, and just recalling ALL the "NOT GUILTY" verdicts given to White police officers here for gunning down unarmed Blacks over wallets, combs, cell phones and pagers...or nothing, at all. Just having a Black face. "Not Guilty!" On ALL charges. Because the government here knows that all they <u>ever</u> have to worry about <u>you and ME</u> doing is getting on the phone and dialing 1-800-WAAAHHH! Or if we get *really* upset, just putting together a bunch of placards, walking around in circles and singing tunes. We get mad and call for "investigations" from those same agencies responsible for the offense, in the first place. Nice going, Gridley. Keep going to one of the seven heads of the dragon to tell it what one of the *other* heads is doing to you!

Sun Tzu...to quote him again, "Know thy enemy/know thyself—One hundred battles/One hundred victories." In order to <u>do</u> something about our situation, you have to know what you can do, what you're not willing to do...and what you're absolutely not <u>able</u> to do. And in true reality, I'm really glad/glad/GLAD that apparently, <u>we're</u> NOT able or willing to "nut up" and "kill White people," as we <u>keep</u> hearing feedback and grapevine talk that that's what they expect us to do any day now. And we just won't do it. We can't do it. It's not in us. You would think that with ALL that's happened to us and been done to us, that if we haven't nutted up and gone berserk *yet* on all Whitedom, with respect to EVERYTHING...then wouldn't it stand to reason that instead of US being the "dangerous animals" <u>you </u>HAVE to believe us to be...that in fact we *must* be the <u>safest</u> (within reasonable treatment) to be around. Sure... and I do mean SURE, we've got Black idiots running around. I, my dear readers, will be the FIRST and <u>foremost</u> to state that fact! We've got some of my people running around that cause *other <u>Black</u>* folks to be ready to take a sheet and cut two eye holes out of it. I know that. Just as you Whites personally know of some of your own kindred, guilty of unnecessary, heinous, grievous actions regularly committed against us that cause *you* to wonder how it is and WHY it is that <u>ALL</u> of us Black folks have <u>not</u> become Colin Fergusons (the subway shooter in New York)...and <u>he</u>

had to be a dern <u>NUT</u> to do what he did. And don't forget, it was a Black passenger that helped tackle him when he went on his shooting spree.

To emphasize the point about "knowing thyself..." there was an incident that occurred in 1977 here in Louisville. Despite all that has been and is being done to keep <u>us</u> out of the financial mainstream, there <u>are</u> those of us who succeed and get ahead, <u>anyway</u>, despite the best efforts of racist society. And no—<u>NOT</u> through drug sales, either! In Louisville in those years, Newburg became a first Black suburb with affluent Black Louisvillians moving there in suburban bliss. As nearly anyone in the know here in these United States can tell you, <u>any</u> Black person, especially with his/her own business who's *made it* and become financially successful—he's been through *Hell*! We all know that. Every means possible...every crooked endeavor and shady, seedy attempt has been made by White society to keep him/her <u>*out*</u> of affluence, no matter what. In the 1920's, if you were financially successful and made a <u>lot</u> of money—you'd be lynched. Despite all the excuses, false or trumped up, no one was in doubt that THIS was the <u>real</u> reason you'd been murdered and made an example of. Because you made *too* much money. Otherwise, government charges and suddenly passed laws and requirements that occurred in the 1940's through the 1970's that was *really* designed to keep <u>you</u> from lucrative business wealth was resorted to when lynchings died down, somewhat—thanks to Ida B. Wells' telling Black people that they just needed to keep a shotgun behind their front doors of their homes. Lynchings went <u>*way down*</u> then! However, die-hard individual pioneers among us got through, *anyway,* and became financially well off, after suffering frightful inconveniences and road blocks thrown up against them. As could be expected, when beaten up on to that degree, one's patience and long-suffering levels have obviously taken some "outta here" turns. And *many* Black people <u>*did NOT*</u> want to be bothered with some of these White folks, anymore. They knew what they'd gone through moving to White Suburbia. They weren't going to stay in the impoverished inner cities. So, in Louisville they moved to Newburg where it became Black Utopia land of these hard suffered, and now *no more nonsense takin'* Black successful people.

Well, in 1977, a White man moved out to Newburg. He was instantly told he was not welcome by the Black residents. This White man was interviewed on our local news programs. He was not embittered sounding. He was not arrogant, bigoted talking or anything like that. He was just a regular guy. Anyway, as he was being interviewed he was talking very sorrowfully. In fact, he began to emotionally break down. He said, "They said they didn't want me out here. One lady said she...she" and he put his hand over his eyes and began to cry as he said it, "...she was gonna burn my house down!" And began sobbing uncontrollably. Well, the response from the Newburg residents was one of immediate reconciliation. They ALL felt terrible. They said that he could stay. The one lady who had made the earlier mentioned comment quickly told him, "I'm not gonna burn your house down!" They felt horrible. You see, *they* had been through the ringer. They'd suffered what they went through and figured, "Here, we can be at peace, bothering and being bothered by NOBODY!" In other words, people, they *meant* to mean it. They <u>*tried*</u> to mean it.

But *that just wasn't them*! In other words, that's just not *us*. Having been exasperated, they *thought* they could play the counterpart to the racisms they'd suffered. But, they just *couldn't*...period. You see, you have to *lose* something to be able to stand to do that to your fellow man. And we just haven't lost it. Despite everything, they just didn't lose out on their souls, their being, their very fibre. Because, once again...that's just not *us*! And White America knows this. I'm not talking about little gangsters or bone thugs who are just as much a threat to their *own* mothers or others within their own communities, let alone others. I mean, just us, period. White people would be more shocked than anybody if we were to actually start trying to be "I don't want YOU around!" racists, just like some of theirs are. Yet, it would appear that this very sentiment is exactly what they seem to be attempting to provoke us toward. We continue now to the 1980's through the 2000's.

With the way that our American Caucasian counterparts just *have* to envision us American Black folks as being that "vision of socially abrasive 'motha fucka' this and 'bitch-ass mo-fo' that" when ever they depict us on screen or in their heads, *that* version or vision as such is only the case *after* so much duress or being needled upon and gotten on to the point of no return. And it does appear that some of our White counterparts do take great pleasure in annoying or trying us. And they don't stop...until WE stop it. And because they are so subtle about doing it, WE look like WE'RE the assholes who can't get along with anybody without going, "MOTHA FUCKA!!" You have to envision a crowd full of people. I mean a deep crowd, packed so tight that only the tops of peoples' heads can be seen. And crouching way down, totally out of sight, is a "mean wittle kid" who keeps stomping on your foot, just out of wicked pleasure and spite. You, the grown up, grit your teeth, squint your eyes, endure the pain until you can stand it no longer. Then you yell out, attracting the attention of every head surrounding you. Then they see you reach down, disappear out of sight, then re-appear with that mean wittle kid grasped between your angry hands as he squiggles and declares his innocence. "Gee, Mister, I didn't do nuthin' wrong! Leggo 'me! Help! Somebody! I wasn't doin' nuthin'!" Everybody in that crowd thinks *you're* the bad guy. "Leggo that young man!" they cry. And you're standing there holding that kid while everybody's looking at *you*...they don't know *what* to believe.

That is *exactly* what our position is here in these United States. Exactly. Things are being done to us. And they keep being done to us. With the doers forever and constantly claiming, "Oh, WE'RE not prejudiced! WE aren't doing anything to those people! We're innocent. In fact, we have a Zero Tolerance policy toward discrimination in our work place!" It's very akin to a dirty and more cowardly version of "Tag—you're it!" Only you can't be "it" and tag back because, "Oh, I was just playing!" or "Now, look here, I'm your boss, you can't speak to me like that!" So what happens? "Tag! Tag! Tag! Tag! Tag!" until you finally erupt and explode—leaving people to think *you're* the one who's screwed up, anti-social, hostile and basically a naturally hard to get along with jack ass. If you see a Black person on the job anywhere, and they're talking to their White management with "that attitude," cuss words, cross, sore, "I've had it up to here!" demeanor...and that White supervisor is just sitting there with that mute silence and combination innocent, yet smug smile on his/her face, or looking about sheepishly as if, "<u>Now</u>, I've gone too far! I think he's/she's gonna hurt me!" you'll know you've just come upon that earlier described example I just gave.

As was pointed out in this particular chapter, the forces representative of the powers that be keep forcing their hand upon those who've been the least likely to have in their possession contraband items at airports, and so on. And no matter how many times their search results garner nothing, these persons are still disproportionately singled out for harassing and insulting searches. Once again, our friends at "60 Minutes" and "Dateline" news story shows covered specials about all the Black women coming back into the States from overseas being singled out and targeted for cavity searches for illegal drugs. Again and again, each woman was innocent. But the predominantly White Federal agents on duty at these airports were regularly targeting them for these invasive searches. The news teams there went so far as to point out the fact that when regular random searches were conducted across the board...it was *White males* who were being discovered with these illegal drugs on *their* person. But apparently such was disregarded by the Federal agents, and they continued to single out Black women.

The news shows pointed out an incident where a dark skinned young Black woman who was pregnant was singled out at the airport by Federal agents, and they absolutely disregarded her pregnant condition. They forced her to take a laxative (not having found anything in her or on her) to force her to do a Number Two to find illegal drugs. They also handcuffed her to a bed while waiting for the laxative to go to work. The ensuing brutal actions on the part of all of these White Federal agents was that her baby was damaged in the process, and she at the time, had a lawsuit filed against the government agents. The response shown to us from these news shows that came from the customs agents was, "We don't feel we owe you any apology, either," along with their dismissive attitude toward what had been done to this young woman. By the way, no drugs were found on her, either.

We've all been lectured and preached to by our parents, grandparents, wiser older heads, etc. about how, "God don't like no ugly!" Now, we Black Americans have patiently and for the most part, silently been putting up with uglinesses to the extremes...mistreatments to the extremes, being kept totally OUT of the money producing processes that have made the nation wealthy beyond its wildest dreams—all on OUR backs and from OUR inventions—the list is <u>TOO LONG</u> to cover. And it just appears that, with the exception of *some* final straw riots, we just don't act. WE just won't revolt. Whites, again, ask themselves everyday—*WHAT'S keeping us* from losing our minds, nutting up and <u>killing</u> Whites everywhere we see them? We've seen evidence ever since I was in High School in the early 1970's that Whites were *looking* for us to come after them. We talked among ourselves about their NRA's, their Rifle Clubs, their unrelenting determination to load up assault weapons and machine guns for their own private arsenals, etc. And some of the more staid students among us would say, "Oh, that's for US! They (Whites) just figure we're comin' after them!" But it hasn't happened. As I said before, wouldn't it stand to reason that if we haven't done anything really significant to you *yet*, why would you keep envisioning "mugger, rapist, killer—mugger, rapist, killer" of our people? But that's getting beyond the following point I'm making. WE haven't acted on such noted actions as the ones so far described in this text. Uglinesses to the extreme, no justification for them, whatsoever, beyond some bent, twisted individuals to enjoy their little moment...continue to be committed. What was described with that Black pregnant lady, while bad enough, if it *were indeed* a case of, "Gee, we made a mistake. We're sorry..." THAT could have been the response. But the response, instead, was one of downright *spitting in her face*, with their statement of, "We don't *owe* you an apology." This statement was in writing, by the way.

Getting back to the Old Folks statement of, "God don't like no ugly"—when wrongs, injustices, and crimes against persons are committed...and the law, as controlled by Man, does not do its job and bring the offenders to justice, and the victims also fail to get justice for themselves...then other forces go to work. Forces unseen by the naked eye or detected by human senses. But their results are undeniable. It's what we call Divine Providence. Commonly called, "what goes around comes around," secularly called, the moment when it's "time to pay the piper," etc., humanity has a long list of descriptions for the time when, "You'll get yours," comes a' callin'. Darlings, we *don't* escape what we do. And there finally comes a time when you've pushed the button on our Creator's patience a little *too* deeply. I love the way Chuck Swindoll, of the radio ministry program, "Insight for Living," puts it... "It's when we go too far and God finally arises from His throne and says, 'Alright, that's enough.' And HE steps in to our human affairs and deals with it." I know there are religious trains of thought out there that feel that everything is ordained by the Hand of God. Even the bad things. The addressing of that philosophical conclusion would take up another two or three more books. But, just in a nutshell, (and I know I'm speaking my own philosophy and belief-oriented thought) the whole thing in this world-wide human existence for us is based on the same process as being a parent. God is the Ultimate Parent—both Mother and Father. We are the babies, turned rebellious teenagers, to more (sometimes) stable, thought-oriented adults, and then parents, ourselves. When you hit your young adult years, you strike out on your own, but your Mom and Dad are there for advice, guidance, etc. And if you decide you don't want to be bothered, Mom and Dad will obligingly leave you alone. God, being the Perfect Parent, won't butt into our affairs if He is not asked. That's the key. He wants to be asked. If He were to just "do" this and "do" that without our wanting it...that would drive us independent-minded young adults/teenagers crazy. Thus, that's one of the reasons for our human suffering down here. I don't have all answers to all things...only the Creator does. This is just learned philosophy and belief as I have been exposed to and accept after and during the years of my own progress. Part of the reason for our human suffering is that we don't want God interfering with our affairs. To the ages' long question of, "WHY does God permit all the *suffering* we go through!?" it's because God is consistent, and will not annoy or bother us if we insist on smoking Cancer-causing cigarettes, drinking liver-damaging booze, gambling our mortgage money away in Atlantic City, New Jersey, etc., etc., etc. And when we suffer the consequences of our actions...well—that's on US! If you have submitted yourself to your Heavenly Parent, given your *entire* will and person over to Him to do with you what He will, asking Him daily to have His own way with you...you ARE making yourself His responsibility. He's been *asked.* And then, whatever happens to you, you'll be able to deal with. It definitely wouldn't mean the *end* of not-so-fun times, but you will be brought through them with His protection, and only by His permission will *some things* be *allowed* to happen to you. But not beyond what you are able to bear...AND to come out shining on the other side of that seemingly bad experience.

However, there *are* some times, as explained, when we go too far. And if you're an asshole who enjoys f'_ckin' with people and hurting people, well—we'd hate to be you when you *finally* get dealt with. And though our Creator will allow you to get by with only so much, at some point, just like a parent with a wayward kid, He just *has* to reach out and "spank" you.

I think this extra-ugly, smug, dismissive attitude these customs agents displayed to this innocent young woman was one of the last straws in permissive allowance on the part of our White racist friends. God, Almighty, is upon His throne, allowing power in the world to shift hands. He observes and views us to see what we will do with it. Of course, and obviously, *some* peoples in power have done horribly worse jobs in the treatment of their subjected peoples than others. In addition, human beings, utilizing what little powers they have in their hands, work and devise strategies in how to either retain or get rid of that so and so, depending upon *how* big an Asshole they are! Egypt's empire lasted over three thousand years. They toppled to others who wanted to rule. Rome's empire lasted from about 200 B.C. to 459 A.D. Greece's empire, thrown upon the world thanks to Alexander the Great, has trace practices and traditions still retained by various world nations to this very day. And that's voluntarily done, as many peoples like and admire the Olympic games, the gymnasiums, wonderful sculptures of the human body, their philosophers' teachings, and so on. The Third Reich Empire under our little Adolph—lasted a full *twelve* years. Uhm, I'm afraid too many different peoples found *their* reign and their practices a bit too unable to be tolerated. So almost all military forces in the world found it necessary to get together and end their Reich...*fast*!

And now the United States is the big bad boy of the block. The majority group here feels that it's the best of all bests. That may be true if you belong to the majority group. While the rest of the citizenry deals with, seemingly unseen by the majority group, those things intently viewed by our Creator as He observes what this country does with all its vast power. Our Heavenly Parent has calmly and patiently looked upon this haughty nation of ours—watching the ruling majority take young Black seventeen year olds and fourteen year olds, and gleefully torture them beyond belief, then burn or hang them for some trifle that they may or may not have committed. While the ruling majority regularly raped and murdered Black women (and have yet to be convicted on such), this very accusation against these young males was one of the primary excuses used to commit these psychopathic acts. On the other hand, in 1921, He has also seen some conscientious and concerned White women form a social group called, "The Southern Women's Society for the Prevention of Lynching," because they were tired of their men *using* them as an excuse to commit these cowardly acts against all these Black men. They met similarly to the way AA groups meet, talking out their upset and concerns, such as, "My husband _knew_ that colored man didn't do anything to me. He just wanted that colored man's property!" When the excuse to lynch was done to many, many Blacks in that period, they would either additionally kill or else chase his surviving family out of town and take the man's property for themselves. God, Almighty, has seen the period of the 1940's and observed when Welfare was established and food stuffs were to be taken to or given to the poor, that milk substitute, "Similac,"was just plain poisoned. Under the Franklin Roosevelt administration, those milk substitutes for babies, and handed out to Black women had properties in it that would cause death. Proof, you say? Bits of that fact have leaked out thanks to certain fact-finding groups and persons connected with the Health industry sub-groups in the U.S. At any rate, the formula, upon its true discovery, was changed in the 1970's, thanks in addition to Dick Gregory's continued exposure of such diabolical chemical additives in other foods as well. Yet, at that time, Mrs. Eleanor Roosevelt was aware of these poisoned properties in this milk substitute, and apparently other foodstuffs destined to come to Black Americans. She used her status and power to intervene, had the foodstuffs and milk substitutes changed for safe and non-dangerous ingredient containing formulas. She did this on her own. I was told this information by our Revenue Agent we nicknamed, "Father Knows Best," because we learned so much wisdom and facts about so many things from him. He told us that White Americans to this day just don't know how they want to feel about Eleanor Roosevelt since she helped save the lives of so many Black people. In addition to that, he told us, for the poisonous foods that did get through to Blacks, God reached His hand into these actions. Rather than stopping it, as such, for every fifty Blacks and Black babies that died, He caused five _hundred_ more to be born. For every one hundred Blacks who would die, He caused one _thousand_ more to be born. "And as for Mrs. Roosevelt...you can bet that wherever she is right now, she's wearing a whole lot of crowns because of what she did on our behalf."

And as our Creator continues to observe His creations do what they do for a time, He determines how long it will be allowed. When He finally sees that despite chance after chance to correct such criminal acts at governmental levels, it just ain't gonna change...that is when (as was mentioned earlier) He begins to give notice that He's on the way—to end it, Himself.

When what was done (along with what *has* been getting done to our people) to this young, Black female airline passenger and her baby, along with the belligerent, dismissive response from the offending authorities, in *this* humble police officer's opinion, THAT was when our Maker, no doubt, sighed and said, "Alright. I've seen enough. Time for this to end."

These "other Forces" going to work, all in conjunction with one another, added up and amounted toward indications that this nation's "protective hedges" are coming down. There is a time, as stated in the Book of Ecclesiastes, for all seasons...a time for all things. While being allowed to remain in power, certain "protective hedges" surrounded that particular power from On High—to give you time to prove what you will and won't be. You'd better stop listening to all this "We're morally superior" junk by self-serving right wing talkers. And NO—you can't blame it all on homosexuals. THEY are not the problem here. The problem is YOU with your screwed up court systems of injustice. We have four systems or levels of justice in these United States: One for the Rich: One for the Poor: One for the Black: One for the White: With subcategories for Black rich/Black poor: White rich/White poor. It's with your hogging up 150% of EVERYTHING for just your own White selves, and divvying out false, phony, counterfeit versions of the real thing to everybody else. It's with your wastefulness...actually *paying* the farmers to destroy overages in their crop or cattle production, so that you can keep prices constant, instead of letting overages out to desperately hungry and needy people. You justify this criminal waste by claiming, "That's Communist!" In all things having to do with how you treat certain peoples for no other reason than who they are, not what they've supposedly done, all these things are being tallied to the three hundred and eighty-sixth year since 1619 A.D. to the present.

When these splinter groups got through customs while Transportation Security was hemming up innocent, passengers, and the country was thrown into the tailspin it was on that particular day in September, the following results occurred: The very "types" of airline passengers regularly singled out for "search and harassment," lo and behold, became the very ones searching and hemming up "majority group" representatives. In other words, in practically one day, the persons smugly and tolerantly watching all these Black women being hemmed up were *themselves* now being hemmed up and searched by "Shaniquas" and "Meeshas" and "Queeshas" and "Neeshas" and "Keetas," etc.! With their long, curling, Fu Manchu nails, their hair unflatteringly described with the "attachments", and so on. And you'd have thought September 11th was occurring daily, in its own varying degrees, to the recipients of these searches. I heard them calling in to the Scumbaugh, Boortz, other right wing shows bleating and crying like slaughtered sheep in outrage. Oh! How DARE they touch **ME**!!! was their mood. "THEY'RE not even qualified to work at MacDonalds!" I heard them crying to the listening ear. "Their nails!" "Their hair!" "I was violated!" "I was insulted!" "How DARE they!" Yes, folks. *That's* an example of Divine Providence. And it's etched in stone. The reactions and some actions taken on the part of authorities to appease the bleating peal of these unhappy "pampered" flyers was such that, as Bill Maher pointed out, they "fired all the Black security agents," which when exposed, I suppose, they hurried up and re-hired some back. But American airline passengers, across the board now, are destined to permanently be stopped and searched, despite the calls by various persons now to "racially pro-file" all Arab types only.

This is not the only obvious Divine example and warning that's due to be. Our Creator always gives us a chance to stop doing what we're doing that we know ain't kosher. Yet, as we see attempts for charges and accusations against other nations begin to spread in order to seemingly justify invasion of *their* countries next—be ye warned: "Whoever is an A__hole, let him continue to be one still. Whoever is lying, let him still lie...by ye not deceived. God is NOT mocked!" (paraphrasing, mine). In other words, just like in the words of our own exasperated parents when WE wouldn't stop being naughty, that's God's way of saying, just before the belt or switch comes out, "...keep it up!"

CHAPTER SEVENTEEN

THE FISH THAT ARE IN THE TRAP BEGIN TO THINK

THE ABOVE is a quote from an old African proverb. As we watched our department evolve and grow, all the time with new faces coming, some old faces going...and some of the new faces leaving as soon as they came, we who were going on our thirteenth and fourteenth year there made a few unmistakable observations. We noticed that every Saturday morning when we arrived for Day Watch, there were NO White sergeants, lieutenants, or majors at work. Those few White regular officers we had with us were barely there. So we remaining Black officers just figured they were all in Stone Mountain, Georgia at Venable Park...the regular meeting/stomping grounds of good standing Ku Klux Klan members. I mean it—NONE of the White officers or their high ranking officials were with us on Saturday mornings. Not that we missed them. We were actually free to talk more relaxed and openly about all the glaring differences in our treatment as opposed to theirs, the various "oreos" in the department...in case you might not be aware, "oreo" is another name given to "Uncle Tom," faithful slave minded Black folks, which of them had written up or fired whom that year, and so on.

Sometimes, there would be wind of, yet again, *another* situation where a well-deserving Black officer who had just outdone Batman on the silver screen got screwed, messed over, unrecognized and finally driven out the door (fired) for some trifle. Or another undeserved promotion of some Klan-type White person or "Yassuh, Boss" type Black person. But more often, it was the new department policy that would just come into effect that was sure to punish (underhandedly) those people needing leave time, overtime, extra-work authorization, etc. It would be so elaborately, yet so obviously done and put into place in order to keep <u>us</u> in a state of suspended animation, while letting all persons who lived way, WAY out in the suburbs and with <u>very</u> recent dates of hire; persons with "other" professional af-filiations so-to-speak, and so on, were given departmental blessings and sure "ok's" that THEY'D be the next precinct commander.

In our own usual, wearily tolerant manner, when news of such would come through to us while in roll-call, some one would start the ending theme song tune of the conclusion of the old black and white Mickey Mouse Club TV show. The same way you spell out, "M-I-C...K-E-Y...M-O-U-S-E!" slowly at the show's end, we would start out with one person spelling, "F-U-C...K-E-D...A-G-A-I-N!" Then we'd all join in, "Fucked again! Fucked again!" And that would be how we'd handle it. I suppose you could call it just getting weary, and tired of having to fight on all sides, in all ar-eas, in all segments of one's life. You get older, you know you need your job, you see the suffering and struggling of dedicated, sincere crusaders who get dead or jailed for their efforts. You have a family, you know you want them to retain the quality of life you've managed to get established for them and yourself. You also know that the choices out there, not only for employment, for a place "where all this kind'a shit ain't goin' on"...aren't very varied. Plus, it's the "same all over!" ALL Black folks working EVERYWHERE where there are (or *were*) well-paying jobs had been putting up with the same kind of horseshit that WE in the police departments had been...and that was doing all that's necessary to keep the Whites at the top, and "us black jellybeans" at the bottom. And ALL of them talked about going to work "some place *else!*" as if there would be a difference in how they'd be treated at a new well paying company. I suppose there's no need to quote White accusations anymore about *why*, after four hundred years of <u>our</u> being here are we still in about the same shape, if not worse, than we were in the 1940's? Why, with the advent of *"other groups"* coming here and making it, couldn't WE do the same? What's wrong with us? With the regularly and on-going exposure of various methods of disenfranchisement practiced here, and as each attempt to address, thus correct it, is shot down, stopped, accused, and other-wise done away with, it appears we don't seem to hear that questioning accusation anymore. When it came to business contracts being awarded out, obviously 100% of the recipients of those contracts were White. When Affirmative Action came into place, not just for jobs, but for a certain percentage of the business contracts to go to Minorities, the Whites simply came up with the clarion call of "Reverse dis-crimination!" and the lousy little single-digit percent of contracts meant to come to us was apparently too much, thus overturned because of "racial discrimination." Thus, Whites again, can get 100% (*maybe* with a fractional percent's exception for "this ought to shut 'em up" money) which gets no complaint—from *them*—about racial discrimination. The home grown leaders we've had, like the formerly known H. Rap Brown, Malachai Z. York, etc. who's teachings and influence were actually dissuading Black people from using drugs, and going on to get their education, were all set up, accused of this or that, neutralized and put in prison, despite evidence to the contrary and witnesses who tried again and again to report that they'd been coerced into making false accusations against them. For those of you familiar with, and therefore, justifying the imprisoning of Mr. York (supposedly for sexual molestation), would you answer me this...? Why in the hell isn't the government going after those Mormons in Utah the same way??? They've even had a news special about them and their **forcing** under age young children to be those dirty old men's *wives*. And the young lady who's committed herself to smuggling them out of their clutches has been openly given death threats...WHY ISN'T THE FEDERAL GOVERNMENT and its authorities stopping *that* <u>DEFINITE</u> statutory rape situation that's on-going? Our own men, for the most part, are woefully absent from protecting their own women and children from street and under color of law violence, their balls too cut off to stop it, or their heads being too caught up in a rap song singing moment. Our own homes and properties, due to financial emergencies, we've practically turned into ATM's with refinancing and refinancing, and doing it again and again until we <u>can't</u> afford the payments anymore—and thus, lose the home. We're losing child after child, son after son, daughter after daughter, parent after parent to violence from each other. Companies and places of employment won't hire us, except for salaries that are what we used to laugh at under the previous administration. The powers that be aren't even pretending anymore to give two bottle caps about us and ours, let alone trying to be fair in their treatment of all citizens. Healthcare for us, even sometimes WITH insurance, is on jokester levels of disinterest toward their patients. The schools and school systems aren't even pretending anymore to try to teach our young people, but only acting as warehouses for them during the day.

To make things *even* worse, these sincere-minded young people who *do* want to do the right thing have observed their own sincere and dedicated parents do everything <u>right</u>...they went to school, they worked hard, they're law abiding, upstanding, employed, etc. And these youngsters watch <u>THEM</u> get burned, anyway. Get screwed, *anyway*. Get fired, laid off, accused of something not really an offense, but rather—a *written in* offense within an office procedure—that no matter *how* asinine or baseless, causes one to get fined or fired. And once again, those NOT in our same pigment tone seem immune to all punishment, except when they fall so low the authorities can't cover up for them anymore. *Then*, <u>they're</u> only moved to an even easier, better paying position or situation than what they had, at first.

And yet and still...<u>*we're*</u> not even supported when we just want to vent. We're condemned and insulted by mainstream U.S.A... "Aww, you people just need to forget all about that and just move o-o-o-n-n-n-n!" *Whenever* Jews want to re-tell the events of their Holocaust, they're ALWAYS accommodated. And this is with not only Germany, but the United States, in addition, regularly sending thirteen <u>bil-</u>

lion dollars in aid/retribution to the State of Israel and to Jewish victims of it. The Cyclorama in Atlanta is nothing but the Civil War re-tellers going over and over and over their experiences during this nation's turmoil in the 1860's. They've got bumper stickers that say, "Forget—HELL!" Everybody else is accommodated. WE get condemnation and total disregard if we even peep about slavery and its non-payment reparations, as well as an iron refusal to even apologize. If you'll note…it's always OUR fault—or somebody *else's* fault. In the 1950's the rationalizations from mainstream U.S.A. was, "We didn't go over there for no slaves, we went over for elephants for ivory—niggers just jumped on the ship! Take me, Bwana! Take ME!" "Naw, Nigger, we don't want you! Get back, Boy!" "Aww, Bwana, take me!" "Alright, Boy, we'll take you. What else you want us to do?" "Put some chains on my leg, so I don't slip off!" *Stolen from Dick Gregory's comments.*

Nowadays in the 2000's, the belligerent excuses are, "Well, *your own people* did it! Your own people caught and sold you to us!" Oh, yeah. You all just went over to Africa, just standing there minding your own business. And here come these native Africans, put you in a Full Nelson, *order* you to and *make* you buy those Blacks…and you keep going back and stand there—hundreds of years at a time to repeat the process-- again and again. Yeah, okay.

At some point, obviously, one begins to do some serious reflection and pondering over these events concerning our sojourn in these United States. *Something* is going on here, both in nature and scope, and in history. Being a Black American woman, myself, I'm obviously going to find my own patience and satisfaction levels as an American citizen who would like to experience the American dream a bit strained due to the constantly thrown up roadblocks by the Caucasoid mainstream. And even in this, they *still* attempt to cast the blame on *us*. "Well, there's this area of 'non-achievement' in the Black community," they say. "They hold each other back by condemning and not supporting each other when they strive for advanced educational levels. So, there's this culture of 'staying dumb', or 'you're being like White Folks'!" they keep saying. Look, folks, my own experience, AND the experience I *continue* to see happening when it comes to "holding people back" is from the White side of business, I'm sorry. I had nothing but support from my fellow Black folks. That was strangers AND acquaintances. Fellow workers all the way from the military to my relocation to Atlanta. In school and in college. I never had a problem of "holding me back" from my own people. ALWAYS, the ones who continually stuck their foot out to trip me, who operated behind my back and before my face with only condemnation and finger-pointing was the Whites, primarily the White males at all levels and walks. Even those other Black folks I've talked with, dealt with and researched, all claimed they suffered the same thing from the same source. And it was always and only when brilliance was shown. If we showed hope, promise and talent beyond the normal school or work mate, rather than be accepted and taken up with the mainstream in and on the job…WE only experienced *panic* on their part, and one thing after another, after another, AFTER ANOTHER was done to us, thrown up at us, written up about us, unfairly accused about us…you name it. In schools, when our young Black males would display *advanced* mathematics skills, it wasn't his fellow school mates who chided him, as the ones really in charge try to pass blame on. It would be <u>*that White teacher*</u> who would pull something like, "How much is 2 + 2, Johnny?" When little Johnny would say, "Four," that White teacher would say, "No—no...that's not what I'm looking for!" That would be done in order to confuse him. Thus, holding him back. In my young cousin's violin class, he's stunned his music professors so much with his ability that at least four music scholarships, one which <u>only</u> *some* types of students get, a rarity where he'll be sent off to some other state to be entered into some previously all-White orchestra team or something to that effect, and ALL expenses paid. All this is due to his parents' relentlessly making him practice on that instrument ever since he was in his single-digit years. And once again, racism came into play from his immediate White female instructor, who once again, falling into that root cause in effect of taking it as a personal affront that 1) he's getting all this scholarship money, and 2) that he's out-doing his contemporary fellow students. To make a long story short about this individual's attempt to waylay and stop my cousin, his parents have had no choice but to *have* to threaten a lawsuit against the school he's attending now due to her antics. The administration of that school, seeing that they have no defense concerning this woman's panicked and insulting actions against this gifted, young Black man, are nervously trying to apologize, make some weak amends, do everything to cover up for this wayward White lady working there, etc. What I'm saying is <u>every time</u> we've experienced problems and hold-up or hold-back in academics when it was a case of truly out-doing all the rest of the class, it wasn't <u>our</u> people notoriously "doing it to us" as you keep wanting to accuse...it's been **YOU** the whole time that was "doing it to us." <u>YOU</u>. So, I'm here to straighten out that *additional* false claim and excuse made by the right wing radio listeners and finger pointers at us. You'll have various *individuals* always, anywhere, that may experience *some* jealousy of you. Sure, we've all run into them. But this *en mass* accusation (and once again, misplaced blame) ALL on US as far as who's doing what to whom in as far as *holding back* and discouraging further learning and educational brilliance...that's been, primarily, a WHITE THING on us. No, you don't *have* to like that I'm saying it. It's just the facts, folks.

Remember that "Primetime" news story in 1994 about that Texas inner city school where the primarily Black student body was outscoring the White students in their respective schools in the 'burbs there? This was thanks to a Black principal's guidance there and who was having progress with his student body. And how the Texas school administrations *had* to decide that there was "cheating" going on there...how *else* could those Black students be outscoring <u>*us!?*</u> And the main reason this story landed on the new show was because the state of Texas' actions were to send in armed police and "troops" on that Black school, practically, to occupy it. Remember that news story? "Primetime" interviewed the White female Texas official who oversaw that action, and when those police, detectives, etc., raided those classrooms, they had video cameras with them in order to capture the surprised looks on the Black teachers' face while they bombarded their teachings in progress. Remember that particular trait about our Caucasian "others" as they enjoy an immense and intense pleasure out of humiliating and embarrassing us? This fact was pointed out by the interviewer of the Texas school administration officials who pulled this little escapade.

How many schools, everywhere, are caught being guilty of having "cheating" going on in their classes, so much so and to the degree that there had to be investigations called? Quite a few. But it never culminated in the feeling the need to send in "troops" to occupy and otherwise be Gestapo-like in their treatment of that school! No. There's something else going on here. It looks more to me like not being a case of, "Stop them...they're cheating!" No, it looks more like a case of, "Stop them...they're *learning!*"

In short, the list is *endless*, as far as non-stop, unprovoked aggression on American Black people. *These* incidences just made the news. There are any number of *thousands* of other actions of this caliber occurring even as of this writing. I know, I know—some of the offenders will want to point out Black incidences on *them*. The primary difference, as I *did* point out at least *twice* in the earlier part of this text is that when you're talking about some hoodlumisms, these guys don't give a damn about their own people, let alone somebody else's people. So, they're a problem to you AND me across the board. The difference is that when they step across the lines and attack YOU, they're *quickly* yanked up off the street and dealt with. Slow progress is made in the capturing and punishing of such Black offenders when their victims are their fellow Blacks.

Remember Emmanuel Hammond, who was convicted of killing Julie Love? He had *killed* TWO other people, in cold blood. But his victims were Black. The first was his girlfriend. The second, a College Park, Georgia man whom he had robbed, then shot. Neither one of these cases got him off the streets. It was only when he killed Julie Love, a petite and pretty young White girl, that he was finally dealt with the way he *should* have been two killings ago. But because our court systems don't consider it worth their time enough to get killers and offenders of US off the streets, if they had done their job fairly, he would have been in prison or on death row way before he'd have gotten anywhere near Julie Love.

As was stated earlier, in my own pondering about just why and what is going on here concerning our sojourn here in these United States, and in becoming more and more flustered with what I see us regularly going through, there are a few conclusions I've drawn about my observations. Those of you who's outlook on this book by now, is one of condemnation, feeling royally like yelling at me the title of these memoirs, and other negatives, all I'll say is that instinctively and truthfully—you KNOW I'm not wrong. You know better than I do, even more and bloodier stuff you're up to that I and the rest of us *don't* know about, that you're *sure* will cause us to lose patience and come after you THIS time, should we find out! No, what you're upset about is not what's being said...but rather, THAT I'm saying it. You're so used to us "suffering in silence," that when anyone even just *talks* about these injustices like police misconduct, *selective* legal enforcement, cherry picking of just who's going to do time for *this*/who's going to "walk" for doing the same, etc., you immediately start your condemnation of the complainer and excuse making for the stated offenses. For you folks who feel like this...whether it's me or anyone else...even among your own who state these things, you were going to have this kind of reaction, anyway. For the rest of my *well*-adjusted readers as opposed to the maladjusted ones, I'll continue.

After being made aware of *one more* racial aggravation against us, having been exposed to even more unresolved crimes and insults committed in the name of White supremacy, etc., I began to have to tell my Maker, outside of prayer time, "You know, I'm getting really pissed off!" The answer I got from Him was that "He (the White man) feels worse." That realization answered about three worlds of questions and solved a myriad of puzzles for me. When you keep your communication open with God, the Creator and you look for answers, you will find them as He sees best for you to be able to be exposed to. And my feeling was, "Oh." Long pause. Then silently to myself, "Okay." In other words, the answer in just a micro-second's worth of time told me all I needed to know.

First...have you seen or heard about these roving bands of women who are not very attractive running around with hooligan males? What they do is when they spot an attractive young girl, they immediately pounce on her, beat her to where she is disfigured in her face and her bosoms, left bleeding and torn up while the homely girl hanging with that crowd will silently say to her, "Now no one will want you." If you really have to have a psychology course to see that action for what it is...on the part of the unattractive woman running around with the band of no-goodnicks, and ruining the looks of pretty young women, then you need to hear that short, sweet saying again of, "Misery loves company." Or, "The only reason anybody would ever hate you is because they want to be just like you." So, since they can't, they'll just take away from you all your advantageous attributes.

We see this highly paid American White man ensuring that his fellow White own have *millions* of dollars routinely in their possession. Every, but everything under the sun is done in order to justify and legitimize their existence on earth with the rest of us...primarily by maneuvering our Black men and women into situations where they can be delegitimized and made to look like scums of the earth, although the rest of the world seems to truly love our product and our ideas we continually come up with that *quickly* get snatched up and enrich everyone else *but* us. All of this money, all of this land and property, everything good and desirable that our White counterparts snatch up all for themselves is to ***give an appearance of something.*** It's a façade. A smoke screen. In reality, this man is *suffering*. All of these clearly seen advantages he puts out for the world to see is to mask something. This man has got **problems**...that you and I will never even *begin* to be able to fathom. I mean, that seemingly little response I got from communing with The Lord told me so many facts about the nature and caliber of the type of individual we're dealing with. Just think about it--WHAT would cause some idiot to go on and on and on and on and on and on and on, ad infinitum, in a non-stop, mindbogglingly burdensome harassment and bloodletting fest of victimizing of one group again and again and again and again...to the point of where once they get their hands on you, they *can't stop* punishing and punishing and punishing and punishing you to the point of where it becomes clear to <u>everyone</u> that, "HEY! <u>You've</u> got a *problem*! There's something <u>wrong</u> with *you!*" That's why the punishments and victimizing of us reaches such unreasonable...and uncalled for degrees of severity. The committers have a *psychosis*.

You'd better look again at *how much* they *claim* they don't want anything to do with a Black skin the whole time they're risking skin cancer by the millions...laying out in the sun trying to turn their skin *some hue* besides that of just "flesh-color." And injecting silicone into their lips for more fullness.

WHY do <u>they</u>...the owners of all cookie factories in existence get so upset and act like it's the end of civilization if WE end up with one broken off piece of a half a cookie? There's something going on here. If YOU can't afford for ME to end up with even a <u>dollar</u> that <u>you</u> haven't got in place for me to immediately *lose* as soon as I get it, then what is that saying about <u>me</u>—and WHAT is that saying about <u>you</u>???

These full of denial inclinations of his has also ballooned out in affecting everything he touches. *Everything* under his production sway—*HAS* to become an artificial, false, phony, counterfeit version of the real thing. <u>EVERYTHING</u>. NONE of it can be real. It ALL has to be "artificial ingredients", "artificial substitute"...etc., etc. EVERYTHING <u>has</u> to have its natural, in-bred and in-built substance done away with and destroyed, and a false version of it put in its place. I'm tellin' ya—psychological prognosis of, "I'M alright—EVERYONE of YOU is wrong! I'm legit—you're de-legit. I have a right—YOU don't have any right. I'm here...YOU need to be *gone*! I'll reject—but I'm gonna stay in demand!" I will note a phenomenon that I've observed concerning that last sentiment of theirs. It's like they can't get enough of doing all they can to make you feel like a cockroach in the salad. They *love* making you feel unwanted and unloved. However, if <u>you</u> at any time make <u>*them*</u> aware that you're not really enjoying *their* company, yourself, and that you're ordering them to go away some place else...have you noticed...you almost have to come to blows with them to make *them* get away from **you**! Don't get me wrong, I'm not saying that some of our people are desiring in their hearts to pay them back in that respect. I'll address that in a bit. Just like with the example of the Newburg residents, it's not a matter of not being able to wait to get them back. It's just a matter of, "Look, you know, ALL that your conversation is about is running down somebody else. It's not positive. You're not pleasant to be around. No hard feelings or anything, but I'd really rather that you just didn't hang around <u>me</u>! I'm not enjoying your company!" They, literally and absolutely <u>will not GO</u>! It's like it's important for *them* to reject/but <u>they</u> don't want to be rejected. They want to tell YOU <u>you're</u> not good enough to be around <u>them/</u> but they want to be desired and pawned over and fawned over by all others.

I was told by another one of our wiser, older heads that Whites here just can't STAND to see other peoples in the world accept us or give us a place. They want to see us as ostracized by them as they ostracize us. And when those other peoples show an interest in us, the powers that be here quickly pounce on them with lies and story telling about how dangerous it will be for them to come anywhere near us because we're "animals." But if any foreign group insists on seeing for themselves and then leaves with a positive report, these folks here go ballistic with condemnation and panic. And then, they give that foreign nation bad press, and talk about *them* in negative, condescending ways saying, "Aw, that nation's messed up now!" because they don't want to, outright, reject you along with these folks here without giving you a fair chance. That will explain why some other nations will be on this nation's "evil" and "bad guy" list until that nation's leader or head of state dies or is replaced with someone who may be more prone to manipulation.

While pondering these things, I also took note of how it seemed that we Black people here were in a position where we had all avenues of escape cut off to us. No matter where we went, no matter what we did, no matter how much we were obviously to everyone's eyes deserving of better and in dire need of some justice...we were NOT GOING TO HAVE IT. We were also not going to get it. We had no place to go, North, South, East or West that would welcome us without making it their mission in life to put us in Hell. We couldn't buy, we couldn't spend, we couldn't work...unless it was the heaviest, dirtiest, poorest paying demeaning work that NOBODY else wanted. If we tried to buy or purchase, the price would be jacked up unreasonably high, and then only for us to have slipped to us foul, fraudulent, undesirable, or inedible stuff, goods or product. We couldn't live anywhere except places where the price was jacked up so unreasonably high that in order to afford it, we had to move friends, relatives, strangers, this or that into already very cramped quarters, and...you know the kinds of problems that can lead to. High incarceration rates, higher number of death row inmates, no justice for us against perpetrators of crimes against us, great numbers of murder victims...We all already know the whole deal with our sojourn here from 1619 until the present. All avenues of escape were blocked. It's as if no relief were to be in effect for us. Why, we can't even complain, talk about or vent our anger or anguish out loud because we'll be condemned for that too. What is going on here, Lord, I wondered.

And, lo, this situation of ours appears in all get out to me to be the Book of Job, revisited. Because, just as with him, EVERYTHING, except his life, was touched in such manner as to provoke him to curse God and die, so has there been nothing, I mean absolutely NOTHING left **UNDONE** to US! And we won't break. And we can't die out, as much as some powers that be would like us to! In as much as has been done to us to the point of staggering the imagination, *still*, with our own unfailing and inexhaustible amount of tolerance and patience, if one of us were to see some little old White lady trip, fall down and hurt herself, we'd knock each other down rushing to her aid and seeing if she was alright. So I do believe that we have passed the test. Our long suffering levels seem limitless. Too bad the people currently running things can't seem to appreciate and reward that. That's one conclusion.

The other is that this situation of ours is also the Parable of Lazarus and the Rich Man.

The African Black man and woman have *been* getting kidnapped, abducted and enslaved by almost every other people on this planet. That's a fact. But it wasn't because of needing dumb, half-human brutes to do all dirty work in societies as the powers that be, today, would have you think. If that was all people wanted you for, then it was much easier to do that to their neighbors in adjoining countries much nearer by. The word, "Cretin" comes from the name of the inhabitants of the Greek isle of Crete. Though they had a very great cultural civilization and produced wonderful works of classic, historical beauty, the other Greeks of their neighboring isles picked on them and used their name as a way of describing the "dumbest of dummies." So, when people use certain descriptive words of those whose intelligence they want to insult, they use the term, "cretin" which means—somebody of low intelligence. But its basis was from using the name of the inhabitants of the isle of Crete.

No, people stole us for a vastly different reason. The country's new Boogeyman, the Muslims, believe in their teachings that the reason God made Man in so many different kindreds, shades and tongues was because all that Man *could* be, and all his great potential could not be contained in just one Race. That was why God made Man in many different races. Every race, they teach, has a particular ability that *they* can do outstandingly among the rest. This, of course, is opinion and some may or may not buy it. In my humble view, _any_ attempt and endeavor regularly practiced by _anyone_ has the potential to be outstanding among the rest. There are some observers of this belief who conclude, "Oh—well...*yeah*, I guess. Uhhh—let's see, hmm! Yeah! White people are good at commerce, trade and industry, and so on. 'Chinese' (meaning all Orientals) are good at math and school studies. Blacks are good with knives, blades, drums, basketball...!" See what I mean? Anybody can be best at *anything* when they work hard at it. Nonetheless, there *were* and are some certain characteristics the Black man and woman had that the rest of the world seemed dead set and determined to get. It's very hard to find and especially to get ahold of, but there do exist some ancient texts and writings that specifically pointed these characteristics of us out. One is by a certain Al-jahiz who in about 1368 A.D. wrote a dissertation about Blacks from not only the African continent, but who populate all the isles between the Africa and China. And it's pretty flattering. He quotes the ancient Greeks' admiration of the jet black body (as their love of the human form, period, can be seen in their sculptures from their civilization), describing the Ethiopian soldiery fighting nearby them as, "Splendid in their blackness." The Africans were usually taken (or sometimes "selected") to fight in other nations' armies due to their fierce loyalty, their bravery, and because they could frighten the dogsh-t out of their enemies! The Greek writings (which had to be transcribed in writing, later, because all their teachings were oratory and passed down the same as with west African Griots) would continue with how when the "Ethiopian general commanded in the midst of the destruction, and they attacked with their superb bodies, the very clouds seemed to be Ethiopians. When they attacked with their spears, bows and arrows and with their blood curdling yells, they spread an unimaginable terror among the enemy." As I said, you will be hard pressed to locate the rest of these texts...they've been deliberately buried, and only exposed thanks to the dedicated efforts of those archeological crusaders who <u>aren't</u> held back by or influenced by White supremacy. The Blacks were also in demand because of their musical ability.

When I took high school band class we had to learn some music history. The instructor was even a not-so-well-inclined-to <u>us</u> individual too. Nonetheless, he taught us truthfully about the comparance of European music to African music... and how the European music just plain and simply *"died"* in popularity when pitted up against the Africans' music. The European music of the ancient and middle-ages' day used one, maybe two instruments, usually consisting of string or maybe a string and a pipe or flute. The African music, on the other hand, would consist of some-times up to twelve different instruments going all at once...string, pipe, kalimba (a hand piano), drum, voice, banzar (banjo), flute, tambourine, horn, and variations and additions to all the above. When the human ear and the human soul are ex-posed to all that variety going on all at once in harmony...the person would discover that their foot was keeping time with the music. Then the hands and arms were keeping time with it. Soon, the whole body would *have* to get up and start moving with it all! In short, it *woke up*, revived and refreshed the wearied, heavily journeyed human spirit. Sometimes the listeners, be they of what other race or group of people, would find themselves shouting and singing with this musical wonderment. That's African music. The basis of ALL rock, pop, blues, soul, gospel, even some country-western—with its own Irish and Scottish influence, as well.

The basis of this reaction to the tones and melodies produced here by the African was the ancients' definition of calling upon "living spirits" to be re-created --recreated, which is how and where the word "recreation," originated. These ancient peoples of that day, as well as peoples today, were dead set and determined to have access to that, no matter what it took to get it. To quote again Dick Gregory as he was talking about the United States (even back during the 1950's and 1960's) going all over the world trying to ram democracy down foreign peoples' throats with a gun, he said, "Anything good you don't have to force on people. They will *steal* it."

You've seen how faithful and loyal we've been to *this* country <u>despite</u> its hor-rible treatment of us from 1619 until now. From the 1700's here right during slavery, it was Crispus Attucks who was the first to die and the fight for American indepen-dence from England. All the way to Dorie Miller during the Japanese attack on Pearl Harbor. He, being Black, was relegated to the status of a cook only, not being allowed into any other higher status field. When the attack was going on Dorie manned a machine gun, not having been trained on how to operate it at all. Yet he positioned, aimed up at the sky, and successfully shot down <u>four</u> of the Japanese planes. The Navy then had an awards ceremony to honor his efforts. When Dorie's mother was passing through the waiting crowd of mostly Whites who were there for it, she had to listen to so many racial insults and horrible condescending descriptions about her son while on the way up to the podium, that by the time she arrived there she was in tears. Then there was Pvt. Henry Johnson and Needham Roberts, who during

World War I were overseas during the conflict with Germany in 1921. They successfully killed/captured over twenty-six German soldiers, single-handed, with Henry Johnson killing four of them, himself, and a wounded Needham Roberts propping himself up on one of his crutches and tossing hand grenades at the advancing German line. It wasn't until about 1986, there or abouts, that these two Black soldiers in the United States Army were posthumously awarded medals of bravery. The accolades, medals of valor and bravery, and a whole host of other military honors were generously awarded to them by the foreign nations whose soil they were serving on. I read about a French army captain who proudly talked about his World War I relic which was a sort of tray or stand made out of the top of a human skull. Pvt. Johnson, in attacking one of the German soldiers just as he was about to bayonet Needham Roberts, buried a knife all the way to the hilt in the German soldier's skull. It was embedded so deeply that all efforts to remove it were in vain. So this French officer made a relic or souvenir out of that portion of the German's skull.

If we're still this devoted to our country here as we've been, despite its spitting in our face and leaving lynched Black figures *while still in uniform*, like they did, it only stands to reason that the nations of old who had Black folks there, either due to immigration, relocation, captured soldiery or slavery, that they were _fanatically_ devoted to their new homelands there, as well. And the surviving memoirs, writings and texts from *those* countries describe such also. The Bokhara were jet Black Africans conscripted into the Morroccan armies of the 1600's and they served as the personal body guard of the Sultans there. They were fanatically loyal. India, of the 1400's to late 1600's had Black soldiers from Ethiopia that were slave descendants from their early time periods. There was an incident in Indian history when Queen Chand Bibi, the Queen Elizabeth of India, was slain by palace rebels, the Ethiopian contingent in her armies would not desert her surviving forces and faithful rulers, though the other Indian rebels who wanted to rule in her place did all they could to bribe them or buy them off. They stayed loyal to her faction until the day that Jolly Ole England came to run things there for awhile. And, during the days of the Roman Empire, as was previously mentioned, Lucius Septimius Severous came to power in 168 A.D. and personally stopped the Praetorian Guard who had grown totally out of their place as bodyguards to the emperors, and into a strong-arm muscle force who put into power, themselves, whoever could pay them. Septimius overthrew them by having them come into the Roman collisium all at once for a ceremony, thus requiring them to leave their weapons outside. Yes, well, I'm quite sure you could garner what happened next! Yet and still, more on the civilized side, Septimius had the entire body of the Guard suddenly surrounded by a ring of steel on all sides from hidden other Roman soldiers. They were then placed on trial...and THEN they were dealt with "Roman action Style"! Thus, that's why he's been known to this very day as a real Roman patriot...because he was the only one who successfully returned Roman rule back to the Roman people. So we were in demand for our absolute loyalty to whatsoever land or group of people we found ourselves newly belonged to.

So now, we come to the era of the United States and its development with

Black slave labor. If you can find truthful and honest coverage of those years, along with picking cotton and tobacco plants, our West and Central African forefathers knew how to make such crops grow…into bumper crop levels. The results were that we were then placed into having to harvest such so that the tobacco and cotton production became wealth producing industries for the United States. Then, after the Emancipation Proclamation and our continued disenfranchisement from the democratic process, WE had to do the brunt of the back-breaking work here that nobody else would or *could* do. Thus, that's how and why WE were the ones who invented all these labor saving devices because we were doing <u>all</u> the work. And Whites just simply sat back, waited, then stole it for themselves leaving the Black inventors to die in poverty and obscurity.

This nation is the bastion and power house of wealth and well-to-do that it is primarily because of our unpaid labor. And they've seen how good a deal it is…for themselves, because to this day they *still* find ways to utilize underpaid skills and labor…from the Hispanics and jobs shipped overseas.

I once heard one of the wiser, learned ones of the present day talking about how White people, in reality, have three patron saints. The first is Adam Smith who taught them how to exploit the masses, and thus become wealthy as a result. The second is Machiavelli who wrote, "The Prince," and claimed that politics is a-moral…apparently so that one can have no conscience about exploiting the masses. The third is Charles Darwin with his, "Survival of the Fittest," claims, so that human beings' being ground up like hamburger in the machine-like chewing up of their lives in servitude and bondage to enrich others can be justified.

Our country here consumes <u>eighty-five percent</u> of the ENTIRE PLANET'S resources, by itself. That's a fact taught to us even in Elementary School by sincere-minded and dedicated teachers who say, "We must learn to share!" That's the very reason why the rest of the world's populace, living on soil so rich in natural resources, are starving to death by the millions every day…they don't have access to their own soil. I found it incredulous to discover that on the African continent, for example, the soil is *so-o-o-o* incredibly <u>rich</u> that precious gem stones just push up through the ground on their own. Yet, if some native or resident standing nearby were to reach down and try to pick it up, somebody's likely to instantly shoot him dead. That's how tightly controlled that land is by foreign forces.

Thus, since so <u>much</u> is *here*, just like with Lazarus and the Rich man, the crumbs that happen to fall from his table are pretty much what so many of the *rest* of us have to rely on for survival. Well, just as Lazarus didn't ask for all that much, but just barely eked out a living by begging and having sores licked by dogs, that Rich man was—spoilt! He had <u>*everything*</u>. And everything, he had <u>*his way*</u>. Sumptuous feasts, sumptuous clothes, sumptuous house, sumptuous servants—the works. And he wanted for nothing.

We-e-e-l-l-l, my readers! Here we have one pampered and spoiled, coddled, babied, catered to always, rich upper class group of, let's just say, "Right-wing Republicans"! I hear that the new slang term used by LAPD in describing their intended Black quarry is, "Democrats"! I think the term "Right-wing Republicans" will do adequately for now. Because, in recalling the words of a very good friend of mine on the police force here, he pointed out some very pertinent truths concerning these political parties. He said, "The Republican party's clearly intended (though unspoken) message is this: 'Vote for us because WE promise two cars in every garage and the niggers back in their place!' And White people buy it every time. And every time, THEY'RE the ones that get hurt!"

During the Clinton Administration you noticed that his approval rating stayed at about sixty-one percent. Apparently, enough Whites realized that *their* problems were not the same problems as Flush Scumbaugh or the bald-headed burglar, or any of the other prophets of Baal whose salaries are in the tens of millions of dollars range. The problems of the rest of mainstream America are the same as your and MY problems...and that is whether or not we're going to have a *job*...that PAYS us something we can live on. Whether or not we have access to adequate health care for when we and ours become sick or injured. Whether our schools are such to where we can be reasonably assured of their ability to teach and educate. And finally, whether we can afford to keep a roof over our heads, AND have quality air to breathe. But since there is, apparently, still a great number of our Caucasian counterparts who are sitting on their haunches along the hinterlands, digging their knives into the ground in a caveman-style drum beat just itching, hungry, and anxious to turn back the clock on racial inter-harmony (do we even *have* that???) that we've ended up with, again, someone who has hinted to them, "*PSSST* –I'll take care of *you*!!! Wink—wink!"

If you **EVER** wake up to the fact that as far as he and his business cronies (who are *really* the ones running the country) are concerned, you fellow Whites are just as much a *nigger* to them as WE are...you MIGHT take certain steps that MAY improve things for everyone again. 'Cuz, it sure ain't gonna happen with just *us*! All we'll get is jailed! You, they might pay a little bit more attention to. Of course, you're going to be "set up" first. You may even be accused of being in league with Osama and his Mama if you look like you're about to effect any real change. But, mark my word...WE aren't going to suffer like YOU all are. Why? Because WE were never allowed to come out from under our disenfranchisement. WE were never afforded or accorded with *real rights*. I mean, if you doubt me, look at how the Voting Rights Act expires in 2007. Why??? Why is the right to vote guaranteed and in place for ALL and EVERYONE **permanently,** except for *us*??? Doesn't that tell you something about this nation's intended plans for *us*? If you're one of these true marshmallows standing on the sidelines going, "Yip! Yip—hooray!" at that news, what the Hell makes you think *you're* not going to be eventually included? Huh? You rich and pampered, spoiled Lazarus's are *not going to do* well when you *finally* open your eyes in Hell. We, Black Americans, who have been saddle-burdened with the brunt of this nation's maladjustments, yet have held up will find that the Justice of God will not allow for beaten up on victims of injustices to suffer with or for *your* crimes any longer. That's right, I said, *your crimes.*

One of the primary psychological occurrences during either lynchings or excessive punishments heaped all on one lone victim who's all by themselves is the phenomenon of the killers ALL placing the blame of _their own_ crimes upon the head and shoulders of their victims, thus causing (in their _own_ mind's eye) YOU to be the biggest rapist/thrill killer/robber/parasite/liar/criminal/enemy, etc. to Man. And in _killing_ you, with afflictions, they're basically making individual Christs out of you. That's right. They're taking individual Black men, women and children... heaping all their sins upon _them_, torture killing and murdering them, then breathing sighs of relief because _now_—they're guiltless in the eyes of each other. Don't get mad at me for being an open-eyed observer. What you'd _better_ do is BE GLAD **somebody's** pointing this out to you now. Christ came only one time. ALL of us are NOT God for you to crucify and pin all your own wrongs upon in order to _feel_ absolved. And your thinking that your standing behind or hiding behind that painting of that German from tenth century Europe is going to "save" you...get ready for a rude awakening, children. When YOU step before that wooly haired, flaming eyed, white-robed Being with the feet and legs as black as burnished bronze (as is described in the book of Revelations) and He sticks his hand out in a barring motion to you as you boldly and straightening your collar approach Him, you've been told innumerable times what you'll hear: "DEPART from me, ye cursed into everlasting destruction. **I** never knew you!" Then YOU'LL be saying—"Wait a minute, Lord...we prophesied in Your Name!" Prophesying that the world was gonna stay White and ruled right by you. "We preached in Your Name!" Yeah, preaching that the world was gonna stay your oyster and the rest of mankind could keep working for you at slave's wages until the end of time. "We cast out devils in Your Name!" Sure—the "devils" of "liberals" whose only message was one of having concern for others who may not have access to the same luxuries as you, but at least a right to _eat_...and have a place to live. Liberals. Devils to the likes of you, because all you unadmittedly saw in their talk was of helping the poor and especially _Black_ folks. Or Hispanic folks. Or other "non-privaledged", i.e., non-White folks.

Then you'll panic when He says, "I was hungry and you fed me not. I was naked and you clothed me not. I was sick and shut in and you came and visited me not. I was homeless and you housed me not. Being falsely accused and you protected me not. Being put on death row and you saved me not. Having my house spray-painted with "KKK" and you defended me not. Being enslaved and worked unto death in the fields and you freed me not. Being beaten by police and you stepped in not. Being mocked and insulted and you stood up for me not..." The list will go on and on. Then, with your poked out chest fallen, your broad, proud shoulders stooped, and your haughty gaze now downward, what can you say but, "When did we do this, Lord?" **"IN AS MUCH—AS YOU'VE DONE THIS TO THE LEAST OF THESE— YOU'VE DONE IT TO ME!!!"**

CHAPTER EIGHTEEN

AND THE KING SAID, "LIVE TOGETHER AS BROTHERS OR DIE APART AS FOOLS"

OR SOMETHING TO THAT EFFECT. One of the vendors we had for a long time at Five Points who seemed to take great pleasure in regularly teeing us off was one "Crazy" Dave Walker. Everybody kept assuring us newer officers that Dave was a *lot* smarter than he acted. That it all *was* just an *act*. I'll dispense with going into descriptions of the oftentimes shouting act some of us had with him. We only noticed that Atlanta P.D. didn't bother him. Other folks he yelled at wouldn't cross him. And it's because with time, when I began to *listen* to him...he <u>did</u> make some sense. And then, he got a radio spot on Ron Sailor's WIGO AM when it was still in effect. I do think that Dave's ratings possibly topped the adjoining talk show line up at that period he was on at 3:00pm. Unfortunately (and I know this without anyone telling me) I do believe that due to Dave's abrasive and combative verbal nature that Ron Sailor kept firing him. But then, he'd have him back, no doubt due to popular demand. This happened three times during WIGO's run. He was just as crazy with the callers too...that's probably why he was so popular. People would call, begin to get angry, then call him a "Nappy head..." ~*click*~ with Dave going, "Thank you," after Dave had just hung up on the caller. One angry, *angry* woman called him, going, "YOU NEED JESUS! YOU NEED TO ACCEPT JESUS! YOU NEED JESUS CHRIST AS YOUR SAVIOUR!!!" ~click~ "Goodbye—witch!" Dave would say as he hung up on her. But every time he wasn't on at 3:00pm, caller after caller would ring up asking, "Where's Dave?"

At any rate, during one of the last times I heard him on radio, he was addressing something very close to what I said at the conclusion of the previous chapter. He was talking about The Lord God, Almighty. And what Dave concluded with was the following: "You keep talkin' about God and Who God is. Man, God is broke. God is sick and shut in. God is homeless. God is in prison. God is poor. God is blind. God is hungry and sick. THAT'S who God is!" In short, all of the despised and unwanted in society. The Spanish girl said to the nobleman, "When you're poor **nobody** wants you!" All of the despised and driven away. Those whom genteel folk snub their noses at. We'd better be careful how we talk to and deal with <u>everyone</u>. As our grandparents put it, "You never know. That could be an angel God sent to you just to see how you would treat him. And when he goes back to Heaven with his report to the Lord, He'll ask him about it. 'Lord, she sure treated me bad! I asked her for something to eat and she just looked at my old clothes and my shoes with holes all in them, and told me to get lost before she called the police!' And the Lord will just nod His head and say, 'Okay'!" Of course, that was in our Grandparents' day when there weren't *as* many folks full of tricks as there are now! With *some* folks, uh, well—yeah. Call us! Even so, you get the crux of what I'm saying. It's hard enough going through Life as it is. Yes, there are going to be "bad hair" days when you're just not feeling good, or someone just yelled at you and you're in a dour mood. That's understandable for anyone. We have to be patient and restrained from "flying off the handle into somebody's stuff" for *every thing*. Some folks are just having a bad time and need a kind word. But don't go out of your way—to screw somebody up because you know you have to fulfill your KK obligations. Trust me, you WILL pay...one way or another.

I believe in leaving people the Hell alone, when I'm not at work. I think that if certain persons *truly* can't stand those of another race, then you know that's not really a problem. I sincerely don't want to force you to hold hands with me and dance around the maypole going "Fa la la la la!" if you don't want to. The problem lies in dealing with people of that sentiment who have direct control over you, and they're not keeping their mood and tone about you to themselves. In fact, they're going out of their way to deliberately make you as uncomfortable as they possibly can. THAT, folks, is the problem. If you want to be in the Klan, then, hey—as long as you keep your claws to yourself that's fine with me. Just don't play some outrage game with me for not being too terribly fond of you *back*. WE probably employ more Klan members, ourselves, than a lot of the rest of America does! Whenever we who *do* actually own successful businesses have to have contract work done...we don't mind driving out to Sticksland, Georgia on Bumfuck road and picking up Billy Jo Bob and Bubba. We'll tell 'em, "C'mere, Billy Jo Bob and Bubba. Put the cross down for a minute. I need to take you into town because I need some carpet taken up, then new carpet installed." Billy Jo Bob and Bubba will gladly get in your truck, 'cuz they *need* the work, they'll go back into town with you...and you know from plenty of experience that they'll take that old carpet up, take care of its disposal, lay the new carpet down...they will have that job completed THAT DAY! And then, you gratefully drive them back out to Sticksland, you tell them if they're running late for their cross burning, you will help them light it! Because, when it comes to *business*, you don't retain it on excuses, slip ups, "things that *keep* happening" to *your* employee, etc. You can't operate that way. The sign in the hair salon says, "Black is beautiful—but business is business!"

As of these times as well as times before, there are certain priorities that some people in desperate situations know that they can't be worried about—survival is at stake. How you feel about me and vice-versa doesn't really count. What really matters is what the hands do. As prices for vitals go up, and quality of product goes down, and as cost of living goes up and salary and wages go down...the times are a' comin' whereby we're not going to really have any choice about whether we get into individual camps or unify across racial and ethnic lines. Your *real* enemy is not the Muslim fundamentalist...his own native people grow weary of that, themselves. Just as we American Blacks here did not look upon Christianity as the Enemy—despite the hatred-filled supremacy groups under its so-called umbrella. Our enemy is only lack of unity.

Just as on the police force, or with the military forces in place—all differences between us and how we feel about each other has to take a second fiddle. *Lives* are on the line. So far, this has been a dissertation on just what some of us devoted, hard working, loyal and patriotic American citizens have to keep putting up with from the very forces we serve and protect...for a reason that these forces continually deny that. I have included facts, figures and undeniable examples of exactly what I'm talking about. Those of you reading this will either take one side or another. It's hard to imagine any of you being totally indifferent.

When I joined the military in 1978 I was twenty-one years old. I had been alive and exposed to enough life's experiences here in these United States to be *very* aware that there was a problem with some people because of who and what I was...a Black woman. And I had noticed that this prevailing attitude permeated just about every level and department I'd been exposed to. But, I was nonplussed and went blissfully and boldly forward despite it all. As I had no other intent except becoming an officer in the Army, when I *finally* managed to get through to training and school for it I noticed to my heart's let down that here in the military—things were *still* being done to lessen our numbers out of certain employment areas. The military classes that were given were of such a nature, in the officer school, that it almost appeared *designed* to not be able to be passed. They'd give you just so many times to flunk one course—then...you were out of the entire army! I couldn't believe it! There was a White West Point graduate who was standing along side of me who had, like me, not been able to pass these tests at first because they were so strangely put together. He was standing there very upset, going, "Ahh, shit!" and again, he was from West

Point. The school commandant authorities took him aside and I didn't see him anymore. I KNOW he didn't flunk out because we knew who the flunk-outs were. Not being a dumb girl, and very observant, I put two and two together and realized they had just simply whisked *him* away from all that hullabaloo and installed or established him elsewhere...the tests apparently not mattering for him. When I saw the room where the people in trouble with passing the tests were—that room was one hundred per cent Black folks. I saw right away... "They're trying to reduce our numbers here in the officer's ranks. There's too many of us, apparently. So our abilities, devotion, education, willingness to serve our country just doesn't mean anything to these people in charge. They just want <u>us</u> gone!" And to my young mind, I was stunned. For I was always taught that if you gave your authority figures *no reason* to be against you, you should be alright. Yet, I saw—color *did* matter. I hung on with tooth and nail, studied their torn up testing methods, none of it having anything to do with commonality or practical methods in the real world. And yes, it did excise a LOT of us Blacks who were about to become 2nd Lieutenants.

Once we got through and successfully made it to our new duty stations, what we Black officers and ones who made Commander experienced was that the other companies forced into our companies their sorry, lazy, pathetic excuses for high ranking White sergeants (E-7's and above) and then wouldn't let us get rid of them, as was supposed to be the commander's prerogative. The lazy excuse I had, even though I was only an XO, which is company executive officer, was an E-7 (Sgt. First Class) whom only I kept messing with. Apparently, everyone else, from the Top or First Sergeant to the Commander was too intimidated by him. I *kept* going across the street on him. "Across the street" was how we referred to Battalion Command. Although they wouldn't support me and *never* assisted me in my drive to remove this guy from my company, those who were sympathetic to me would tell me in private, "I've been hearing good things about you across the street. They're saying it seems that you're the only one at that company who's stopped and paid attention to the fact that you've got a fucked up NCO over there, and you're <u>*trying*</u> to do something about it!" These E-7s (Sergeant First Class) were usually older White guys who were established, used to running things, unbothered, etc. And if they didn't feel like doing what they were supposed to do, few were able to challenge them. So, there were a *lot* of E-7s and up who were forced upon us new Black commanders and executive officers because they'd been regularly kicked out of other companies. And it was hard to do anything with them. Even so, this experience of mine made me aware of what to expect should I attempt a management or leadership position anywhere else. Because when all was said and done, not only did upper-*upper* management completely override <u>my</u> write-ups of this screw-up...but they just plain spat in my face and <u>*ordered*</u> me to write this joker a good evaluation. That told me a lot of things, right there. That no matter <u>*how*</u> wrong they were/and no matter *HOW* right I was...I was NOT going to be supported or backed in my efforts to discipline one of their White own. That is a completely demoralizing experience. WHY should I bother then? What's the point if I'm only going to be supported if I want to burn somebody they don't like…such as one of my own fellow Blacks, but they're going to trip over themselves running to protect their own sorry, lazy, screwed up individuals from *me?* That was the main reason I never sought a leadership position in the police department I was employed with, though I apparently had ALL the qualifications and traits necessary to be promoted as such, and these qualifications and qualities were obviously apparent to my higher ups…thus sparking that little comment that some conscientious and sympathetic somebody exposed to me. I was already able to observe what some Black sergeants and even lieutenants were experiencing in the police department not long after I got there.

What really caused me to have some degree of mild alarm at all the racism everywhere was just that point—that it was *everywhere*…even in Government, which was supposed to be in force as the last bastion of protection for ALL rights. And even here, the United States Military, an arm of the government, was actively practicing it at obviously high, high levels. It made me *seriously* consider the feasibility of enacting Paragraph II, there or abouts, of the Bill of Rights in the United States Constitution. This is where, after it says that, "We hold these truths to be self-evident, that ALL men are created equal, and endowed *by their Creator* with certain <u>inalienable</u> rights." When this fact of "inalienable" rights is mentioned, it means those rights are God-given. You don't have to work for them. You don't have to earn them. It says and means that we are <u>*born*</u> with those rights…the right to life, liberty and the pursuit of happiness. Well, paragraph II continues with, "And when these rights are destroyed…over <u>long periods of time</u>, it is your DUTY to destroy or abolish that governing entity." At any rate, the rogue elements of that governing entity dedicated to *our* destruction, at least.

Yet, I knew I could never be involved in something *sudden* like that…that's not <u>me</u>. Rather, I'm hoping this book of memoirs in pointing out some distinct wrongs in our government's actions toward some of its citizens on an ongoing basis will be instrumental along with whatsoever other forces out there are at work in seeking to stop it.

You readers of these memoirs who are probably mad at me for these exposures and criticisms of it—don't worry your pretty (ugly) little heads. I'm just one lone woman who is no threat to *you*. I'm just little ol' me, <u>not</u> pretending any longer like everything is peachy-keen. You big, strong Black men out there, you'd better start paying attention to the tide coming back in to the shores. Not only are you woefully absent from protecting your women, the powers that be are testing the waters. They're starting to police-taser your <u>children</u> now. This is <u>your</u> children that this is being done to. The first two cases that were exposed as happening to these youngsters still in their single-digit years did not immediately have their race revealed. There were a lot of White parents calling in saying, "You let 'em taser MY child! There'll be HELL to pay!" As I said before, the powers that be KNOW that. It was <u>our</u> youngsters, and a Hispanic girl, that were the victims of this. AND WHERE WERE **<u>YOU???</u>** Don't you realize, Black men, that if they see that you all are not even going to protect your own **<u>children</u>** from this kind of uncalled for senselessness, they'll <u>know</u> it's safe to come after YOU next! And I don't mean just to jail. But *en mass* to those closed down military facilities.

Time-Warner knew what it was doing in only being willing to finance these rap songs that were concentrating on calling all Black women bitches and "ho's." Malcolm X said in 1963, "Why, Good God, man, what's happening to your woman. They're making her a harlot. They're making her a charlatan, because you and I won't stand up and be MEN! You and I will NEVER be respected, until we get some respect for this Black woman!" These powers that be know that if you don't respect and thus, won't protect your women, YOU will be very easy targets for them to pick off. That's one of the first things you need to do if you want this kind of racism foolishness to stop. Start protecting your woman. Stop being the source she has to be protected *from*.

These authority figures are put in place to <u>*serve*</u> and <u>protect</u> you and your interests. Apparently, you all seem to have let that little fact slip from your minds. You know what the real problem is? YOU won't stand up and seize the authority back that you gave them in the first place. You keep *asking* them to please punish that mean old group of officers who shot 47 times into that unarmed man. You keep *asking* the Columbus, Georgia authorities to please punish and/or deal with that old Deputy Glisson who put two bullets without provocation into the back of the skull of an unarmed Black man he had on the ground. You have the *right* to <u>demand</u> that. Don't ask. TELL them to. It will fall into the same category as when the priest is exorcising the devil out of a person's body. The devil and Satan has very vast powers, alright. But he MUST bend and capitulate to whoever ORDERS him in the NAME OF <u>GOD</u> to "git!" Yes, YOU don't own weapons of mass destruction or have access to nuclear reactors and big Tomahawk missiles. But then, you don't *have* to. <u>Order</u> your police department to make these improvements and to do its <u>job</u>—serving citizens, <u>not</u> victimizing them. You've had the wool pulled over your eyes in that regard too. The current forces running the show now are not running it by right...but by default. YOU are going to have to be the ones to give the orders. And don't let them continue to make out like you're buffoons. You'll be buffoons alright, if you keep letting things go as they are. Realize that despite *their* deepest wishes...<u>you have RIGHTS</u>. Seize those rights. Otherwise, what's going to happen is that when the "balloon" goes up, and everything comes crashing back down to earth, <u>he</u>, the new Rich Man in the Lazarus parable will lift up his eyes being in torments in Hell, where his pain and his flame will be so bad that even a *very* <u>*little*</u> succor from just a drop of water will be *some* relief. And you, Lazarus, with your ever forgiving, cheek turning, enemy-loving heart, will attempt to run and rescue him out of his misery *as you've always done* throughout this nation's inception. But...since it will be the Day, even if it is not THE Judgement—it will be <u>his</u> (the rich man's) judgement. And when The Lord is ready for you to suffer judgement, guess what...<u>*you*</u> ain't gonna be allowed to help or rescue him any longer. That's why there will be that great big chasm that was described in that parable...to keep you from getting to him to offer relief. That is why the Scriptures say it is a *fearful* thing to fall into the Hands of the Living God.

And as one of our ministers pointed out—you'll notice that even in Hell, that rich man was <u>still</u> trying to boss Lazarus around and give him orders. "Father Abraham, send Lazarus to dip his finger in cool water for my burning tongue!" "No, Lazarus ain't gonna do that anymore!" "Well send Lazarus to do this/to do that!" "Nope, Lazarus ain't your servant no more!" "Well, send Lazarus to tell my brothers not to come to this place!" "Look, Lazarus ain't your slave no more. He ain't your boy no more! He's here with me...you're there in Hell with the devil. Plus, even if Lazarus wanted to, he can't 'cause there's this great big chasm between us. So, I guess for this point—*you're* screwed now!"

In the meantime, Lazarus, as you are taken to your new destinies, the rest of the Planet Earth will be exposed to some things they probably suspected all along. With YOU in charge, Lazarus...could it be that—*maybe* <u>you</u> won't find it necessary to hide from the earth actual cures for diseases that have been kept bottled up by the rich man, previously. You might actually want to see Human Beings being cared for and cured...rather than suffer and suffer, then just be *treated* for current sicknesses and diseases—in order to clear a profit. YOU, Lazarus, just may take out of existence the *artificial shortages* created by the previous bunch of buffoons of all foods, crops, precious commodities, etc., once again to just be able to charge a higher price for what God, in His generosity, has placed in *abundance* on this earth. *When Hurricane Opal blew through Georgia and left its devastation, one of my pecan trees was knocked down. I was astounded at *how many* pecans were on that <u>one tree</u>! I, and every squirrel in Atlanta, could have subsisted for twenty years on those pecans, alone.*

Could it be, Lazarus, that THIS was what the previous powers that *were* and now are not, did not want the rest of the world to discover concerning the real difference between <u>you,</u> and vice-versa with *them*? You might actually be content to "live and let live."

As far as being "highly in demand" for their company, once it's no longer necessary to have to crawl to *them*, begging for a job, trying to buy goods out of their stores only to be followed, harassed, insulted, then arrested—let alone being charged a greater price for lesser quality, and otherwise being forced into a position where *they* have to be approached for their crumbs...what will be the result of our no longer being dependent on him?? Will he and his be at the mercy of rampaging hordes just itching to pay them back for their myriad of unfairnesses? Will they be chased down, strung up, lynched and castrated in retaliation once their guns, assault weapons and nukes are no longer in their possession? Or might they be relegated to a secondary position in society where *they* have to take a back seat to all, or any other number of fears and concerns they had as when we were first freed in 1865 and ALL reprisal they thought they'd have to suffer from us turned out to be nil?

Or is it more a case of our Caucasian counterparts finding out, to their horror, that not only is no one really interested in them enough to make it their mission in life to *find* them and *deal* with them and make <u>them</u> the center of attraction, positive OR negative...just so <u>they</u> count! Might it be due to the rude awakening on their part that no one is bothering with them, one way or another, but just leaving them alone and going on about their own personal and private affairs...which would indict their guilty consciences further about their holding their foot on the rest of the world's neck, because they were just <u>sure</u> that WE ALL were <u>so</u> preoccupied with <u>them</u> that we just couldn't live without them...even if it meant negative attention as opposed to positive attention? That, people, is the earmark of a rebellious particular angel who wants to be God and thus, worshipped...only is he NOT GOD!

CHAPTER NINETEEN

"WELL, IF YA DON'T LIKE IT, WHY DON'T 'CHA LEAVE?"

I SAW A VERY DISTURBING SITUATION that was profiled on "Dateline," one Sunday earlier in the year in 2006. It was about this very devout family man who was the head of an organization in Arizona that was boot camp-like called, "The Buffalo Soldiers," and named after the Black cavalrymen who fought Native Americans on the behalf of the very government that was screwing them both. To make a long story short, one very disturbed and out-of-control White kid who had been sent to them (you guessed it) died while in their custody. The kid was highly suicidal and violent with his mother, and on a variety of medications for mental imbalance.

Initially, it was ruled accidental and all things were left as was because the kid intentionally swallowed fistful after fistful of dirt in a suicide attempt, and the camp heads took him into the showers to try to wash it out, called an ambulance, yet the kid died. Well, I guess for Texas authorities and with that usual Caucasian mood of, "A WHITE person's died! SOMEBODY has to PAY!" Even if nobody _is_ responsible— "somebody's gonna be held responsible!" They decided to bring charges in court. The whole "Dateline" program was about _how much_ these grateful Whites in the Arizona community concerned whose wayward young men had been successfully straightened out by this Buffalo Soldier program just *kept* finding the camp head not responsible. And the Arizona authorities just *kept* trying the case and pressing the issue until finally an all-White jury found the camp head, "Guilty," in the young man's death. He was sentenced to the sound of his six year old daughter's sobs in the background to six years in prison. **FOR WHAT???** The "Dateline" interviewer talked to one of the jury members who said he didn't like what they had to do to him. The camp head *wasn't even* **there** when the young man swallowed all that dirt! If Arizonan authorities just *had* to have a pound of flesh due to this kid's death, they should have *put his mamma* in prison for sending him to that camp with all that medication in his system, and then only half-telling them about that fact in the first place. That did come out during the trial, too, and that his own mother could be held liable in this case due to that reason.

ALL of those medical and legal experts who were testifying at his trial brought up instance after instance that showed that **nobody** *did* anything to him or directly caused his demise. Yet, they found this man "guilty." Any ONE of these panel of experts' findings would have kept *anybody else* out of prison...in other words, you get my drift...a White guy out if the victim were Black. And if you don't think so, you've seen, I hope, that video footage that was apparently *eased* out to public view of a Florida boot camp were about five White camp guard personnel were surrounding, beating, choking and shoving onto the ground the usual *one*, lone young Black male...and *he* died. No charges. "Not Guilty," was the verdict. They were allowed to say, "He had sickle-cell!" and they all walked.

That Buffalo Soldier camp head has NO BUSINESS being locked up! None, at all! I mean they weren't kicking and beating on this kid. They didn't leave him abandoned and neglected or anything like that. They got him indoors. They put him into the showers to cool him off. They called an ambulance for cryin' out loud! And somebody had to be found "guilty" because of this??? Once again...*another* Black male father and provider—yanked out of the home and away from his family. As it's turned out, now the White boot camp heads in Florida are supposedly having to re-face the music about the death of that earlier described young Black man. It *could* have something to do with the fact that if this man has to do prison time behind that kid...how can they continue to hide their hands? However, you might as well be aware—this is probably *just show*...and the powers that be may have NO intention of letting any real jailable offenses be charged in *their* case. Or they'll drag it out until the case is forty years old and really too late to do anything about.

It was just like with those "Walmart Kids," as they came to be known in Georgia some time in early 2000. These young White employees of the Walmart there committed theft of the merchandise and rigged the computers to reflect paid-for-sales, which amounted to nearly a *million* dollars or more in losses. The store did absolutely nothing to them about it in the way of charges, jail, etc. Well, all these angry Black parents and relatives of their own young people and kin made a storm out of it. They angrily talked about how *their* kids had been jacked up, backed up, jailed up, etc. over stolen shoes, radios, other types of smaller merchandise, you name it.

Since these were the days of "new denial-levels" among our Caucasian counter parts the parents and so on didn't use "color of skin" as the basis of their accusation. They said, "If *those* kids of theirs lived in a different <u>zip code</u>, the results in their treatment would be vastly different." Of course, the meaning was clear. And in addition to "new denials" of that accusation, also, the powers that be did put those "Walmart Kids" on trial. But it was only a show. Because, once all the anger and heat from all these Black parents died down, the charges and court times died down too—and everything went back to what they were originally doing with their own thieving kids...**nothing.**

You fellow Americans of mine who are suffering through this outrageous gas price hike debacle had better realize it's the same thing with this supposed "investigation of possible price-gouging" that George Bush Jr. is having to go on. IT'S just a show. Absolutely <u>nothing</u> is going to be with it or about it. All this is to just calm us down and shut us up. And when you do—they'll have gas prices up to $20 a gallon. Why not?? What's your pain and suffering to ***them***?

As 2006 is about to wrap up and 2007 comes along, remember—the Voting Rights Act that was enacted to guarantee us Black Americans the right to vote expires. Everyone else occupying this planet from Tibet to South America—upon successful immigration and acceptance of American citizenship has this right naturally and permanently. WHY are there time limits for <u>us</u>??? I can't help thinking that this previous 2000 election was only a test—to see what our reaction would be to <u>our</u> votes being arbitrarily thrown out, disallowed, "lost" and otherwise not counted. Let's face un-fun facts, folks. What happened in 2000 was a coup. ALBERT GORE was the one who was truly elected to the Presidency of the United States in 2000. The Supreme Court handed one George Bush Jr. the office instead. I have a theory about why this was allowed to happen.

We American citizens had enjoyed relatively much better relations with the rest of the world and a whole hell of a *lot* more prosperity and affordability of items and goods here under the unjustly maligned President Bill Clinton. The very folks who "have it all" and whose four hundred prophets of Baal everyday on rightwing radio were running him down unforgivably everyday for his trying to be fair to all did nothing but complain, complain, complain. Being a strict Baptist-Fundamentalist raised southerner, Ah do b'lieve in praisin' and listenin' to the Lawd. As you've seen in the Old Testament with the Exodus of the Hebrews, our Creator does not appreciate chronic complainin'...not when He's been taking reasonably good care of you and yours. Our Hebrew brothers of the period also complained that they wanted a king to rule over them just like the other surrounding nations did. To get right to the nitty-gritty, the Israelites were made to wander the desert for forty years until all the complainers were gone. The Israelites also got King Saul as their ruler during their later Land of Canaan occupation-period as well.

Well, we had it pretty good under Mr. Clinton. We had jobs that paid us salaries all across the board that we could actually *afford* to buy nice things with, have enough to pay health-care co-expenses, keep the economy growing with spending/

buying power, et.al. And gas prices were .93 to $1.12 per gallon. Well, complain, complain, complain said the rich. Complain, complain, complain said the wife-cheatin' hypocrites. Complain, complain, complain said the bigots about the darkies' not bein' satisfied with their crumbs. Yet, Mr. Clinton's approval rating across the board from Americans remained in the 61% to 63% range. Well, a man who would, in this author's humble opinion have continued the good to better roads--Mr. Clinton's vice-president--appeared to be a shoe-in, no? Well, since the rest of America couldn't openly acknowledge the relative peace and calm it enjoyed (and possibly for a few other reasons), we've ended up with who we have now. The hundreds of billions of dollars surplus that the country hadn't enjoyed in over 30 years (along with the additional $256 billion surplus in Medicare monies) disappeared in less than the first eight months of Mr. Bush's reign. No more discrimination lawsuits were given validity. The Reverse discrimination suits filed by Whites were entertained and given audience constantly. All of the safeguards put in place by Bill Clinton to protect the working man were instantly done away with. I could go on. You live here too, and you've been through and are going through everything I'm pointing out.

The following statement, I've been roundly and soundly chided and castigated for, yet I'll say it again, anyway. September the Eleventh *may* have come and gone, uneventfully...just "another day" here, under Pres. Al Gore. **But**. Those *same* complaining elements, not appreciating their good blessings, refusing to acknowledge any good *he* was doing, and in reality—*probably* putting him through the same kind of horse mess and scandal over something comparatively frivolous or just down right **stupid** may have been the prevailing news story and public thought of the day. For those of you, though, who just *have* to believe that things of that magnitude happen thoroughly unprovoked, in lands that have bought and paid for leadership courtesy of *this* leadership here...keep believing that. And if you think that the spying and tapping of our phone calls and so on are for the finding of Osama and his Mama instead of, in reality, keeping an eye on **YOU**, the American populace (in case any of y'all out there are plotting an effective strategy that might successfully put in new American leadership and reclaim the Constitution and its protections)...then I've got some Lunar property deeds I want to sell you. I can't understand why people here are acting as if this is the first they've ever heard of wire-tapping and spying by our government upon us American citizens. Joseph McCarthy, J. Edgar Hoover, President Nixon, the F.B.I. and C.I.A...the list is ad infinitum. We've **been** getting spied upon.

As things under the present leadership worsen, and the rallying cry for you all to keep taking it is, "Terr'r...Terr'r...Terr'r!" and international relations, now with friends as well as people who may not have previously been, but sure are enemies now, ponder the following:

Suppose the new pressing problem as of the date of this writing, Iran, comes to a successful conclusion (like Iraq's not). Do you really think that's going to be the end of our leadership's international paranoia? I'm already hearing distrusting talk among senate and congressional leadership about Burma. Indonesia could be the next nation of ill view. Or next, Pakistan. I'm tellin' ya...it's not going to stop with Iraq. Iran. Ya' think they'll finally get the balls to confront North Korea? *Where* will it end? Observant eyes and inquiring minds want to know. Of course, as I know, *I'm* not supposed to say such or talk like this because...**I** don't have the right. But, if enough of you klan-minded folks out there can get past your klanishness enough to realize--what I'm talking about (and also reserve the **right** to do) is everybody's SURVIVAL. You have to realize, a machine like this that is Corporate big business, knows nothing else except money. Money. Money. That's ALL. There's not a thing wrong with wanting to make a profit, either. I'm not a communist. I don't get emotional about the word as most Baptist-Fundamentalist southerners do. But this thing of, "From each according to his ability—to each according to his need"-- uh, thank you, but **I'LL** decide how much of something I need! I'm grown. I don't need you telling me how much of something I can have. I'll get as much as I can afford! I believe in *that*! If I have a voracious appetite for something or some product, I, by myself, *cannot* exhaust the world supply! If I have a *problem*...and I have to exhaust the store's supply...not to worry. They'll have more by the end of the day on Wednesday. If I'm somebody who just can't get enough...my *body* will step in and take over. Either I'll get deathly sick, or pass out cold, which will stop my insane drive for whatever it is that I cannot consume enough. Do you get my point? All of us—everybody has a drive, a taste, a desire, a talent, a dream, the list is infinite. God has created us this way—lots of diversity. And we're ALL in each others' service! I can't paint a room to save my soul. I've tried gardening and planting things *"guaranteed"* to grow—that not only didn't. It died. That's just *not* my strong point! But if you talk numbers and lecturing, biography and tutoring (as well as preparing a mean steak dinner), come see Mama! And some of us do have talents great enough to be able to make a *nice* living. The problem is that the powers that currently *are*-- keep interfering with and halting the good service to others we are capable of producing—if it looks like it's going to compete with the worthless, counterfeit, mundane and unoriginal *crap* we're all forced to have to make due with. Medicinal herbal products, natural and originally produced food product combinations, etc. are routinely and suddenly knocked off the market when they appear...again, supposedly, due to some "problem" that can't be worked out with the buyer. Ways and means of support for smaller business owners and farmers are being sucked up out of existence by the conglomerates so that the vast majority of us are condemned to be "worker bees" only.

Whether it's 1919's United Fruit Company, notorious for barging into South America and Haiti, controlling ALL their land resources and making them harvest fruits and goods...and then paying their workers so little that they literally starved to death... Or whether it's the mining companies of late 1890's to the same early 1900's time periods here in the United States, where the working conditions were so dangerous and the pay again so low, that deaths among these workers were astronomical...it's all thanks to the same animal. G-R-R-E-E-E-D-Y big business interests! Of course, the conditions, being thoroughly unbearable caused revolts during those years. Haiti revolted against United Fruit Company and the U.S. Marines were sent in to quash it. Lots of Haitian deaths. Likewise, the oppressed miners in the U.S., mostly poor and downtrodden Whites, tried to organize protests and unionize. THEY were met with violence and death at the hands of the Pinkerton company strong-arm men called in to quash their opposition to oppression. The same lawless violence against oppressed working men/women whether Blacks, Hispanics or Whites, as well, was immediately and ruthlessly resorted to by our corporate benefactors.

At least twice in pre-1930's America, out-right _Ku Klux Klan_ members willingly sat down next to Black Americans in meeting rooms of mixed races, organized and headed by Blacks, themselves, because these Whites realized that they had a problem that was ***not US***! And if _they_ wanted to thrive and **survive**, something was going to have to be done about being taken for a ride by uncaring big business forces running the show. But, the usual scare tactics were resorted to by those forces' minions about how Blacks would, "Come through your bedroom windows! Burn your churches! Rape your wives! Kill your kids with Bowie knives!!!" And the races were successfully pitted against each other once more.

I hope you're seeing the familiarity about today's situation as those days' prior ones. It has not changed one iota except in product, place and today's particular catch-phrase names.

This is MY home. America is where I live. I've got just as much to lose as anybody else if our land goes down the tubes. And I wish more of you out there would hear and respond to the rest of the world's beleaguered inhabitants, Muslim and Christian, even many _communist_ countries, who tell us over and over again that they truly have nothing against us ordinary American citizens. That they downright _like_ us. They have. And they still do. Apparently, _most_ of you know how to be cordial and get along with people...especially being visitors, sightseers, and _tourists_. Those _some_ on the other hand (you know who you are) whose attitude is that "all those sorry bastards would be toast without us!" are the ones who make the rest of us seem arrogant and a chore to endure, tourist dollars or not. Remember the old sayings and wisdoms through the ages. The foot you step on today might be the foot you have to kiss tomorrow. If things are not _corrected_ before they become any worse, just as someone managed to punch their way through this nation's defenses in September of '01...there _may_ be someone who will make all this administration's "seeing enemies everywhere" a self-fulfilling prophecy. Should that happen, beloved citizens of our purple mounted majestic land, and we're seeing how many of us The Lord allows to escape with our very lives alone...you ain't gonna like hearing those citizens in lands we're having to escape to for safety tell _you_— "Well if you don't like it here, why don't 'cha _leave_?"

Thank you for your cooperation.

Printed in the United States
By Bookmasters